A Johnny Reb Band from Salem:

The Pride of Tarheelia

A Johnny Reb Band from Salem:
The Pride of Tarheelia

Harry H. Hall

Office of Archives and History
North Carolina Department of Cultural Resources
Raleigh
Revised Edition, 2006

COVER: The original members of the Twenty-sixth North Carolina Regimental Band at Salem in the summer of 1862. For identification of bandmembers, see page 46.

In Memory of the Twenty-sixth
Regimental Band, N.C. Troops, C.S.A.

Contents

Illustrations

Field Sketches of Alexander C. Meinung

Acknowledgments

Those persons and institutions that helped to make the publication of the first edition of this book possible are again recognized for their contributions to the present work. To this number are added the individuals and organizations whose help and resources have been invaluable to this new edition.

I would be remiss in failing to single out two persons in particular who had a very special part in helping with my initial research through the final typescript of the first book. Their contributions at that time carry over to the present in many ways. First, to the late Donald M. McCorkle, Ph.D., first Director of the Moravian Music Foundation, I owe a special debt of gratitude for his having introduced me to the vast area of Moravian music. It was his enthusiasm and special interest in the Twenty-sixth Band and its rare collection of music that intrigued and prompted me to make this segment of Moravian wind music a special topic of study. Second, I owe much to the late J. Isaac Copeland, Ph.D., then (1960s) Librarian of Peabody College, Nashville, Tennessee, and subsequently (1967) Director of the Southern Historical Collection and Professor of history at the University of North Carolina at Chapel Hill. His personal friendship, enthusiastic support of the early research, and encouragement were of immeasurable importance to me during the preparation of the typescript for publication—first submitted as a four-part article to the *North Carolina Historical Review*, which then passed it on to the North Carolina Confederate Centennial Commission.

Many of my contemporaries and institutions have, in their special ways, contributed to the preparation of this revised edition. I wish to express my deep sense of appreciation to Margaret Leinbach Kolb of Winston-Salem, N.C., granddaughter of Julius Leinbach, who kindly granted me permission for the unqualified use of her grandfather's extensive wartime documents. This material, much of which was unavailable at the time of the earlier publication, is now deposited in the Southern Historical Collection, Manuscripts Department, Wilson Library, University of North Carolina at Chapel Hill. It has been my pleasure to have enjoyed a long-standing friendship with Ms. Kolb, recognized for her many contributions—personal and official—to the Moravian Music Foundation since its inception in the mid-1950s. It is therefore especially gratifying that she has shown a personal interest in the publication of the present edition.

To Nola Reed Knouse, Ph.D., Director of the Moravian Music Foundation, I am deeply grateful for her help in so many ways during the preparation of this edition. By making available the vast resources of the foundation, Dr. Knouse has provided the means for expanding the scope of my research and expediting the completion of this work. Her enthusiastic support of this project warrants a special note of appreciation.

The gleaning of records pertaining to many aspects of Moraviana naturally led me to explore the wealth of material located in the Archives of the Moravian Church in America, Southern Province, Winston-Salem. To C. Daniel Crews, Ph.D., Archivist, and to Richard Starbuck, Assistant Archivist, I gratefully acknowledge their assistance and cooperation in the search for and use of the special documents in their care.

Pictorial illustrations and similar material add much to any historical writing of this nature. In this regard I gratefully acknowledge the valued contributions of several divisions of the Museum of Early Southern Decorative Arts (MESDA), Horton Center Museums of Old Salem, Inc., Paula Loclair, Vice President. To Martha Rowe, Director of MESDA's Research Center, I am particularly appreciative of her kindness and cooperation, and for having placed the extensive research facilities of the center at my disposal. A very special word of thanks goes to Jennifer Bean Bower, Manager of Photographic Resources, for her assistance in locating the many photographs and written miscellanea that have added much to this history. Her observations regarding the assignment of dates and places of the various photographs have been especially useful.

For their financial contributions to defray the cost of the many illustrations in this edition, I wish to thank the following: Richard M. Henderson, Margaret Leinbach Kolb, Charles W. Miller, David Hagen Pfaff, and Fred Pfohl—all of Winston-Salem—and Robert S.

Simon of Clemmons, N.C., whose contribution is in memory of Dr. Frederick Fennell.

My sincere thanks go to John White, retired, former Public Services Assistant of the Southern Historical Collection, Manuscripts Department, Wilson Library, University of North Carolina at Chapel Hill, for having given generously of his time and help in connection with the Julius Lineback Papers. His ready assistance in making available material from these papers and his various suggestions for their usage have been especially helpful. I would also express my appreciation to Harry McKown, North Carolina Collection, Wilson Library, for his courteous and ready responses to numerous questions regarding the search for sources of historical information. The selection and inclusion of the maps from the atlas to the multi-volume *War of the Rebellion* have been with the aid of Celia D. Pratt, Map Librarian, Maps Collection of Wilson Library. For her assistance in this important task, I wish to express my thanks at this time.

Ancillary material with a special significance to the Twenty-sixth Band's wartime service has come from many sources beyond the folds of Moravian records. In this respect I wish to acknowledge the help of Molly Rawls, Photograph Collection Librarian, Forsyth County Public Library. Molly has come to my aid a number of times, readily locating various items of special interest.

For providing photocopies of selected Confederate band muster rolls, I am grateful to the South Carolina Department of Archives and History, Columbia. My thanks are extended also to the Mississippi Department of Archives and History, Archives and Library Division, Jackson, for locating and providing me with photocopies of two significant biographical items: the grave registration and death certificate of William H. Hartwell, who contributed many of the tunes in the Twenty-sixth Band books.

To my good friend of many years, Hubert P. Henderson, Ph.D., Lexington, Kentucky, Professor Emeritus, University of Kentucky, it is indeed a pleasure to express my appreciation for having read most of the manuscript. His encouragement to "keep at it" has been most significant and largely responsible for my pushing ahead to completion of what began as a kind of pipe dream several years ago.

I owe the Historical Publications Section, North Carolina Office of Archives and History, Raleigh, a special debt of gratitude for their work in preparing the manuscript for publication. To Donna Kelly, Administrator, and her staff, I am extremely grateful for their interest in seeing this revised edition brought to fruition. A special word of thanks goes to Kenrick N. Simpson, Supervisor of the General Publications and Periodicals Branch of the section, who served as primary editor. His careful readings of the manuscript, preparation of the index, and many suggestions and valuable criticisms along the way have been the result of long hours of work. Susan M. Trimble, as digital editor, has skillfully scanned the many illustrations and has been responsible for their placement in the text. For this important task, I acknowledge her service with gratitude. She also was responsible for typesetting the entire book. To other members of the section, specifically Lisa D. Bailey, who has been of assistance in proofreading, I express my appreciation.

Finally, I fondly remember my late wife Jane in connection with this book in many ways. Her contributions to the first edition, too numerous to list—time, sacrifice, work, help—carry forward to the present. Now, in retrospect, it was her encouragement in recent years that prompted me to consider, though remotely at the time, preparing a revised edition. Not until her passing a few years ago did I regrettably take her encouragement to heart and undertake the present project. To you, Jane, I am immeasurably grateful.

Introduction

The American Civil War has inspired more writing—historical and fictional, good and bad—than any other single event in the history of mankind. The centennial observance of this conflict in the early 1960s brought forth a spate of literature and projects that touched on nearly every aspect of this tragic chapter in American history. All have had something for most everyone—from the "buff" and casual reader, to those who have made a special study of this period in the nation's history. In view of the important role of musicians, North and South, it seemed entirely fitting that at least one act of the commemorative drama pay tribute to the "Johnny Reb" bandsman, an unsung hero who, through his signal talent, infused a good measure of spirit and hope into the Confederate cause.

My own contribution to the observance was a paperback edition of the present book, published by the North Carolina Confederate Centennial Commission in 1963. The limited number of one thousand copies was sold almost immediately. A hardcover reprint was released by Da Capo Press in 1980. There appear to be no copies presently for sale except perhaps in some rare bookstore.

The major source for this edition, revised and enlarged, remains the Civil War notes and recollections of Julius Augustus Leinbach, or Lineback (1834–1930), a musician from the nineteenth-century Moravian Church community of Salem, North Carolina, and a member of the Twenty-sixth Regimental Band, North Carolina Troops, C.S.A. The "Lineback" spelling of the surname—retained by the writer as it appears in original documents—was used for a number of years, including in the writings of Julius, who has left us a fascinating story of the band's service in the Confederacy for a little more than three years.

The original Leinbach manuscript was thought to have been lost or misplaced when research for the first edition began in the late 1950s. It was my good fortune to become acquainted with Miss Caroline E. Leinbach, daughter of bandsman Julius, who kindly gave me access to her personal scrapbook containing a series of newspaper clippings based on her father's wartime experiences. Entitled "Extracts from a Civil War Diary," these appeared as a series of articles in the *Twin City Daily Sentinel* (Winston, N.C., ca. 1905).

My recent search in the Southern Historical Collection, Manuscripts Department, Wilson Library, University of North Carolina at Chapel Hill, led to a surprising discovery: Julius Leinbach's wartime material, identified as the JULIUS A. LINEBACK PAPERS #4547. Deposited in the Manuscripts Department in 1982 by the late Clarence T. Leinbach Jr., grandson of Julius, ownership of the three-volume collection has passed to Margaret Leinbach Kolb of Winston-Salem, the musician's granddaughter.

Volume 1 is a small notebook (approximately 6 cm. x 10 cm. x 1 cm.) of about two hundred pages, printed by Philip J. Coznans, New York. Titled "POCKET DIARY. FOR 1861," it was used initially by Leinbach to record daily occurrences and business accounts from January 1 into April of that year. Tuesday, April 21, was the date on which Leinbach changed the printed year 1861 to a penciled 1863, and began recording his on-the-scene wartime notes. In the entry for that date, he mentioned the Twenty-sixth Regiment having returned to Greenville in eastern North Carolina, where the band played several concerts. The last entry for the year was Thursday, December 31; on that day, the band remained up until midnight to usher in the New Year by playing Tune 146, *Nun danket alle Gott* (*Now Thank We All Our God*). The remainder of the booklet, designated "Memoranda" (n.d.), appears to be devoted primarily to business matters.

The general appearance of Leinbach's manuscript bears close resemblance to the German script found in old Moravian diaries. Many comments in the volume were written so closely together that they are difficult, if not impossible, to read, even when enlarged above the 5x setting for microfilming. Only by comparing these entries with parallel statements in the handwritten notebook (Volume 2) can we determine some of the information.

The band's performance of music during the Battle of Gettysburg, according to Leinbach, was on the second day, Thursday, July 2, when the Twenty-sixth Regiment and the rest of Pettigrew's brigade were not engaged. The closing sentences of Julius's diary notes at that time stated: "At 6 o'cl. we are ordered to brigade. Col. Marshall in com'd. wants us to play for troops. We and 11 Band double on several pieces—heavy firing going on during the time. Got back to hospital after dark." That little mention was made of the band having played music during the sanguine three-day encounter can be understood in view of the circumstances.

But why were Julius's wartime comments of 1863 inserted amidst his business notations for the year 1861? A far more intriguing puzzle centers on the absence of firsthand accounts for 1862 and 1864–1865. Were there once other similar documents to the pocket diary? Although Leinbach indicated having had access to various original materials (as noted below), none of these have thus far surfaced in various collections, including letters in possession of his descendants.

Volume 2, a hardbound notebook, contains the complete handwritten narrative of 390 pages, the source for Leinbach's series of newspaper clippings that comprise Volume 3, the scrapbook. (Several microfilmed pages were duplicated for clarity.) The title page reads: "The 26th Regimental Band, Being a History of the Military Band Attached to the 26th Regiment, No. Car. Troops, Pettigrew's Brigade, Heth's Division, Hill's Corps, Army of Northern Virginia, 1862–1865." The second page of the "Preface" states:

The story has been compiled from parts of diaries, incomplete in themselves, a very few of the many letters, that were written that have survived the times, and the personal recollections of some of the participants that now after the lapse of 40 years, have become hazy and indistinct.

The illustrations are copies from "Sketches of Camp life," made on the spot by our artist, Mr. A. C. Meinung, for whose kindness in leaving them for this purpose, I thankfully acknowledge my obligations.

To S. T. Mickey & J. E. Peterson, I am also greatly indebted, as well as to others of "The Band."

[Signed] J. A. L.

In addition to the written narrative, the volume contains a variety of supplementary material: camp sketches, photographs, letters, a section of newspaper extracts, and other associated items of interest. The document is signed by Julius A. Lineback of Salem and dated February 27, 1904.

Volume 3 is another hardback, loose-leaf notebook of nearly two hundred pages of newspaper clippings, apparently from the *Sentinel*, titled "Extracts From a Civil War Diary." Page one has the inscription, "Clarence T. Lineback from father, 1915." The contents are based on the handwritten account in volume 2, supplemented by other newspaper clippings and a miscellanea of relevant material, including copies of Alexander Meinung's camp sketches interspersed throughout. Of special interest are two articles: "Some Reminiscences of a Store Boy of 60 Odd Years Ago," and "Some More Reminiscences of Muster Days before the War."

Of the many major engagements in which the Twenty-sixth Band saw service, the Battle of Gettysburg heads the list. Notwithstanding the Battle of Malvern Hill in 1862, it was the regiment's first major encounter. The bandsmen were in the thick of battle. Aside from their limited opportunity to play music, they served the troops in other ways as needed. Theirs was a regiment that, after having lost almost 90 percent of its personnel—a casualty toll of over seven hundred members—acquired the fitting epithet, "The Bloody Twenty-sixth."

An account of the band's experience at Gettysburg was first made public by Leinbach in a paper titled, "Scenes at the Battle of Gettysburg," read before the Wachovia Historical Society in Winston-Salem during the early part of the twentieth century. In the late 1950s, an edited, abridged version was prepared by the late Donald M. McCorkle. Titled "Regiment Band of the Twenty-sixth North Carolina," it appeared in *Civil War History*, published by the State University of Iowa in 1958. A reprint was issued as *Moravian Music Foundation Publications* No. 5 (Winston-Salem, 1958). Of particular interest is the special supplement, "Repertory of the 26th Regiment Band," compiled and edited by McCorkle. It is a list of music comprising five of seven sets of manuscript part-books—not all complete—used by the Twenty-sixth musicians and now preserved by the Moravian Music Foundation.

No richer treasure of Civil War band music exists, except perhaps a "Yankee companion," *The Ingals Book,* located in the Library of Congress. Referred to as *The Port Royal* [S.C.] *Books,* these were first used by the band of the Third New Hampshire Regiment, directed by the enterprising Gustavus W. Ingals. Ingals and his band were later assigned to the Union's Department of the South as the Second Brigade Band, Tenth Army Corps.

The music from these two collections was first brought to public notice in a set of recordings by the late Frederick Fennell and the Eastman School of Music's wind ensemble in the late 1950s. The set, with associated materials, was released as a compact disc recording in 1990. Copies of music from the two collections have become staple items in the repertories of a number of reconstituted Confederate and Union bands at various festivals and period reenactments throughout the country.

While the Julius Leinbach account remains the primary source for this edition, the inclusion of additional material lends a broader historical and sociological scope to the work. A major new feature chronicles a detailed history of Salem's first formally organized band, formed in 1831 as an adjunct to the local militia. Of special interest is the source of this history: the journal of Johann Heinrich (John Henry) Leinbach (1796–1870), father of Julius.

An additional supplement is another firsthand account of the Twenty-sixth Band: the fragmentary diary of the Moravian Samuel Timothy Mickey (1839–1914), who was credited with having organized and led the band throughout the war. This was indeed a surprising discovery, for at the time of my original research, the Mickey diary was believed to have been lost; when last seen, it reportedly had experienced extensive damage. Fortunately, the partial remains have recently been located and are now preserved in the Moravian Archives at Old Salem, the restored section of the original town. A typescript of this portion, with many missing words and incomplete sentences, has been meticulously prepared by

Grace S. Robinson of the Moravian Archives and made available to me in preparing this edition.

Notwithstanding the fragmentary nature of the Mickey document, it is a valuable supplement to the Leinbach record. It includes several items omitted in the latter; at the same time, the two accounts contain almost word-for-word descriptions of many events. Minor differences between the two sources are no doubt the result of both men having been partially dependent upon fading memory when writing.

Music of some kind has been associated with organized warfare through the ages. With its wide range of appeal to emotions, sentiments, and attitudes, it has served primarily to bolster morale on the battlefield, as well as on the home front. In times of armed conflict, music might well be regarded as the oil that makes the wheels of war machines run smoother. In the front rank stands the military band. Whether performing martial airs or tunes of a popular variety, it is regarded as one of the more effective means of evoking feelings and emotions during the turbulence of war.

Most of the musical fare of the soldier and civilian during these periods is a product of circumstance, here today and gone tomorrow. The two major conflicts of the twentieth century brought forth an effusion of timely favorites. The majority of these special ditties served their purpose well, then passed out of mind almost overnight, and this was just as well. On the other hand, a few special tunes and lyrics, not specifically geared to the conflict at hand, still linger in present-day society. They poignantly recall deep feelings reminiscent of their time and still provide listening pleasure more than half a century later! Consider, for example, the seasonal favorite, *White Christmas*, or the romantic, *As Time Goes By,* both enjoying a degree of popularity by means of tapes, compact discs, and occasional television reruns. These ballads and similar ones of the time have become "standards" and owe their longevity in large measure to advances in media technology, especially in the recording industry.

There is no way to determine just how long the musical output of the Civil War lingered in the minds and hearts of soldiers and civilians in postbellum times, though probably not fifty or more years! But today, thanks to the preservation of various musical collections, one can revisit those days through the performances of a growing number of reconstituted Civil War bands. Their presence, most with restored, over-the-shoulder period instruments playing from copies of the original band books, is a distinctive feature of Civil War commemorative ceremonies and reenactments throughout this country and abroad. We are able to recapture the spirit of the era on hearing many rollicking favorites of that day: e.g., *Rappahannock Polka*, *Easter Galop*, *Cape May Polka*, *Here's Your Mule*, and the ever-popular *When Johnny Comes Marching Home*. The stirring medley of *Dixie* and *The Bonnie Blue Flag* never fails to rouse a crowd and most always elicits some "Rebel" yells.

One might wonder how members of the Twenty-sixth Regimental Band, born of a religious lineage with conscientious convictions against warfare and political embroilment, became active participants in this national conflict, in which relatives and friends were sometimes set against each other in mortal combat. Suffice it to say that by the mid-nineteenth century, external influences of the time had gradually eroded many of the Moravian Church attitudes and restrictions of previous years. By the opening guns of the Civil War, these were no longer a controlling influence over its members.

Among some questions that might be asked at this point include: "Who are these Moravians?" "Where did they originate and what part did music, especially that of wind instruments, play in the lives of these early emigrants to America?" "Why did these peace-loving people with their instruments and music, so rooted in an aversion to warfare, form bands of music in the American military?" Answers to these and other questions will no doubt become apparent as the story unfolds.

PART ONE

BACKGROUND FOR A TRADITION

1 *The Eighteenth-Century Antecedents*

The modern period in Moravian Church history dates from 1722, when a small band of religious refugees from Moravia, surviving an underground existence during the Thirty Years' War, established the village of Herrnhut on the east Saxon estate of Count Nicolaus Ludwig von Zinzendorf (1700–1760). Here, in 1727, the little band of evangelical Christians formally reestablished their Church, a renewed branch of the pre-Reformation *Unitas Fratrum* (Unity of Brethren). With Herrnhut as their center, the Moravians launched a worldwide program of missions: to North and South America, Africa, and Asia. A fervent desire to Christianize the heathen whites and Indians brought them to colonial America to establish permanent settlements in Pennsylvania and North Carolina. The hardships of frontier life notwithstanding, these hardy churchmen's ingrained love and verve for music blossomed into a vital art that came to challenge the best of this country's cultural centers for three-quarters of a century (ca. 1760–ca. 1835).

One important aspect of the Moravian musical tradition is the preeminence of brass ensembles, generally indicated in early church records as *Blasinstrumenten* or *Bläser-Chor*. The designation, *ein chor Posaunen*, is used to identify an ensemble of trombones. No doubt reflecting a Moravian predilection for these instruments, the term "trombone choir" has been used rather freely by some American congregations to identify any combination of trumpets, horns, and/or trombones. Even so, the designation has become generally recognized as comprising the complete family of trombones: descant (soprano), alto, tenor, and bass.

Although the Moravian musical tradition took root and flourished in the early classical environment, the trombone choir is one of the few remnants of the baroque absorbed into this tradition. Adopted at a time when the ensemble had practically fallen into disuse in Europe, its appearance in this country in the mid-1700s was completely foreign; the inclusion of the soprano instrument, especially, has been identified only with the Moravians.

Employed in similar fashion as its immediate predecessor, the seventeenth-century *Stadtpfeifer*, the Moravian wind choir, whether of mixed instrumentation or as a consort of trombones, has served to announce almost every event of community interest, both religious and civic. The body of music has consisted mainly of the traditional Lutheran-Moravian chorales. The trombone, by virtue of its tonal quality and slide action to affect a portamento style of playing, was ideally suited mechanically, acoustically, and aesthetically to accompany congregational singing, which was a distinctive aspect of Moravian faith.

Many uses of the early wind choirs have long since been discontinued, but two distinguishing customs remain: the traditional Easter morning sunrise proclamation, and the special, threefold announcement to the congregation of a member's death. This announcement is reserved for members of the Moravian faith with

Page from an eighteenth-century Moravian chorale book. (Image courtesy of the Moravian Music Foundation, Winston-Salem, N.C.)

one notable exception—the death of the president of the United States, in which case the middle section of the announcement is modified to include the National Anthem in place of a special tune identifying the particular congregational division or "choir" of the departed member.

One of the earliest dates that can be assigned with certainty to any use of wind instruments—horns and the first, recently acquired trombones—by the Moravians prior to their emigration to America is May 12, 1731. On that date, about forty residents of Herrnhut traveled to nearby Berthelsdorf to help celebrate the birthday of the Lutheran minister, Johann A. Rothe.[1]

Although the Moravian use of brass instruments took firm root in the American congregations of Pennsylvania and North Carolina during the mid-eighteenth century, a beginning note had been sounded earlier in the short-lived settlement in Savannah, Georgia (1735–1740). Unfortunately, we are not informed as to how or when these instruments were acquired and first used in the colony. It is within reason to suppose that they were among the belongings of early arrivals, when enthusiasm for establishing the Savannah mission was at its peak, not during the latter years when, with each passing day, adverse conditions, such as internal disputes, contentious neighbors, sickness, and threatened invasion by the Spaniards in Florida, pointed toward the congregation's impending dissolution.

The final note may have been sounded at the funeral of one Michael Shober on August 10, 1739. Despite the depleted mission, instrumentalists were no doubt available to announce the death. This appears confirmed in an interesting letter written by the distinguished Moravian leader Peter Böhler (1712–1775) from Savannah the following December. He related that Gen. James Oglethorpe

bought the Brethren's trumpets and hunting horns and gave them ten shillings more than they asked. He positively wanted to persuade Brother [Johann] Bohner to become his trumpeter, and promised him 110 shillings per month. When Toma Chachi [*sic*] was buried, he also wanted to pay the Brethren if they would play music, but they refused him.[2]

Böhler's letter, identifying the instruments (probably no more than two of each), is important for additional reasons. First, it appears to be the only known primary source, Moravian or otherwise, referring to the Georgia ensemble. Second, it implies that a good relationship existed between Oglethorpe and the Brethren, something almost completely lacking in the settlement's dealings with many neighboring settlers and Indians. Third, we may infer that Johann Bohner (1710–1785), a Moravian carpenter, was obviously an able performer to have been tabbed by Oglethorpe for possible duty with his troops. (Bohner left for Pennsylvania in January 1740.) Fourth, the purchase of these instruments suggests that a pressing need for money influenced the Moravian decision to make the sale. How ironic that these instruments of the devout churchmen would pass to the British military! Finally, of special significance, Bohner is the first player thus far identified with American Moravian wind music—perhaps all Moravian music in this country.

In April 1740, the six remaining Brethren of the ill-fated mission, accompanied by three non-Moravians, left to join fellow residents in Pennsylvania—first at Nazareth, then Bethlehem and Lititz—thus closing out the Moravian enterprise in Georgia.[3]

A shift in location by American Moravians has never seriously impeded the growth of their musical endeavor. The process began in earnest during the late eighteenth and early nineteenth centuries, as population and resources grew with the constant arrival of Brethren, music, and instruments from Europe.

By the time the Moravians reached North Carolina in November 1753, brass instruments were already becoming an integral part of life among the Pennsylvania congregations. In the central area of Carolina, known today as the "Piedmont," the church had acquired about 100,000 acres of wilderness land, to which was given the name "Wachovia" (die Wachau) because of its topographical similarity to the first settlement in Germany. The governing center would become Salem (now Winston-Salem), first settled in 1766, but not assuming full leadership until 1772. The earlier satellite villages of Bethabara (1753) and Bethania (1759) were primarily farming communities. The subsequent settlements of Friedberg (1772), Friedland (1780), and Hope (1780) completed the communal design in this wilderness region.

The piercing sound of a watchman's "conch" in Bethabara on November 20, 1753, though having no musical significance, might

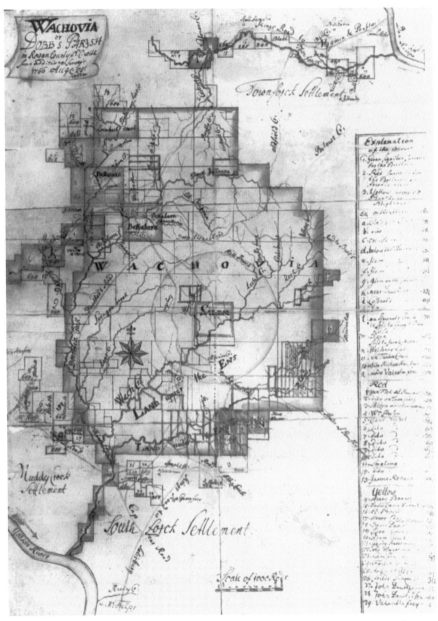

Map of the Wachovia land tract by Philip Christian Gottlieb Reuter, 1766, with some additional surveys. (Image courtesy of the Archives of the Moravian Church in America, Southern Province, Winston-Salem, N.C.)

be considered as having ushered in the wind tradition of the Wachovia Moravians.[4] The following year a wooden trumpet (an ersatz zinke or cornet?) was ingeniously fashioned to announce the traditional love feast in this first settlement. More significantly, a later entry in the church diary for July 22, 1755, stated that for "the first time at morning prayer we have used the trumpets which the last company brought with them from Pennsylvania."[5] Then in November, two more trumpets were among the effects of about twenty Brethren arriving in Bethabara from Bethlehem, Pennsylvania, in three wagons. One member of this group stated that

after morning prayers we took up our last days journey toward the Wachau. . . .We reached the boundary . . . at 11 A.M. . . . About five o'clock in the afternoon we met the first of the Brethren. . . . From our party Aust and Opitz rode ahead, blowing on their trumpets . . . , and the Brethren of the Wachau were not slow to answer with their trumpets, and to welcome us from the peak of their new house.[6]

Later diary entries mention flutes (probably only a pair) having been played at a Sabbath love feast on November 15. Excluding the flutes, those wind instruments available in Bethabara at the end of 1755 might have been four trumpets and one horn. Approximately ten years later, on August 14, 1766, an inventory of church-owned furnishings lists only two trumpets and two horns.[7] The record may be incomplete because some personal ownership of items was allowed and may have included additional trumpets and/or horns. This makes an accurate accounting of all such portable instruments impossible. Trombones were not acquired by Bethabara until 1768; they were used for the first time on July 4 to announce an infant's death, and again at the burial the next day.[8]

When Salem, with a population of approximately 120, became the Moravian governing center in North Carolina in 1772, it assumed leadership, if not outright control, of all things musical. Significantly, this included a restrictive view by many church leaders permitting the performance of only a limited amount of secular music.

The first official document thus far discovered that refers specifically to secular music in early Salem appeared, interestingly, during the community's first year of leadership. This was an admonition directed primarily to the musicians; but it also served as a

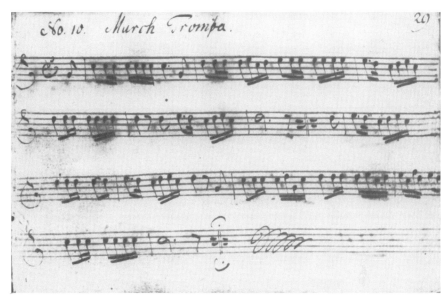

The *March Trompa*. Moravian musicians were forbidden to play marches. (Image courtesy of the Moravian Music Foundation.)

reminder for the *Gemeine* (Church-Community) that certain activities were forbidden on the Sabbath. The notice, dated December 1, 1772, stated:

Dear Brethren and Sisters of the Aeltesten Conferenz [Elders Conference]:

We think it would be well to abide by the Helfer Conferenz [Ministers Conference] concerning playing on Sunday. In connection with the subject of Sunday we desire to say that in business nothing ought to be sold on Sunday, nor charged, neither should work be taken in nor given out. Neither should the musicians play Minuets, Polonaises, Marches, or other worldly music, but rather confine themselves to chorales.[9]

This brief statement discloses an emerging Moravian distinction between sacred and secular music. That playing this kind of music on Sunday was considered inappropriate comes as no surprise. More importantly, though, is the implication that performances of such "worldly music" *would be tolerated* by some church officials at other times.

Of special historical interest is the music singled out in this instance. The remains of these compositions quite possibly exist today in two leather-bound, treble-clef manuscript books for natural trumpets and/or horns in the collections of the Moravian Music

Foundation. Although the approximate date assigned to these two books is 1780, the contents—about forty chorales and many short minuets, polonaises, and marches—suggest their use a decade earlier when singled out by the church elders.[10] Thus the Moravians may have registered another of their many firsts in the history of American music: the germ of a modest trumpet-horn group (possibly more than one to a part) playing some of the earliest, if not the earliest, so-called "band" pieces in this country. These single-page, secular tunes no doubt proved to be a diversion for the players, if not for the community at large.

Sometime during this period, two collections of a more distinctive genre of brass music, certainly more advanced in many ways than that of the trumpet/horn books, found their way to Salem. These provide additional insights into contemporary practice and taste. The first is a group of eight, Baroque-type sonatas for two natural trumpets and two trombones. In the hand of an unknown copyist, these works are identified only by a small superscription on page one of the first trumpet part: "*8 Sonaten die Weber.*"[11]

A more startling discovery of this period, no doubt of later vintage, are six pre-classical sonatas for the unique choir of soprano, alto, tenor, and bass trombones! As with the Weber pieces, the composer and copyist remain unidentified except for a superscription in the upper right-hand corner of the soprano part to Sonata No. 1: "*6 Sonaten auf Posaunen die Cruse.*"[12] If the sonatas of Weber and Cruse pose intriguing questions as to their composers and origins, one thing is fairly certain: they underscore the idea that the performance of secular music was at least capturing the interest of the brass players, if not a segment of the townsfolk.

A number of late-eighteenth-century records, including various receipts, reveals the constant arrival at Salem of personnel, instruments, music, and accessories from Europe and the Pennsylvania settlements. One document is a detailed statement of items ordered from Germany in 1783 and received in 1785. An intriguing thought is that the listing of "Trombone sonatas and 2 horn books," priced at £2.20, might include either the Weber or Cruse compositions. This shipment received notice in the Salem diary entry for October 26, 1785, which stated that "several wagons arrived from Charleston [S.C.] and we finally received the box of musical instruments which have

Left: "Tromba Primo" of Sonata No. 1, *8 Sonaten die Weber. Right:* "Discant" (trombone) of Sonata No. 1, *6 Sonaten auf Posaunen die Cruse.* (Both images courtesy of the Moravian Music Foundation.)

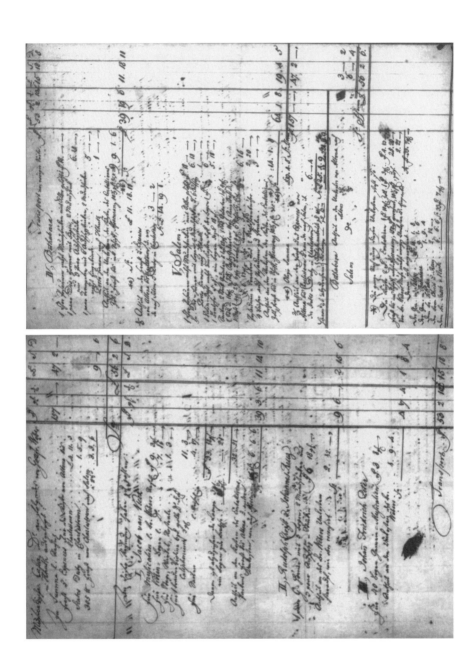

Musical Bill paid by Gottfr[ied] Weber in Herrnhut [ca. 1785]. . . .
     I. Jacob van Vleck. . . .
     II. Rudolph Crist and Johannes Reuz
1 pair of G horns with 3 crooks, 2 mouthpieces and 3 pairs
of mouthpiece [tuning bits?]. . . .   £ 6.18.___,
     III. Johan Friedrich Peter. . . .
     IV. Bethabara
1 choir of trombones with silverplated mouthpieces   18.___.___,
1 pair of D# [E-flat] horns with crooks, 2 mouthpieces and   6.___.___,
3 pairs of mouthpiece [bits?]
1 pair of trumpets with 6 mouthpiece [bits?], 2 mouthpieces
together with wrapping [probably separately packed]. . . .
                                             5.___.___.

     V. Salem
1 choir of trombones with silverplated mouthpieces   18.___.___,
1 pair of D# [E-flat] horns with crooks, 2 mouthpieces and 6
mouthpiece [bits?]. . . .   6.___.___,
Trombone sonatas and 2 horn books   2.___.___,
4 chorale books for trombones. . . .   3.___.___.

Left: Account for Moravian music order, ca. 1785, submitted by Gottfried Weber, Herrnhut, Germany. From a miscellaneous collection of accounts and receipts in the archives of the Moravian Music Foundation. (Image courtesy of the Moravian Music Foundation.) *Above*: Author's translation of portions of the Weber account pertaining to wind instruments and music billed to Bethabara, Salem congregation, and the two individuals, Crist (primarily a hornist) and Reuz (trombonist). Some personal property was allowed to Salem Moravians during this period.

been waiting for an opportunity of shipment for some time."[13] A general subscription provided funds for all items except those purchased by individuals. The contribution by Salem exceeded its share of the total order by £2.[14]

    Little time was wasted in pressing Salem's new instruments into service. An ensemble of trumpets, horns, and *two* choirs of trombones announced the Festal Day of November 13, 1785.[15] Representing perhaps the largest group of brass instruments to perform in an American Moravian settlement, the instrumentation probably included at least eight trombones, four trumpets, and four horns.

Eighteenth-century natural horn in E-flat with decorative inscription by the maker, "Johann Joseph Schmied machts in Pfaffendorff 1784." From the Collection of the Wachovia Historical Society. (Image courtesy of Old Salem, Inc., Winston-Salem, N.C.)

With the acquisition of trombones for Bethania on January 16, 1790, the three principal congregations in North Carolina apparently were supplied with four complete sets of these instruments: two at Salem, and one each at Bethabara and Bethania.[16] If one adds to these a conservative estimate of eight trumpets and horns—two of each in Bethabara and the same in Salem—the available brasses in Wachovia may have numbered at least twenty-four by the close of the century.

Trumpets and horns received little or no mention in the church diaries during the last two decades of the century; at the same time, significantly, trombones and organs became the principal instruments of the Church and, therefore, received primary notice. Information on the natural or valveless instruments derives from a miscellanea of official accounts dating from the mid-eighties. These indicate the arrival of trumpets, horns, and a few strings. By 1788, Salem reputedly had the embryonic orchestral nucleus of "at least three

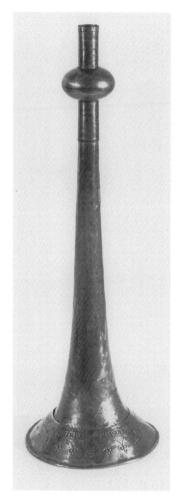

Left: Eighteenth-century natural trumpet, inscribed by its maker, "Johann Joseph Schmied machts in Pfaffendorff 1784." From the Collection of the Wachovia Historical Society. *Inset*: Close-up view of decorative rim inscription. (Images courtesy of Old Salem, Inc.)

violins, a viola, a violoncello, flute, two horns, and two clarin trumpets."[17]

These modest resources marked the beginning of the *Collegium musicum Salem*, a choral-instrumental group patterned after the old German amateur music societies. The *Collegium musicum*, officially organized in 1786, had an impelling influence on the musical scene almost immediately. The community then had the means for performing many of the compositions, both manuscript copies and printed works, constantly being added to Salem's collection of anthems, oratorios, symphonies, and chamber pieces. Thus the *Collegium musicum* capped the musical activity in Salem during the last decades of the eighteenth century; it also heralded a period of unprecedented musical growth during the decades ahead.[18]

Sketch of Salem, ca. 1819–1820, from a lithograph by W. F. Neuhauser. (Image courtesy of Old Salem, Inc.)

2   *The Nineteenth Century to ca. 1860*

The dawn of the new century witnessed the constant flow into Salem of considerably more resources for making music—personnel, sheet music, instruments, and accessories. Significantly, clarinets and bassoons, the first woodwinds besides flutes, were obtained in 1805, followed by similar acquisitions shortly thereafter. With an enhanced instrumental capability, there was an increase in the performance of large secular works by the local *Collegium musicum*. Of particular interest was the acquisition of a number of *Parthien* (*Pièces d' harmonie*) calling for a basic instrumentation of two clarinets, two horns, and one or two bassoons. This ensemble and its sprightly music rapidly gained favor among the Salemites as both indoor and *al fresco* entertainment at a time when the eighteenth-century genus in Europe was in its eventide. An intriguing thought is that the performance of these classical miniatures by the Moravians may have prolonged the life of the esteemed woodwind divertimenti well into the nineteenth century, at least in America. This brings to mind another interesting thought: was there a time during these years when this ensemble also served as the community "band?" Of course there was no military connection, but the group at least mirrored the instrumentation (minus a drum) and, to a degree, the function of its military antecedents: the small eighteenth-century European ensembles and the more recently formed United States Marine Band.

The Church's negative attitude toward the performance of secular music, notwithstanding the increasing signs of moderation, is nevertheless reflected in official records of the period. These practically ignore such performances, especially those of the *Collegium musicum*.

On the other hand, certain references indicate a separate group then serving more nearly as a medium of social utility and interest. This group appears to have included, on occasion, the revered trombone.

With the surging currents of early-nineteenth-century secularism effecting radical changes in almost every phase of Moravian life, nowhere was this more readily apparent than in the local music scene. The high tide of Salem's musical culture, as revealed especially in the secular performances of the *Collegium musicum*, devolved more into the popular fare of the day, a crowd-pleasing plethora of martial music, operatic airs, and overtures.

As the line of demarcation between sacred and secular musical performances became more pronounced, an increasing distinction between the religious and temporal functions of wind instruments became more clearly defined. The functional distinction failed to hold when it came to the matter of personnel for a simple reason: the musicians, because of their instrumental versatility, "crossed lines" when it came to performing. For example, it was not at all unusual for a trombone player to appear with the church wind choir at some religious observance and, later that day, reappear in concert on trumpet or as a cellist with the *Collegium musicum* orchestra.

The restoration of peace following the War of 1812 was an occasion for rejoicing by North Carolina Moravians. On July 19, 1814, following the celebration of the Fourth, the Church admonished the younger generation for excessive exuberance, a definite sign of things to come:

Disapproval is expressed concerning the behaviour of certain of the younger people on the fourth of this month, who made a noise by shooting in the Square and out of the Brothers House. In addition they have repeatedly occupied themselves with marching, soldier fashion, with drum and fife, near the town and in the evening, which must be considered disorder and must be suppressed so far as possible.[1]

Although there was an expression of displeasure, it was mild compared to what such "antics" would have evoked just a few years earlier. A more conciliatory attitude might be considered to have been in the wind by the following year. If so, what a difference a year made! A report for March 1, 1815, stated that the musicians did not fail to increase the rejoicing by playing appropriate melodies on the wind instruments, as they marched all over the town; then they stopped on the green Square in front of the chief buildings where most of the Brn. and Sr. had gathered, and there in a true spirit of brotherly love and genuine thankfulness to the Lord they sang "Now thank we all our God." . . . Then all present joined in singing a number of verses from the English Hymn Book, the musicians playing the accompaniment.[2]

On April 13 there is further evidence that a musical group of brasses and woodwinds possibly contributed to the growing feeling of national allegiance:

This day was noteworthy because of the solemn celebration which the President of the U.S. recommended as a festival of thanks and joy. . . . At daybreak a solemn, thankful note was sounded by the playing of stirring melodies on the trombones and other wind instruments.[3]

There is no indication of what constituted the "stirring melodies!"

Outdoor gatherings then included concerts, welcome additions to the local ambience. One major event—an occasion of even greater proportions in later years—was duly acknowledged in the official records of July 1816: "The anniversary of the Declaration of Independence was observed in Salem; and in the afternoon wind instruments were played from the church balcony and on the Square, giving pleasure to the congregation and the visitors."[4] It now seems certain that a nondescript ensemble of mixed winds assembled to perform on special occasions prior to the 1820s. Although the organization of a military band was more than a decade away, its immediate predecessor may have been a civilian group formed in 1822. On April 15 an official statement from the Church revealed that

several of our musician Brn. ask for the Collegium's permission to purchase a large drum. So far the *band* [author's italics] only comprises blowers. The Collegium could not give its permission, since we wish to avoid all matters at which people could take any offence.[5]

This brief excerpt is significant for several reasons. First, it is one of the few church records according any special attention to the practice of secular music prior to about 1835. Second, this was the first official recognition of the existence of a band. Third, in spite of increasingly strained relations between the Church and town, even a sense of independence on the part of the citizens, the influence of the former over activities of the latter was still very much in evidence. Finally, the request for a drum indicated that the musicians wished to keep pace with contemporary trends, especially those already established in the companion settlements of Pennsylvania.[6]

With the lessening of church control and support of the *Collegia musica* in Moravian communities, aesthetic ideals were, to an extent, sacrificed; musical culture soon became a pedestrian state of the art. Within this setting emerged the Salem Band, the spawn of newly imposed militia demands. The turn of events is somewhat paradoxical because the majority, if not all, of the band's personnel were also members of the *Collegium musicum* orchestra or singers.[7] Thus these same musicians, while heralding the approach of a new era, were quite literally, though unintentionally, sounding the death knell of the community's zenith of musical culture.

The early months of 1831 were a time of notable consequence in the lives of North Carolina's Moravians, a time when the Wachovia residents first felt the impact of a recent state order rescinding their coveted exemption from military service. The citizens of Salem realized that it was to their advantage to organize a volunteer militia company, complete with its own officers, regulations, and uniforms. An adjunct musical group capable of performing at company drills, parades, and special ceremonies—all to the enjoyment of the large crowds usually in attendance—was an absolute necessity. The constitution of these companion bodies, the Salem Light Infantry Company and the Military Musical Band, was the end result.

The details of the organization and activity of the two units, especially the band, were recorded for more than a decade in the previously mentioned journal of Johann Leinbach, prominent citizen-musician of Salem.[8] This is the single most important document thus far discovered that chronicles the Salem Band history for an extended period of time, from January 1831 to December 1843. This entertaining narrative truly captures the spirit of the times, an era that witnessed the emergence of a totally secular community, with its band a prominent means of musical entertainment.

Tintype of John Henry (Johann) Leinbach, ca. 1865. (Image courtesy of Old Salem, Inc.)

The following journal excerpts, unedited for the most part, provide but a glimpse of this history as it unfolded. For the sake of interest and completeness, some of the more lengthy entries appear in their entirety.

Taking special note of the situation in which the Moravians and those of other faiths found themselves following the revocation of their coveted exemption from military service, Leinbach commented on a number of town meetings in early 1831:

Jan. 12. In the evening at half past seven attended a meeting of the young men, & such of the married men as came within the grasp of the militia laws of the state, which were passed by the last legislature [first week in January], compelling the Moravians, Quakers etc. to perform military duty. The meeting was organized by calling Mr. E[manuel] Shober to the Chair, & Mr. Oppelt secretary. Not much business was transacted, except appointing a comittee of five to make enquiries as to the duties of volunter companys &c. We shall have another meeting, probably next week.

Jan. 24. At half past seven p.m. the muster company had a meeting; transacted some business & determined to hold an election for officers to morrow evening. Col. [Joseph] Winston attended also.

Jan 25. In the evening the muster company met again for the purpose of electing its officers. Mr. E. Shober & D[aniel] Welfare were run for the Captain's commission, on the first ballot Mr. Shober was elected having twenty six votes, which was a majority, Mr. Welfare had nineteen. Mr. Welfare was elected first <u>Lieutenant</u>, & Mr. P[hilip] Reich, second. Mr. Boner was elected <u>ensign</u>; adjourned at a late hour till tomorrow evening.

The body of musicians, quickly following suit, held their own meeting on January 27:

This evening the Musicians met in the school house for the purpose of forming a Military Musical Band. I had the honour of being called to the Chair, & [August Heinrich] Shultz acted as secretary. After considerable conversation we arranged matters to the best of our understanding; at the conclusion we proceeded to elect a Captain of the Band, when, contrary to my wishes, the company thought proper to elect me as the leader, for which, I told them, I owed them <u>no</u> thanks. I did not desire the honour of being Captain of the Band. I think it of right belongs to the first Clarionet and <u>not</u> the Flute.[9]

The next evening a band committee met to discuss the important matter of trappings for the uniforms, probably to be obtained locally. The principal order of business focused on types, availability, and

Page from the journal of John Henry (Johann) Leinbach, January 1831. (Image courtesy of the Archives of the Moravian Church.)

cost. A mark of distinction for the bands of this period was an ornate attire, and the local musicians were inclined to be in style—military caps with red ostrich plumes, bright sashes, shoulder ornaments, silver cords, and wide neckpieces. It was decided that these would be ordered from Philadelphia through Jacob Blum, the local congregation/general store manager. These Moravians considered the manner of dress essential to establishing a *military* image. Indeed, the word "military" appeared in a number of Leinbach's statements. There then seemed to be no fear of retribution from the Church for openly expressing such worldly thoughts!

With the matter of acquiring uniforms and accessories under way, the boys wasted little time in getting prepared for their role with the militia, as "in the evening [January 29] the Military Band commenced practicing in order to be able to appear in a Military shape." On the evening of February 2, the group met again and "made Military marches." A few days later there was an important afternoon meeting of the militia, at which, Leinbach noted, "Capt. Cooper drilled our Officers & some others who are desirous of acquiring a little knowledge of drilling as soon as possible." The band was not mentioned, but it would have served the members well to have attended the meeting. It would soon become obvious that drilling, particularly playing on the march, would require special attention.

Although formally organized, accoutered, and drilled as a military band, this was a civilian organization reflecting the status of most town bands of the era. Besides routine appearances with the local militia, the band began making excursions as an independent organization, but in military dress and playing customary martial airs. There was much music to be learned—for many, an entirely different style—that required rehearsing, which the band did on average about twice a week. All of these activities, plus daily business pursuits—most, if not all, bandsmen were leading businessmen and prominent in musical activities of the church and community—added up to an exacting schedule that would challenge the energy of many professionals today!

The more ambitious members, including Leinbach, devoted some time and effort toward improving skills on their respective instruments. One of the earliest such practice sessions appears to have been on February 8.

At noon to day, as several times before, myself, H. Ruede [George Heinrich Reid, b. 1812], & T[imotheus] Holder made music in my shop. T. Holder is trying to learn to beat the drum, & I think he will succeed, he appears to have a turn for it. H. Ruede is having to blow the trumpet, all for the Military Band. I hope we shall succeed.

Success appears to have been assured. In less than a month, on February 19, the townsfolk had the opportunity to see their militia and military band on parade for the first time. It was noted that they "were much <u>praised</u> for . . . <u>regularity</u>, & <u>uniform</u> appearance." There is every indication that the two units, especially the band, were well on their way to becoming featured attractions in the community. Not only local residents, but also those of other communities as well, were afforded many opportunities to see and hear "Salem's Pride" in the coming months and years.

No Independence Day celebration of the period would have been complete without its manifold of patriotic exuberance—grandiose speeches, interminable toasts, pompous military drill, and stirring martial music. July 4, 1831, was no exception. The report of activities failed to mention the band at the outset, although there is hardly any doubt about its presence. It does appear rather strange, though, that director Leinbach failed to include his group in the opening sentence:

Being the <u>great</u> day of American Independance the Salem Light Infantry company appeared for the first time in full uniform. We met soon after four oclock [A.M.] on our muster ground, fired thirteen rounds in honour of the thirteen good old States; after which we marched into town & were dismissed till eight oclock when we met again, & marched to our muster ground, where Capt. Shober & Let. Welfare spoke to the company, after which divers movements were performed, soon after nine oclock we returned to town again & were dismissed; at ten Mr. [Gotthold Benjamin] Reichel delivered a very good sermon. Soon after 1 oclock the Band had Vesper in School house, male. At three paraded again before the Male Academy, from whence we again marched to the muster ground. A large number of people having collected by this time, they crouded on us, & it [was] difficult to keep them at a proper distance; also on the muster ground they could not be induced to give way till several men were ordered to clear them off to a proper distance.

Top: Part for clarino, *General Brown's March*. *Bottom*: Trombone militaire part to the *Salem Light Infantry Grand Parade March*. Examples of marches that were probably performed in parades. (Images courtesy of the Moravian Music Foundation.)

There is little doubt that the American eagle did indeed scream in Salem on that day!

To be outfitted with the best affordable uniforms, obtained as soon as possible, was a major objective; at the same time, there was equal interest in adding to the group's instrumental resources. Receiving special mention during the following months was the acquisition of clarinets, the band's first keyed or Kent bugle, horns, a bass trombone, and a bassoon. Curiously, there is no indication, in either the written record, music, or museum pieces, of Salem having acquired the popular ophicleide and the upright, double-tubed brass bass horn (both counterparts of the keyed bugle), as well as that ineffectual oddity, the serpent.

Despite the band's busy schedule during this period, there appear to have been some "goof offs" or "soft peddlers" (the latter an expression used by members of one band in which the author served during World War II). This was cause for concern, at least for John Henry, as implied in a statement on August 29 that

this evening we had [been] appointed to make Military music, so few musicians attended however, that we abandoned the design in despair. The musicians from the lower town are continually complaining of head ache or the lax.

Within a month, however, all appears to have been back to normal as preparations were made for attending the general muster at Germanton (Germantown, approximately nine miles from Salem) on Saturday, September 24. As recorded, "the Band has been invited to attend the drill muster on Friday also, & in the evening to repair to Col. Winston's." Following the afternoon's activities, Leinbach observed that "the Spectators, & all the Officers were well pleased with the band, & we . . . were treated to wine by three different Officers." During the evening visit to the Winstons' home, a good time was had, but John Henry was not impressed with the coffee, and even less with the colonel's wife: "Col. Winston's lady is not of the first chop as I think."

Not long after the turn of the year, on January 3, 1832, Leinbach mentioned "yesterday a patent Bugle & a pair of French-horns arrived here for the Band, for which I wrote last summer already." As the bugle was an unfamiliar instrument, its player would require special instruction.

While generally applauded for their musical contribution to various events, some band members seemed to think at times that their efforts were unappreciated, that they were being treated in a manner unbefitting their status. One such occasion was the celebration of George Washington's birthday in 1832:

Feb. 22. The Salem Light Infantree [sic] company met at half past five this morning on the muster ground, ushered in the day with firing, after which we marched through town to the Tavern, where we were dismissed. The weather was too cold this morning for the musicians to make much music; we got stiff lips & finger . . . Thermometer 26. Nearly the whole company took dinner at the Tavern. . . . The company was too large to sit at the table at once, some had to wait, this lot fell to the Band; we got the skeletons of two turkees, the better part which was on them had disapeared [*sic*]. Besides we [had] beef, ham, & chicken pie, we undoubtedly had plenty to eat but every member of the band felt that he had been put at the tail of the dinner.

Not all comments in Leinbach's journal were about the band, music, or the militia. A little over a month after the above episode, an interesting tidbit appeared in the journal: "Jacob Reich wants to have a bed-fellow, by the name of Nancy Geiger." The couple was united on April 12, 1832, and had only one child—William Augustus, born July 16, 1833. "Gus," as he later came to be known, became the bass drummer for the Twenty-sixth Regimental Band during most of the group's period of service for the Confederacy.[10]

Beginning in 1833, there is a noticeable decrease in Leinbach's coverage of the band. Surprisingly, just four entries appear in the journal for that year, and only one concerns the local infantry company. On February 6 a single sentence about the musicians stated that "in the evening the band met again for the purpose of making music." A brief comment for February 22 simply mentioned "Washington's birth-day; no celebration, no, not even music. The band met, but did nothing." An even more dismal report, suggesting the possibility of some dissension in the ranks, surfaced for the biggest secular event of the year:

Jul. 4. The Salem light infantry company were cutting their shines to day again. The band rather weak, only five of the members being present. In the morning I had a little brush with C[harles] Levering, in consequence of his obstinacy.

There are no references to the band in 1834, perhaps another indication of a state of decline. Something positive must have happened to turn things around by the middle of 1835. That the group was fast gaining local acclaim is not too surprising, but the celerity with which its popularity extended to other parts of the state is quite astonishing.

May 20 was a great day in Charlotte, as crowds gathered to commemorate the signing of the historic "Mecklenburg Declaration of Independence." It was undoubtedly an occasion long remembered by the Salem bandsmen. They certainly attracted considerable attention, according to a local newspaper:

On seats higher than those of the audience and overlooking them, sat the Salem Band, who had kindly volunteered their services without reward, and who contributed in a high degree to the enjoyment of the occassion. They were gentlemen, handsomely dressed in uniform and performed with skill and ability seldom if ever witnessed so far in the interior. Those who participated in the festivities of that day will not for long time remember it without a passing thought on the fine music of the Salem Band.[11]

Writing in retrospect, Leinbach provided a more colorful, detailed description of the trip. His opening statement suggested no reason for the hiatus in the record since the pitiful state of affairs on July 4, 1834, but it appeared that a new, more active era had then begun.

I take my pen in hand to write something again after a long period. On the seventeenth of May last, the whole Salem Band left here for Charlotte, to assist with our Music at the celebration of the North Carolina Declaration of Independence. We were invited by Gen. [Thomas G.] Polk, & the people of Charlotte agreed to pay our expenses, which amounted to seventy-three dollars. We had a grande spree & were respectfully toasted. There was a public dinner, where we also made music to the toasts. Gov. [David Lowry] Swain, Senator [Willie Person] Mangum, Gen. [Duff] Green, Gen. [Joseph] Graham besides many other great bugs attended; wine was plenty, & the dinner party did not break up till dusk. On our return through Salisbury, some of the Citizens there prevailed on us to stay with them one night & give them some music; they paid our supper, nights lodging & breakfast. They were highly pleased with our music, & we with them.

A glance at some of the musical fare leaves no doubt that the musicians were then playing to and, in some cases, composing for their audiences. Selections for this particular occasion, as listed in the newspaper account, included *Hail Columbia*, *Washington's Grand March*, *General Polk's March*, "March" from *The Marriage of Figaro*, and *Governor Swain's March* (David Lowry Swain, governor of North Carolina, 1832-1835). Although not specifically mentioned, three other appropriate pieces from the band library almost certainly had a special place on the program: *Mecklenburg Grand March*, *Senator Mangum's March*, and *General Graham's March*.[12]

Providing further insight into the musical library of the period is a full-blown newspaper account of Salem's celebration of Independence Day two months later. As usual, the ever abundant, well-worn rounds of toasts were interspersed with rousing music by the band.

Left: Bugle part to *Mecklenburg Grand March*, composed for the Salem band by Johann Christian Bechler (1784–1857). *Right:* Bugle part to *General Polk's March*, another Bechler composition performed by the Salem band in Charlotte, May 20, 1835. (Images courtesy of the Moravian Music Foundation.)

Clarinet parts to marches composed by Johann Bechler to honor Gov. David Lowry Swain and Sen. Willie Person Mangum at Mecklenburg Declaration Day, 1835. (Image courtesy of the Moravian Music Foundation.)

In addition to the selections that had delighted the audiences in
Charlotte and Salisbury a few weeks earlier, a number of period
favorites were played, including *Sax Coburg's March*, "March" from
The Battle of Salamanca, *Dresden Body Guards* [*sic*], *Andrew Jackson's
March*, *Cincinnati Quickstep*, and *Home Sweet Home*.[13]

Increasingly in demand during the 1840s, the bandsmen continued
to oblige North Carolinians in fine fashion. Significantly, a change in
leadership had taken place since the visit to Charlotte in 1835, and
before a return engagement to Mecklenburg County (presumably in
Charlotte) in 1841. The new leader was Joshua Boner.[14]

Arising from this particular jaunt was the questioned propriety of
receiving monetary compensation for out-of-town appearances. The
Church Elders Conference, in particular, still harbored "misgivings
and feared possible detrimental effects might come from such
expeditions."[15] The question apparently was settled with the band's
new leader. Although the details of agreement are unknown, it
appears that the official position of the Church was becoming more
tolerant in such matters. Within a relatively short time, performances
for monetary compensation became fairly common.[16]

Notwithstanding the change in leadership—there is no indication
when this occurred—Leinbach continued to record events in his
journal for a couple of more years, resuming his story in the middle
of July 1843. The first extract is especially interesting because it
reveals at least one reason for the break in the chronology since the
Charlotte trip nearly ten years earlier. The community was
experiencing a financial depression, and John Henry's business
suffered accordingly:

I will make another attempt at keeping notice of passing events; although I
am fully concious of my inability to do the thing in a "workmanlike
manner." For the first I will notice the times, & money hard to be got at, &
after a person puts his hands on some of the needfull it is yet <u>more</u> difficult to
make it stay at home. The prospect ahead for my business is by no means
encouraging; shoemaking is completely run aground at this time; shoes have
to be sold almost at ruinous prices, & that on a long winded Cost.

The torpid state of affairs continued, according to the following
statement on September 10:

Sunday. By some unaccountable neglect I have come to this day without much trouble; last week passed away without any thing extraordinary excitement or trouble, except on Thursday, when the spirit moved the town to take the fire engine in hands & make a little display with a view to forming of a fire company, in order to get rid of military trainings.

The novel experience of being identified with the local militia had apparently lost its appeal, but making a break from the association had become more difficult than had been anticipated.

The following entry marks the end of Leinbach's remarkable record. It is significant to note that music, at least playing the flute, was apparently no longer an important avocation for him. On October 28, 1843, a simple sentence told it all: "At night went to concert, played the flute the first time in several years." But the band's history continued to be reported in other sources, and in time there appears to have been a noticeable change for the better.

Perhaps few appearances by Salem's band attracted more attention during the 1840s than Henry Clay's visit to the North Carolina capital on April 12, 1844, a stop on a political tour. An advance notice indicated a musical welcome would be extended the Whig presidential candidate by "the delightful band . . . from the staunch Whig town, Salem, Stokes County."[17] Commenting on the band's passage through Greensboro on its way to Raleigh, a news item reported that

there was a constant stream of travelers on horse back and in carriages of all descriptions passing through our town towards Raleigh for the purpose of meeting that splendid man of the times, Henry Clay. The Salem Band tarried all night at Col. Gott's Hotel and enlivened the night with a few soul-stirring tunes.[18]

The following week a reprinted account of Clay's visit, appearing in the Greensboro newspaper, implied that the occasion proved to be quite exciting for the small-town Moravians.

The last has been a glorious week. . . . As early as Wednesday evening the principal hotel (Mr. Yarborough's) was filled, and early in the day on Thursday, every house of entertainment was crowded to overflowing. . . .

But to proceed—On Friday morning the Salem Band was escorted from Mr. Litchford's Hotel (where they were entertained during their stay with us)

Salem Square in winter, 1850, from a lithograph by Elias Vogler titled, *A Winter View of the Church, Academy, etc. at Salem, N.C.* (Image courtesy of Old Salem, Inc.)

to the Capitol, where they regaled the tremendous assembly in front of the western portico with two or three most splendidly executed pieces of music. . . .

The afternoon was spent in preparations to receive Mr. Clay, who, according to the plan of arrangement, was expected to arrive on the [rail] cars at 5 o'clock. At 3 o'clock the procession formed at the tented grove and moved thence to the place of reception in the following order:

Wake [County] Cavalry,
Raleigh Guards,
Committee of Reception,
Soldiers of the Revolution,
Salem Band,
City Whig Banner,
Heads of Departments,
Intendant and Commissioners of the City,
Citizens and Visitors of the City.[19]

Implying a continuing military image, without actual drill and other distasteful activities, are various references to the Salem bandsmen throughout the 1840s. While the lively strains of their martial airs continued to please audiences, these same gems were, on occasion, the objects of deep concern to certain church leaders. Within the official administration, an interesting point of disagreement arose over the type of music to be played during examination week at Salem Female Academy. Attributing recent disorders directly to inappropriate music, the Elders Conference touched off a heated controversy with the suggestion that "instead of playing the customary military music," the bandsmen should "play more subdued pieces."[20] Quickly coming to the musicians' defense, the influential and probably partial *Aufseher Collegium* was quick to respond:

In order to improve discipline among the visitors for the examination, the Elders Conf. made the suggestion to hold English sermons during examination week in the evenings, and instead of having a military kind of music, some other music should be played—or none at all. The Collegium does not believe that the kind of music so far played during examination week had contributed to the general disorder among the visiting guests, but rather believes that the cause of the disturbances is mainly the exaggerated drinking of liquore. No music during those evenings would also be an insult to the musicians, whose only opportunity for making some extra money for the purchase of additional instruments is their playing at examination week evenings. We do not believe that the visitors will like other than military music.[21]

The church records make no further mention of the subject, which suggests that a decision was made in the band's favor. It seems all the more likely since the musicians had such strong support from this influential body of officials. With the *Aufseher Collegium* apparently on their side, the bandsmen undoubtedly had an advantage then and in the future.

The official church records offer little as a guide to what subsequently transpired in Salem Band history, even by way of the usual reprimands. Fortunately, however, we are able to pick up the historical thread by other means, primarily from newspaper reports in which there was ample coverage.

Reflecting the general trend in this country, the tonal complexion of the band had changed by 1851 from the early-century woodwinds or mixed woodwinds and brass to all brass.[22] The local newspaper report of the celebration of Washington's birthday includes the "Salem Brass Band" in the order of march for the day's parade.[23] A few months later, an account of the parade on July 4 makes special mention of "the 'Salem Brass Band,' in their splendid 'coach and four,' moving through our streets, hailed the day of Jubilee with their 'soul-stirring strains.' "[24]

During the remainder of the 1850s, newspaper coverage of music in Salem, especially that of the band, indicated a flourishing period of activity. In May 1853, the group's "eloquent strains of music" were noted at the dedication of the new Salem Lodge Hall.[25] On Washington's birthday the following year, the local citizens were reminded that "our far-famed Brass Band, is seldom ever found wanting, but generally ready to pour forth its patriotic strains on appropriate occasions, which entitles the members to special regard."[26]

Similar reports continued to indicate that the band had indeed become a fashionable medium of musical expression. As civic and social life continued to expand, demands upon the ensemble, conceivably the most active, popular musical group in the community, were greater than ever. One event in particular would seem to signal its position in the musical hierarchy; it also might have been a significant "first" for the bandsmen, sharing at least one program with a companion group of musicians in June 1857:

The long contemplated Concert of the Salem Classical Music Society, came off last Saturday evening, and was attended by a large audience, who were for several hours delighted with good music. The pieces were performed most admirably, and their music will compare with any in the South. We were glad to see that they were so well encouraged, and we hope that it will not be long before they again appear, and be again as liberally patronized, both for the object they have in view, and the fair musical taste which they are endeavoring to instill in some of the rising generation.[27]

Strangely, there is no mention of the band in this opening paragraph, but its presence is noted in the printed program that followed. Of the eleven selections listed, five were performed by the "Orchestre" and six by the "Brass Band."[28] By that time the Salem Band was in step with other bands of the era; its library was typical and included military music, as well as a potpourri of popular swill *en vogue* at the time. It was this music that found great favor with audiences, though music that, in the not-too-distant future, would sound the clarion call to arms for many of the town's citizens on the eve of a more telling period in Salem Band history.

Eastern North Carolina. Detail of "General Topographical Map. Sheet III," in George B. Davis, et al., *Atlas to Accompany the Official Records of the Union and Confederate Armies* (Washington: Government Printing Office, 1891–1895), Plate CXXXVIII.

PART TWO

THE WAR YEARS:
A CALL TO SERVICE

3 *Response to the Call: A New Way of Life*

On the eve of the Civil War, Salem and other towns throughout the country were experiencing various degrees of concern for the immediate future. From the *Memorabilia of Salem Congregation*, 1857, word came that

at this very moment the western sky is overcast with ominous clouds, and well-grounded fears intrude themselves involuntarily that they will not scatter before brother shall have lifted up sword against brother and fellow citizens shall have engaged in a fierce and bloody civil strife.[1]

These fears were realized in the spring of 1861, as the curtain lifted on this country's horrific four-year drama. The opening scene began with the Confederate attack on Fort Sumter at Charleston, South Carolina, on April 12, 1861. On May 20, North Carolina became one of the last of eleven states comprising the Confederacy.

Johnny Reb came from all walks of life and answered the call to arms for two main reasons: patriotism and thoughts of adventure—but not necessarily in that order. Regardless of his motive, the Reb was itching for a fight!

The distinction of being the first musicians from the Salem area to become Confederate bandsmen belonged to a group that enlisted in May, shortly after the beginning of hostilities. Initially they were members of the "Forsyth Grays," a unit later assigned as Company E to the Eleventh Regiment, North Carolina Volunteers, a twelve-month body, organized and mustered into service at Danville, Virginia, on June 18, 1861.[2] During the fall of 1861, North Carolina infantry regiments were renumbered to eliminate the confusion

occasioned by the double set of numbers that designated state troops
(1-10) and volunteers (1-14). On November 14, the Eleventh
Volunteers became the Twenty-first Regiment, North Carolina
Troops, and served under that banner for the remainder of the war.[3]

The early part of 1862 witnessed other significant changes that
impacted the soldiers of this command. A general order in April
affecting all troops—unpleasant for some, and downright resented by
others—stated that all twelve-month regiments would be reorganized
to serve for three years, or for the duration of the war.[4] This resulted
in a significant change for the band, still carried on the roll of
Company E. On April 28 this company and Company B were
detached from the regiment and redesignated Companies A (now
including the band) and B, respectively, of the First Battalion, North
Carolina Sharpshooters.[5] Although a separate organization, the
two-company battalion remained with the regiment until after the
battle at Winchester on May 5. It then rejoined its former brigade
under Brig. Gen. Isaac R. Trimble and served in Lt. Gen. Thomas J.
("Stonewall") Jackson's Army of the Shenandoah as it fought the
Federals up and down the valley.

Unlike the Twenty-sixth Regimental Band, whose service career
can be derived mainly from personal accounts, a history of the
"Sharpshooter Band" thus far remains scant. The names of band
personnel appear, nevertheless, with the field and staff of the new
battalion, as well as on the roster of Company A.[6]

Shifting operations of the battalion, including brief return periods
to the regiment, create much difficulty in establishing an official
assignment/duty for the band—Twenty-first Regiment or First
Battalion of Sharpshooters. There were also times when the
musicians appear to have served as a brigade band. (Julius Leinbach
mentioned this in at least one instance.) That they must have served
predominantly—perhaps even officially—with the sharpshooters,
seems to be supported for several reasons. First, the names of
bandsmen are absent on the four extant rolls of the Twenty-first
Regiment.[7] Second, a published history of the regiment fails to
mention a band.[8] Third, on one occasion a member of the band
requested that relatives in Salem send his mail directly to the First

Battalion, then located at Kinston in eastern North Carolina.[9] Finally, and most importantly, recent research gives credence to the idea that the original members of the Eleventh Volunteers became the band of the First Battalion, North Carolina Sharpshooters, after April 1862.[10] Further evidence supporting this belief may yet be found. In the meantime, we are safe in assuming that these bandsmen served both the battalion and the regiment in various ways until the war's end. One thing is certain: they continued to be known, popularly if not accurately, to their friends in the Twenty-sixth and back home as the Twenty-first Band.

Following this group of locals into service almost immediately were nine musicians, most if not all Moravians, primarily from neighboring Bethania (approximately seven miles from Salem). Enlisted at nearby Pfafftown, they joined the "Confederate Stars," a company formed in Forsyth County during July and August 1861. On October 30 this unit was mustered into state service as Company F, Thirty-third Regiment, North Carolina Troops. Upon the regiment's transfer to the Confederacy on January 9, 1862, the company was redesignated Company I and remained with the Thirty-third Regiment throughout the conflict.[11] From its inception, unlike the earlier twelve-month regiments of volunteers, the Thirty-third was a regular "war" body of troops, formed to serve at least three years or for the duration.

The writings of Oliver J. Lehman (ca. 1839-1937), prominent community bandleader and a member of the Thirty-third Band, add a personal touch to his group's wartime story. Prior to entering the service in July 1863, Lehman visited the regiment several times to assist the bandsmen. One occasion occurred after their instruments had been confiscated following the regiment's encounter with the enemy at New Bern in March 1862. Lehman stated that he was called back to Kinston in April; this time he indicated that replacement "brass instruments" were purchased at Danbury, referring perhaps to the seat of Stokes County.[12]

Several facts relating to band personnel may be gleaned from the extant official records of the regiment. For example, of the nine original members mustered into service, only four were with the seven-piece group when the regiment surrendered at Appomattox.[13]

As the fires of war burned brightly in early 1862, other Salem musicians would enter the fray to form the Twenty-sixth Regimental Band. They had witnessed their fellow musicians departing for service under the Stars and Bars; likewise, other acquaintances, Moravian and non-Moravian, touched by the first glow of patriotism after the outbreak of hostilities, were joining the ranks almost daily. Thus the constant departure of lifelong friends had, understandably, a strong emotional effect on the future Twenty-sixth "boys," an effect that might easily have been tinged with feelings of envy, to be mollified only by an exchange of Salem "civies" for Confederate gray. In contrast to the relatively quiet existence in the little Moravian community, a stretch in the army might be just the thing to add a little spice to the tedium of small-town life.

Probably no motive kindled the desire of Salem's remaining bandsmen to don a uniform more than the rising tide of war fever, inspired in part by their own music making. On numerous occasions in 1861, they were called forth to arouse the citizenry and "blow spirit" into some newly formed military company.

Capt. Kinyoun's [John H. Kenyon] Company from Yadkin County, the "Yadkin Boys," passed through this place [Winston, N.C.] on Monday evening last and encamped just beyond Salem. They were met on the Outskirts of the town by the Salem Brass Band . . . and a large number of citizens.[14]

Very often the musicians were summoned to perform for local benefits connected with the war effort. Although the following announcement failed to mention the band, its presence was almost a certainty: "On Friday, 10th September a CONCERT will be given in Salem, for the Benefit of our Forsyth Volunteers. The Ladies' Relief Society will appropriate the proceeds in a judicious manner."[15]

Something less than patriotism might be ascribed to many similar events—*propaganda*! Actually, much of what transpires in this manner during wartime is unmistakably propaganda.[16] In this regard Salem's bandsmen, while infusing spirit into their audiences, were also victims of their own music making; they not only set the mood for the crowds, but they also were stirred by their own efforts. Some were thus sufficiently primed for enlisting in early March 1862; others appear not to have been overly enthusiastic. Julius Leinbach had this to say in the prefatory remarks to his handwritten account:

> I was not wanting to shirk any duty that called me; at the same time I was not anxious to become a target for bullets fired by any one. I was open for some other engagement, and therefore, when an offer came to me to become a member of a band that was being organized in Salem, N.C., to go into service with some No. Car. regiment, I accepted, resigned the situation I had of book keeper of Haw River Mills, in Alamance Co. came home, and became one of the "Band Boys."

An added item of interest appended to these written statements is a note by John Henry Leinbach, father of Julius and, as indicated in a previous chapter, a leading figure in founding Salem's first official band in 1831. It read:

> 1862 March 5th. Today at one half past two o'clock a Brass Band left home for New Bern to enter the service of Col. Vance. The members constituting the Band were, Sam Mickey, Jos. & W. H. Hall, Aug. Hauser, Ab. Gibson, Dan Crouse, Alex Meinung & Julius A. Lineback. Edward [my son] accompanied them.[17]

There followed this postscript: "Taken from an old memorandum book of my father's. J. A. L."

In comments to the Wachovia Historical Society years later, upon reflecting on experiences related to the enlistment, Julius stated that

> Mr. S. T. Mickey had been mainly instrumental in getting up this organization, and was naturally chosen as leader or captain. He had made arrangements with Col. Z. B. Vance, of the 26th regiment, North Carolina troops, and his officers, for the band to become attached to their command as an independent band, under their pay, without being regularly enlisted. Having completed our arrangements we left Salem on March 5, 1862, our destination being Camp Branch, some four miles below New Bern on the south side of Trent river, between the railroad and Neuse river. We reached the regiment on the 7th of March, and were kindly received by the officers who took us into their tents for the first night.
>
> Next morning the ground was covered with a light coat of snow. During the day we were furnished with tents which we put up nearby the captain's, outside of the guard lines.

Samuel T. Mickey, ca. 1850s. (Image courtesy of the Moravian Music Foundation.)

Prior to the band leaving Salem, Mickey probably had made a personal reconnaissance of North Carolina troops in the Kinston area until he found a regiment for his band. This would seem logical rather than having the group leave town with high expectations of latching onto some regiment.

That Sam was successful in his search for an assignment seemingly bore fruit, but not with the Twenty-sixth Regiment. Reportedly, the band was originally headed for a battalion that was captured at the Battle of Roanoke Island in early February, a favorable quirk of fate that subsequently landed the boys in Vance's outfit.[18] The circumstances are quoted in a history of the Twenty-sixth Regiment:

> I was sitting in the lobby of the Gaston House, New Bern, when a man wearing a Colonel's uniform came in with a loaf of bread under each arm. This was Zeb Vance. I spoke to him and told him my errand. Colonel Vance replied: "You are the very man I am looking for. You represent the Salem Band. Come to my regiment at Wood's brick yard, four miles below New Bern." Next morning (March 1862), I went down to the camp, was met by Captain [Alexander H.] Horton, of Company C, and as the result of my visit, the band was engaged and at first it was paid by the officers.[19]

This passage seemingly indicates the existence of a now missing first section of the diary, or at least that the writer had access to some of Mickey's personal notes. Nevertheless, the musicians found a home and served, with a few additions in personnel, as the

The original members of the Twenty-sixth North Carolina Regimental Band on their first furlough, July–August 1862: (*left to right*) S. T. Mickey, A. P. Gibson, J. O. Hall, W. H. Hall, A. L. Hauser, D. T. Crouse, J. A. Leinbach, and James M. Fisher (substituting for the ailing A. C. Meinung). This image was reversed in the first edition. (Image courtesy of the Moravian Music Foundation.)

Twenty-sixth Regimental Band throughout the war. The original members were:

Samuel T. Mickey (leader or "Captain")	E^b cornet
A. P. Gibson	1st B^b cornet
Joe O. Hall	2nd B^b cornet (later, bass)
Augustus Hauser	1st E^b alto
William H. Hall	2nd E^b alto
Daniel T. Crouse	1st B^b tenor
Alexander C. Meinung	2nd B^b tenor
Julius A. Lineback	E^b bass (later, 2nd B^b cornet)[20]

Though small in number, the group lacked only drums to complete its relatively balanced, brass band instrumentation.[21] The omission of drums at this time is difficult to understand. Their inclusion in bands was essentially the order of the day, whether for hometown performances or as an integral part of a military unit. There is no doubt about the Moravian musicians being in tune with the times. Thus the absence of a drummer in this instance remains one of the more tantalizing puzzles of the story. Probably the Salem player was unavailable at the time or not quite ready to become a Reb. Another explanation is that the bandsmen, once established with the regiment, could not locate a capable replacement for a former member. Be that as it may, the following sequence of events is interesting.

Having gotten the musicians assigned to the Twenty-sixth Regiment, Mickey apparently canvassed other units in search of a drummer. This is revealed in the second section of his comments, which opens with two incomplete sentences. Even with critical words missing, these remarks are informative, and are included as they appear with some speculative editorial fills:

[The] Drummers [were] together, and choose a Bass [word missing] and Band. I took Daniel Hackney for [word missing] and Jos. Long then Major Drummer of [Co. I as] our Bass Drummer on trial. In a few days [ha]d to turn off the Bass Drummer, and get a better one which I soon got[;] his name was Calvin R. Boyd. Fifer of Cap[tain] Carraways [K] Company. We practiced regular every day in public road near camp, and near a house where some very nice ladies lived. Several evenings we had the pleasure of being at the house, and enjoying ourselves in plays with the young ladies; and one by the name of Miss Sallie was the beauty of the flock who appeared to be taken in with a certain Capt[ain] of the Reg[iment].

The fragmentary beginning of this excerpt reveals that Sam Mickey was probably familiar with military regulations and knew that the best source for locating a drummer was no doubt one of the infantry companies nearby. Each would normally have had, if not a band, at least its own field musicians—a drummer and a fifer.[22] Mickey might even be so lucky as to locate his man in a drum pool or corps.

The names of Hackney, Long, and Boyd, curiously, never appear in Leinbach's account, and their mention by Mickey indicates that at least something was being done toward acquiring a drummer for the band. Although the attempt appears to have been fruitless, the subject is interesting and adds to the mystery of the drum situation—even to this time. At any rate, regardless of who was chosen, his service was at best short-lived.[23]

Prior to leaving Salem, whether as a unit or individually, the boys packed as many luxuries as possible, including "a mess-chest . . . in which were various light cooking utensils, . . . bedticks, . . . blankets and quilts a camp stool apiece, etc." In addition to this array of household necessities, each member had his musical instrument, perhaps the most treasured possession.

In an effort to provide themselves with all the physical comforts of home, the bandsmen gave special attention to their "military" dress—uniforms made from "Fries best cadet jeans, with brass buttons."[24] The Salem Rebs could have shown no more pride in their appearance had they been decked out in the elegant trappings prescribed by Confederate army regulations.[25] Nevertheless, their irregularity of uniform followed the pattern of many Johnnies throughout the Confederacy. Deviation in the soldiers' manner of dress seemed the rule rather than the exception.[26] This situation is more readily understood when we consider that the twelve-month enlistees in volunteer regiments were expected to provide their own uniforms.[27]

On March 7, according to Leinbach, the band reached the regiment, then encamped about four miles southeast of New Bern "on the south side of Trent river, between the railroad and Neuse River." A cordial welcome, mentioned by Leinbach, included an invitation to share the officers' tents that first night. This friendly relationship between officers and band continued throughout the war and was evident on numerous occasions. Mickey wrote that

we reached Newbern [sic], and about dark we arrived at Camp Branch; which was 4 miles below Newbern near Woods Brick yard. The first evening in Camp, we played Slumber Polka [author's italics] and etc. and while playing we had almost [all] in the Regiment around us. Mr. E[dward] W. Lein[bach] [made] the trip with us, but did not intend to remain. The first night we were in Camp it [snowed].

An immediate challenge was learning to play while on the march—shades of a problem with the band's predecessor of the 1830s! Many military bandsmen will agree that this can be quite a frustrating, if not distasteful, experience. It was something the Salem boys mastered only after long hours of practice that obviously produced many amusing results, as indicated by Julius:

One of the most difficult acquirements was to keep step as we marched up and down the lines at dress parade. Our natural gaits were very dissimilar, and, as our attention must necessarily be given closely to our music, we would sometimes forget our feet and they would naturally go at their own accustomed gait, until one or the other of us would suddenly discover that he had lost step. The parade grounds were sometimes imperfectly cleared of all stumps and runners or inequalities of surface, so that now and again some unsuspecting musician would encounter a snag, or his foot would go into a hole, causing him to execute maneuvers not laid down in Hardee's [Infantry] Tactics. However, we drilled ourselves in marching and countermarching, and gradually acquired the art of dividing our attention between music, feet and the ground.

The lighthearted frame of mind with which the Salem musicians entered the army was quickly dispelled in the late afternoon of March 12, when word was received in camp that the enemy had landed an amphibious force about seventeen miles below New Bern and was advancing northwesterly along the Neuse River in the direction of Camp Branch. The next morning, Vance's men

Slumber Polka, played by the Salem band its first night in the camp of the Twenty-sixth North Carolina Regiment in March 1862. (Image courtesy of the Moravian Music Foundation.)

assembled into line quickly to the long roll of company drums. As the band played them off, the troops left to engage the approaching enemy. Leinbach stated that they "had not expected to so soon run up against the serious side of army life, and heartily wished that the disturbing element had kept quiet some time longer." Fears mounted, he reported, when word was received that a large enemy contingent was advancing on land "while the gunboats were coming up the river, shelling the woods as they advanced." With cannon booming as the forces clashed at the breastworks about six miles below New Bern, the musicians realized for the first time that this was war indeed!

Overwhelmed by superior numbers, the Confederates, including Vance and most of the Twenty-sixth Regiment, began a retreat that would eventually take them to Kinston, about forty miles to the west. During all of the confusion, instructions were received from the regiment for the band to "put the officers' baggage on the train, take it to New Bern and there await further orders." Now aware that their troops were in full retreat, Leinbach stated that

we were only too glad to obey the orders we had received, and accordingly put the officers' and our own baggage on the train, went with it across the river to New Bern, and stored it in the railroad depot.

We could hear the sound of the heavy guns, but knew nothing of the state of affairs across the river.

Next morning the unwelcome sound of cannonading greeted our ears, continuing all the forenoon. And after a time we were startled by seeing the railroad and county bridges in flames. We knew that this indicated disaster to our forces. The bridge had been fired by citizens to prevent the enemy from crossing the river. We knew that our regiment either had been captured or was retreating up the south bank of the Trent river.

There was great excitement in the city. Citizens were flocking to the station; train after train was run up the road.

In all the confusion of preparing to depart, the band boys finally boarded a flatcar, supposedly about to leave. Not surprisingly, they and the rest of the troops then played the old army game of "Hurry up and wait!" Expressions of impatience and frustration included "Why don't the train start?" and "I wish they would hurry up." No doubt there were other outbursts best not repeated. All of the delay afforded the opportunity for Julius and his companions to make several trips to the station for their belongings. He stated that

we succeeded in getting on board nearly everything that we had in charge, our mess-chest and instrument cases being all of our own property that we left. . . .

At length the train moved off, greatly to our relief. After going a few miles the train stopped for wood and water, the engineer not having taken time to supply his engine before starting. We did not know what to do nor where to stop and so remained on the train until it reached the end of its run to Goldsboro.

Here we found a place to store our baggage until we could hear something from our regiment and know what to do with it and ourselves. We knew, of course, that New Bern had fallen into the hands of the enemy.

We remained in Goldsboro a couple of days and then went back to Kinston, expecting that whatever troops had escaped being killed or captured would be most likely to strike the railroad at that point.

Sam Mickey, though not as descriptive of the existing confusion, included some interesting details on the arrival at Goldsboro and subsequent return to Kinston.

We left New [Bern] about noon and reached Goldsboro about Dusk where we left the Baggage that was in our charge, and took up Quarter's [sic] in Charles Parmelee's tin shop, and remained in Goldsboro, until, the 16th and arrived at Kinston about dark and put up in a small room at Stevenson's Hotel; room was about, 8 x 10[;] we heard the news that our Regiment had made their escape, and were coming up by the way of Trenton. Sunday morning the 17th we heard that Col. Vance's regiment was near the town, and we immediately got our Instruments, and marched out to escort them in. When we met them we found them very much fatigued from their March, and heard that the Regiment lost 12 killed[,] wounded and taken prisoners. Major [Abner B.] Carmichael was killed behind the Breastworks, and several drowned in trying to swim a creek. The Col had his hand somewhat bruised; and was not able to use it for some time. We marched in[to] Kingston [sic] playing.[28]

Almost immediately the entire command was organized into brigades. The situation appeared somewhat stable, and Kinston would be the general area of operations for the troops. Leinbach reported that "the other regiments of this command having settled down too, brigade review was had soon after, and our band, being the only one in the brigade, played for the first time on such an occasion." In the absence of any action for the troops at this time, reviews became rather common and required the band's presence. Other performances, of which there were a number, would prove to be less taxing and no doubt more enjoyable.

One of the more significant occasions for the bandsmen was playing their time-honored chorales on Easter Sunday, April 20. The Moravian tradition of ushering in the Day of Resurrection at an early hour probably caused considerable comment among the troops, particularly those to whom the realm of Morpheus seemed more inviting. In addition to this special observance, the band played many times for various camp church services during its army career. These musical calls to worship were very much welcomed by the chaplains in their efforts to combat the spiritual indifference that beset a large number of the Confederate soldiery. Many Southern soldiers who had been active in church life before the war were becoming increasingly apathetic toward matters of religion.[29] In contrast, the Moravian attitude simply reflected the essence of a long-standing, deeply imbedded expression of faith.

An order received in Kinston about April 21 stated that all twelve-month regiments would henceforth serve for at least three years or for the duration of the war, one of many major developments affecting the fortunes of the various regiments, including the Twenty-sixth and its band. Many men throughout the command were counting on returning home and had to be coaxed into remaining in uniform. At this point Vance and his band rose to the occasion. The colonel, a political stump-speaker of no little renown, was just the right person to head up a campaign for encouraging reluctant Rebs to reenlist. When he requested the band to join him on this mission, there was a ready response. This proved to be one of the more enjoyable times for the musicians; they felt flattered, said Leinbach, "and consented to blow as much war spirit into the men as we could." One such occasion was singled out by Mickey:

Col. Vance and the Band were requested to visit the 27th Reg. Camp, N.C. T[roops,] Col. Sloan's Reg. Col. Vance made a speech, and explained, and gave his views about the state of the Country, and urged them to remain in the army and fight for the South and etc. after the speech we played some and returned to Camp. This Camp was Camp Rest; but the Band did not have much rest as we had much blowing.

Although the leader's record is sketchy at this point, sections indicate that some interesting sidelights were taking place. One note concerning personal hygiene can be appreciated by any soldier who has spent an extended time in the field, whether on maneuvers or in combat. The situation in this case indicated that the uniforms were evidently becoming fairly rancid. Mickey stated that they no "doubt would [give] us trouble if we should have worn them longer; we did not rest untill [sic] all the Clothes were Boiled and were shed of them." Continuing with more pleasing subject matter, he stated at length that

Col. Vance's wife came on a visit to the Reg, and while with us we went up to the Col's Quarters which was a tolerable good house, and gave his wife a serenade, after which we received an introduction to her. We practiced in a pine grove a short distance from Camp, and while at this camp we practiced *Col. Kirklands March* [author's italics], and practiced marching to Waltzes. After practicing, one day one of the Capt's invited some [of] us to his tent, after which some of us were <u>resting</u> and etc. The old field seemed to be most too hot and disagreeable, and we moved over to a nice pine grove. At the Camp we were thrown out in the sun where it was too hot for us, and by permission of the Col., we moved our tent outside the Guard lines in rear of Field and staff. Gen. [Robert] Ransom was very strict and kept all the men in Camp unless they had business to attend to which called them away and while he was our Gen. a great many letters came through from Newbern [sic] by flag of truce, and some were German[,] Danish etc. He found out that A[lexander] Meinung could translate the German letters and often sent for him at such times. While here . . . O[liver] Lehman came down and spent one day with us, and helped us eat some fresh shad which were caught in the Neuse River. We had not been in this camp long before, one man had the misfortune to shoot himself in the arm which was amputated; and one opening [evening?] while 2 were eating Supper, one struck the other under the chin, and knocked him down, and [he] died in a few minutes, and no one knows whether the fall or the fist that struck him killed him.

There followed what seems to have been a rather common occurrence in the Confederate ranks. Many women would cut their hair and make obvious physical alterations to appear as men, in order to serve with husbands or boyfriends, or as camp tagalongs. In some cases, the deceit would last for long periods of time before being discovered. Sam Mickey mentioned one such instance in the Twenty-sixth Regiment: "For 2 weeks we had a Female Soldier [in] camp and as soon as her Husband was discharged she applied for a discharge but did not succeed until she made herself known her name was Blaylock." A slightly different version was given by Leinbach, who indicated a much longer time for the sham.

Amongst the new recruits coming to our regiment were two young persons from Caldwell county by the name of Blalock, who called themselves brothers. For some time they did full military duty in a satisfactory manner.

March composed by Edward W. Leinbach to honor Col. William W. Kirkland, who led the Twenty-first N.C. Regiment before succeeding to command of Pettigrew's brigade after Gettysburg. (Image courtesy of the Moravian Music Foundation.)

After a couple of months one of them showed such symptoms of its health that he was discharged from service. It then developed that the supposed brother was a woman and the wife of the other. Of course she was discharged also.

A brief excerpt from Walter Clark's regimental history stated that "a man and wife, L. M. (Keith) Blalock and his supposedly brother,

Samuel, were enlisted in the 26th for a time without the woman's identity being found out."[30]

About this time (April 20), Mickey noted that the band was near the First Cavalry Regiment of North Carolina Troops, who

had a Brass Band, from whom we got *Annie Laurie Medley, Band March, Be Kind to the Loved Ones at Home* and *Cottage by the Sea* [author's italics]. . . . We had several Reviews, and one Day had a Review twice . . . and one evening we gave General Ransom a Serenade at his Quarters, and after playing his favorite Marseilles, he made a short address and thanked us kindly for the Serenade. Another evening we had permission to go to a House near Camp and take Supper which had been prepared for us, after supper we passed off the time in the yard playing some pieces for the family.

Mickey stated that "the first payment we received from Regt. was the 3d of May." (Initially, payment of the band had been the contractual responsibility of the regimental officers.) A second payment by the regiment was made on May 10 while the unit was stationed temporarily at Camp Magruder, about a mile from Kinston. Having been paid only a week earlier, the bandsmen and the troops no doubt experienced quite a surprise at becoming so affluent in this short span of time! (Leinbach failed to mention either payment.)

Encamped near Kinston for several weeks, Leinbach thought it was "perhaps the most pleasant time of all our army life, though it must be confessed that it was rather indolent in character." Food was plentiful and, most importantly, the band had several opportunities to display its musical talents in a tranquil setting. He added that "our relations with the officers were of the most cordial nature, our duties were light, and we were under very little restraint." He described the ambient setting:

The opening spring season was most delightful. The woods and fields were bright and odorous with flowers, many of them new to us. The wild crabapple with its pink and white blossoms, with other flowering shrubs, made the woods seem almost like a garden, while the snow-white bloom of the baytree, or bastard magnolia as it was sometimes called, filled the air with a fragrance that we had never known before.

Even in this relaxed state, the Twenty-sixth Band, the only one in the brigade, appears to have had a full schedule playing for reviews and reenlistment tours with Vance to the regiments, and providing numerous serenades for the men of various commands. Julius stated that "nearly every evening there would come out to our camp numbers of ladies and gentlemen from Kinston, and we were vain enough to imagine that our music was a large part of the attraction for them." Consequently, he continued, "while here, we conceived the idea of giving concerts in Kinston, and being encouraged in it and having the consent of Colonel Vance and General Ransom, we made arrangements to do so in the not quite finished Methodist church." The series was intended for both citizens and soldiers and was set for the evenings of May 16, 17, and 18. The following account indicates that the concerts were not only very popular with the large audiences, but also gratifying, and some very lucrative, for the performers as well:

On the first night the house was filled to its utmost capacity, while a great many soldiers were unable to gain entrance. There was considerable disturbance. A guard was unable to control the crowd until Col. Mat[t] Ransom, of the 35th regiment, went out and ordered the men to their quarters, telling them that the concert would be repeated, and that they should all have an opportunity to hear it. After this there was no further trouble.

Those concerts netted $420.65 which sum was equally divided between the six regimental and the brigade hospitals.

According to Mickey, "the first night we played, Mr. E[dward] A. Brietz assisted us by playing B flat cornet; he came down [from Salem] on a [?] and on the 17th left." In addition to "a crowded house the first night [there were] about 12 or 1500 outside that could not get in." After the unruly crowd was under control,

we opened with a National [?] Air, and performed for several hours. We performed 3 nights; and the proceeds of the 3 nights perform[ance] was between $450.00 and $500.00; the expenses we had were very light, and $420.00 we presented to the Hospitals of the Brigade; there were 6 Regimental Hospitals and one General Hospital. The last night's Concert a great many ladies were in . . . owing to the heavy rain, after we had finished our programme, we played some more pieces, and had vocal music. . . . After the Concerts Julius Transou joined our band, and played 3d E flat Cornet. After the heavy rains, we had fine weather and of a moon light night we would go up to Kinston and Serenade the young ladies, and often Serenaded Gen Ransom whose quarters were on the road.

Leinbach failed to mention the brief visit by their friend Brietz, but he stated that "about this time our number was increased by the arrival of Julius A. Transou, of Pfafftown, who played leading cornet for awhile and later became our solo alto player." That the new member played 3d E-flat cornet, as Mickey stated, seems questionable, primarily because the sets of original band books fail to include this part in the group's instrumentation.

While the Salem musicians were thus enjoying themselves, they were probably unaware that, less than thirty miles away in Yankee-occupied New Bern, "Billy Yank" was not lacking in high quality musical entertainment. The Twenty-fourth Massachusetts Regiment boasted one of the best bands in the country.[31] This truly superb musical group played under the direction of none other than Patrick Sarsfield Gilmore.[32] The high esteem with which Gilmore and his band were regarded was expressed by one Union soldier, who wrote:

I don't know what we should have done without our band. It is acknowledged by everyone to be the best in the division. Every night about sun down Gilmore gives us a splendid concert, playing selections from the operas and some very pretty marches, quick-steps, waltzes and the like, most of which are composed by himself or by Zohler, a member of his band. . . . Thus you see we get a great deal of *new* music, notwithstanding we are off here in the woods. Gilmore used to give some of the fashionable concerts we had at home and we lack nothing but the stringed instruments now. In their place however we have five reed instruments, of which no other band can boast.[33]

Even on the edge of battle, this flamboyant Irish bandmaster brought the height of entertainment to the troops until his regiment, a twelve-month organization, was mustered out of service in August 1862.

Much of the time the Twenty-sixth Regiment and band were located in a swampy area with most disagreeable weather. Yet unlike many of their fellow soldiers, the bandsmen had thus far remained fairly healthy. Mickey's opening words in the following excerpt, unknowingly, contained a warning of conditions to come:

Alexander Meinung was taken sick at Camp, and after we advised him to go to a private Boarding house in Kinston, he went to a Mrs. Dunn; who paid very good attention to him, and nursed him well, and would not receive any pay for her trouble. All the boys enjoyed tolerable good health at this camp, and fared tolerably well, we sometimes had Chicken, and Mutton, and never ate our rations of Flour, and sold a Barrell while at this Camp. We had very hot weather, and after I had performed my duty, I rode over to 2nd N.C. Cavalry Camp and taught that Band to play several pieces of Music for which I received but little pay.

In commenting on the general combat situation, Leinbach had this to say:

Since the Federal forces had captured New Bern they seemed to be satisfied for the time being, and made no further demonstration in North Carolina.

Our camp life therefore was a quiet one, and the men became restive and anxious for more active and exciting occupation than the double daily drill and dress parade afforded, and often expressed the wish that they had something more to do.

The wish became a reality in a very short time. As part of upcoming operations, the troops were transferred to Camp Johnson about eight miles above Kinston. They were there for just a few days. On June 20 an order was received to begin moving toward Petersburg and the immediate defense of Richmond. Vance addressed his regiment: "Fellow soldiers, it gives me pleasure to announce to you that we will leave for Richmond, Va., tomorrow morning by daylight to take part in the vital struggle now pending before its walls, etc." Mickey described leaving Camp Johnson:

The 20th of June we left our Camp and marched out to the Rail road, and waited for the train; and when it came, only 8 Companies could get on, and the other 2 were left behind. We left, Camp Johnson about 9 o'clock in the morning, and about 11 o'clock we were on the train travelling towards Goldsboro; and when we reached Goldsboro the Band struck up on *Luto Quick Step* [author's italics] and when opposite the Griswold Hotel the train run off the track, and the car before us broke down, and Abe Gibson in attempting to jump out of one of the Windows almost ruined his instrument; which he had in his hand, and hit the first valve against the Car. We had to remain here for several hours, and while there I worked on Abe Gibson's instrument in C. Parmalee's shop until I got the valve to work.

The train was overloaded and, after several breakdowns, reached Petersburg after dark the next day. As the troops were marched off to bivouac in a nearby market, the band and several officers spent the

The *Luto Quickstep*, part for the E-flat cornet. (Image courtesy of the Moravian Music Foundation.)

night in a local hotel. This was a luxury not to be enjoyed much longer, as the privations of war became increasingly worse. The next morning the Twenty-sixth Regiment, headed by its band, marched through town, crossed the Appomattox River on the Pocahontas Bridge and made camp at Dunn's Hill on the outskirts of Petersburg. While there, Mickey "heard some good music by the 20th Virginia Band which was in sight of our Camp." Although the stay at this location was brief, it made a good impression on Sam, who stated that

we had plenty to eat, . . . and a great many Darkies would come out with Baskets full of pies and etc, and buckets of Milk, and as long as we have money it generally is spent for some thing good to eat. We had splendid Water while here, and were near a splendid Dwelling House which had a splendid yard before it with magnificent shade trees under which some of us would spend our time during the heat of the day; and one day some of the men behaved very badly, and all that were in the yard were taken up before Col. [Vance?] and 2 of our Band were in the crowd of "prisoners" [author's quotes].

During this brief stay several new North Carolina units were added to Robert Ransom's brigade.[34] Only just settled in, the troops

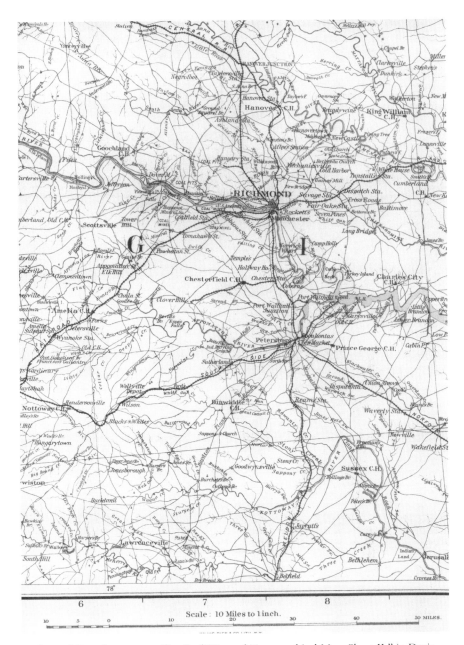

Richmond–Petersburg sector. Detail of "General Topographical Map. Sheet II," in Davis, *Atlas to Accompany the Official Records*, Plate CXXXVII.

received orders to start for Richmond. They left Petersburg about
10:00 P.M. on June 24 and arrived at the capital soon after midnight.
Leinbach picked up the story:

We marched through the city trying to play several pieces, not doing
ourselves much credit thereby, as some of the boys were not very good at
memorizing music and therefore could not play much without notes.

We went to the capitol square. Here we were halted and, as we thought,
waited to be taken to some quarters to spend the rest of the night. No
invitation came. . . .

With a deep sense of personal injury at the thought of sleeping out of
doors without even a fly to keep off the dew, we tried to make the best of a
bad situation, rolled ourselves in our blankets and lay down on the grass to get
what sleep we could.

Sam Mickey's account of the move included a little more detail:

Monday evening we received orders for Richmond; Teausday [*sic*] morning
early we left camp for Richmond Depot and did not get off until late in the
Afternoon. A[lex] Meinung remained at Petersburg as he was unable to make
the trip. When we reached the city of Richmond, Abe Gibson lost his mouth
piece, and had it not been dark we may have found it in the Car we were in.
Going through the city we played the *Salem Grand March* [author's italics]
until we reached the square, where (the band) slept the first night without
tents. Early in the morning we were aroused from our slumber by the long
roll, and as day was breaking we saw that there was more than one Reg. In the
Square We marched out main Street . . . blowing with our knapsacks on our
backs; and when we were out of the city we were thankful that we did not
have to play again with our Burden upon our Backs. We marched about 5
miles from the city.

Before moving on, the band and part of the regiment halted and
awaited further orders. The sound of cannon fire in the distance was
disconcerting and suggested major action ahead. The bandsmen were
told to not be alarmed, that this was not at all unusual. Perhaps not,
but having already been introduced to cannonading and its results in
eastern North Carolina soon after entering service, the boys from
Salem regarded these sounds as a portent of coming events—and
soon! Again quoting Leinbach:

At length orders came for our regiment to move forward to the breastworks,
a portion of our brigade having arrived some time before us and being already
in position and in the fight.

Possibly the music for the *Salem Grand March*, composed for the Twenty-sixth Regimental Band by Amelia A. Van Vleck. (Image courtesy of the Moravian Music Foundation.)

Our men marched off while we played "Marseilles" with seven pieces, Meinung having remained at the hospital at Petersburg, and one of our leaders [Abe Gibson] having lost his mouthpiece in the confusion last night.

Our colonel instructed us to remain with the surgeon at his quarters. Soon after the regiment had gone, wounded men from the other commands began to pass by on foot, most of them being wounded in the hand or arm, some few in the head. A little later ambulances came on with the more severly [sic] wounded. Our regiment did not get into this action the first day, but was put on picket duty that night. . . .

When the wounded from our brigade began to come in, we assisted the surgeon in every way we could.

A quick conversion from "windjammers" to "pillrollers" might describe the transformation to an entirely new role for the Salem musicians. There was no time for music making as the battle casualties began to mount. The Confederate troops kept pressure on the retreating enemy, and as the intensity level of fighting increased, so did the need for more medical attention, some of which proved rather unpleasant.

In describing the next day's activities as medics, Julius supplied this account:

We came within hearing of heavy cannonading, about 4 o'clock in the afternoon, and in another hour came to the last temporary hospital of our troops. Here the slightly wounded had their hurts dressed and were sent on foot towards Richmond, where the more severely injured were kept until it came their turn to be hauled in ambulances.

We at once went to work helping the [brigade] surgeons, having by this time gained some little experience in dressing slight wounds as well as helping the surgeons with more serious cases, such as amputations, etc. We carried wood and water, too, kept up the fires and fed the helpless wounded. Almost the entire night was thus spent and we got but little rest.

On Tuesday, July 1, 1862, the Battle of Malvern Hill, last action of the weeklong struggle known as the Seven Days Battle, was fought. In Leinbach's words, "the battle having moved still farther forward, we carried the helpless wounded men into a house and made them as comfortable as possible before following our men as was our duty to do." The account of the day's events continued on the lighter side, with an oft-repeated, perhaps apocryphal, tale about one of the colonel's remarks:

As the line was moving forward at one time a rabbit was flushed, and as it went bounding off amid the yells of the men, Colonel Vance exclaimed: "Go it, Mollie Cottontail; if it wasn't for these shoulder straps I'd be with you!"

During the next couple of days, the intensity of fighting gradually abated, and the Yanks were unquestionably on the run! As they fell back to their gunboats on the James River, they left a scene of almost total disaster: dead men and horses, knapsacks, and many personal items of value scattered everywhere in sight. One semblance of order was the well-constructed system of breastworks, abandoned by the enemy while hastily evacuating his position. This was quite unexpected and difficult for Sam Mickey to understand: "We were surprised to see that the Yankees had left there [sic] strong fortifications." Other sights, some quite vivid and gruesome, no doubt left lasting impressions on the Moravian bandleader and his friends:

It was a horrid looking sight as we were going along seeing some men only half buried and but little dirt thrown on some of them. At these Breastworks we halted and found many valuable articles, knapsacks etc. which we helped ourselves to. At these Breastworks it was very dirty and filthy, and it seemed as if a human being could not stand being at such a place any length of time. Judging by the cards and bottles that were lying under the yankee Banks they must have been a hard sett [sic] of men.

Among the spoils of battle acquired by the band, one item was put to immediate use, according to Leinbach:

One man of our regiment found a fine brass bass horn which had been left by some member of the enemy's band, which he presented to our band, and which was used by our base [sic] player all thru the rest of the war, it being a better tuned instrument than the one we had brought from home.[35]

Mickey recorded that the "Bass Tuba" was for Joseph Hall; he also mentioned "occasionally finding some Band Music." In addition, "we found an E flat Alto which was slightly damaged; we picked it up; and thought it might be of some service when we could have it repaired."

While there, Mickey noted, "Sam Hall and Dave Murchison went with us over to our Wagons." Their stay was brief, though, and Mickey indicated that "when we got near the Battlefield, . . . [they]

left us and as we got there, their wagons were leaving." The two musicians were among the group of original enlistees from Salem in May 1861 who had become band members of the Eleventh Regiment of North Carolina Volunteers, redesignated the Twenty-first Regiment, North Carolina Troops, in November 1861. At the time of this visit by Hall and Murchison, they and the remainder of their band were listed as "Band" with the field and staff of the Sharpshooter Battalion; their names also appeared on the roster of Company A of the Twenty-first (see Appendixes A and B).

As the Twenty-sixth continued to follow the retreating enemy on Friday, July 4, the bandsmen witnessed many more unusual sights. One in particular that caught the boys' eyes was an abundance of live projectiles that had misfired when shot from the enemy gunboats. Mickey and Leinbach made a special note of these in their accounts. Both referred to the missiles as "bombs" and gave the same estimates of their size: eighteen inches in length by ten inches in diameter.

The band moved at a more leisurely pace after most of the enemy had crossed the lower Chickahominy River. (Some had boarded their gunboats, still anchored in the James.) The boys felt fairly safe as they made camp near the river on Sunday, July 6. It was a time to relax and think more about food, which, said Julius, consisted mainly of hard crackers and bacon, "washed down by coffee made of parched corn." Among the available delicacies was an abundance of blackberries.

On Monday morning the group started back toward Richmond and made camp in late afternoon within a few miles of Drewry's Bluff, at the frequently crossed pontoon bridge over the James River. Crossing it the next morning, they soon reached the Richmond-Petersburg turnpike, and "from this place the wagons were sent back for the men's knapsacks, etc., and the band was directed to go on to our permanent camp on Dunn's Hill, near Petersburg." A little humor colored the opening remarks by Mickey in setting the scene, notwithstanding what might have been a disaster!

After the Wagons had left us; a negroe [sic] Boy came along with a 2 horse wagon on his way to Petersburg, and which we hired . . . as I was not able to march. We had not drove more than 4 or 5 miles before the Bridle but [bit?] broke of one of the Horses and the Horses were going down grade, and both were blind and in a few minutes we were in a ditch aside the rode [*sic*] which turned the wagon over, and threw the driver out, and sprained his wrist. We soon got both horses out and had them hitched up and traveling. We got to our old Camp before Sundown, and found the 48th N.C. Regiment near our Camp. We had been away . . . 2 weeks, and whenever we reach our permanent Camps, it seems almost like home. Wednesday we took a good wash in the river, and put on our best clothes, and had the pleasure of having nothing to do as we had our Cook to do all the work and wait upon us.

Having suffered through the exigent demands of the campaign since the latter part of June, Julius expressed the group's relief to finally arrive back in camp, "a very pleasant location." He spoke highly of Mr. Dunn, owner of the property, as "a very genial gentleman . . . [who] became our very good friend." He continued: "On his beautiful lawn, under the fine large oak trees, we would lie about and sleep or play as the mood took us. It was only a short distance from the city, where we loved to go when any of us had any money to spend."

At this location the band was joined by its second recruit, W. Augustus ("Gus") Reich, who became the much-needed bass drummer. In addition to his musical talent, Reich was quite a sleight-of-hand artist who, before entering service, had adopted the sobriquet, "Wizard of the Blue Ridge." Almost immediately he became an added attraction of the band, invariably performing his "wonders of magic" at concerts.[36]

While there the band also received unexpected boons—pay and a furlough! On Thursday, July 10, Mickey went to regimental headquarters at Drewry's Bluff to get money and furloughs for the band members. He returned the following day with these important items and a "Bass Drum." Amazingly, all of the music performed to that point appears to have been played without a drum, bass or snare. The latter would subsequently be supplied with the addition of the youngest member of the Twenty-sixth Band. Mickey's earlier statements concerning his search for a bass drummer remain a mystery awaiting verification.

After hasty preparations for this first visit home since their enlistment, the boys left camp at Drewry's Bluff for Weldon early Sunday morning. Following an all-day train ride, they arrived in High Point around 11:00 that evening. Even in their haste to reach Salem (approximately twenty miles away), the group woke up the neighboring town with a little music, not as an act of mischief but to "work off . . . exuberant spirits." The remaining distance was covered by stage, with arrival in Salem at an early hour on the morning of July 14.

The members had hoped to favor the home folks with an abundance of serenades and concerts while they were on furlough; however, the sickness of Mickey and several others limited their music making. Painfully, the first musical performance on this visit was in connection with the funeral of bandsman Bill Hall's young son, Gustavius. After the customary death announcement from the church cupola, the band played appropriate chorales at the interment.[37] This grievous experience saddened an otherwise happy reunion with loved ones.

The musicians received an extension of their leave as a result of the continued sickness of several members, especially Sam Mickey, and, perhaps more importantly, because of their anticipated help to Zeb Vance as a candidate in the forthcoming North Carolina gubernatorial election.[38] Their former colonel had called upon the band in the spring to join him in a tour of the regiments in order to boost morale and encourage reenlistment as the one-year terms of volunteers were about to expire. Confident of *his* boys' ability to blow many a vote his way during the upcoming political rallies as well, Vance was undoubtedly more than glad to honor the band's request for a furlough extension.

On August 13, after exactly one month at home, most of the band left Salem for camp. They were accompanied by the newest addition to their group, Ed Peterson, who became their trombone player.[39] Meinung, Transou, and Bill Hall remained in Salem a few days longer because of persistent illness. Shortly after returning to camp, the band membership was increased again, when Edward A. Brietz joined his friends to play E-flat alto.[40] (It will be recalled that Brietz had visited his musician buddies earlier while the band was at Kinston.) With this addition the group now had a roster of twelve members, its maximum strength—though all were present for duty only at times—during the period of service.

The matter of war had settled down to routine camp life by this time, and the greatest concern for everyone was the impending departure of Colonel Vance to assume his duties as the new governor of North Carolina. (He had won a decisive victory over William J. Johnston while the band was on furlough.) The highly popular Vance delivered his farewell address to the troops on Friday evening, August 15, the day the band rejoined the regiment. Final good-byes were exchanged with the men the following morning, prior to the colonel's departure for Raleigh.

Vance's resignation led to the succession of his second-in-command, the youthful Lt. Col. Harry King Burgwyn Jr. (1841-1863). This routine promotion was to prove very significant in the lives of the Twenty-sixth Regiment. For the Salem bandsmen it was another major turn of fate in their army career.

General Ransom reputedly stated that he "wanted no boy Colonel in his brigade."[41] This remark, as might be expected, was considered something of an insult by many who had come to like and admire the leadership of Burgwyn as a regimental officer. As a result, Burgwyn requested that the regiment be reassigned to another brigade. Subsequently, the Twenty-sixth Regiment and its band, with Colonel Burgwyn as their new leader, were transferred on August 26 to the command of Brig. Gen. James Johnston Pettigrew (1828-1863).[42]

Soon after the transfer, the band received a special invitation to furnish music at Vance's forthcoming inauguration. In addition to their request for permission to play at the Raleigh ceremonies, the musicians asked for a few extra days in order to give a series of concerts in several eastern Carolina towns. As the campaign around Petersburg was somewhat static at that time, the boys had little difficulty in obtaining another furlough extension. Pettigrew, their new brigade commander, appears to have already developed a liking for his "band boys."

Governor Vance's Inauguration March, composed by Edward W. Leinbach and performed by the Twenty-sixth Regimental Band in Raleigh on September 8, 1862. (Image courtesy of the Moravian Music Foundation.)

Even during the time of war, Leinbach indicated that the Raleigh jaunt proved to be quite an event, especially for the Salem crew:

We polished our instruments nice and bright and on Saturday [September 6] before inauguration Monday, we left Petersburg, arriving at Raleigh the same evening. The committee of arrangements met us at the station with a large bus, in which we rode thru the city discoursing some of our best music. At the Yarboro [Yarborough] Hotel we were given good rooms and received excellent treatment.

On Monday, inauguration day, the boys who had been at home had rejoined us, together with several friends from Salem, bringing us some decent "home clothes," more suitable for the occasion than our soiled army wear.

As the hour drew near, we marched from the hotel to the capitol, took our assigned places on the west side of the building and played while the large concourse of people were gathering.

The Governor's address was short, but good, and seemed to please his hearers. After he was done speaking, we again played to dismiss the crowd. After dinner we made arrangements to give a concert in the deaf, dumb and blind institute chapel, which some friends had secured for us. We had a crowded house, repeated the concert [and] again the chapel was full. Gus Rich [as he liked to be called], "The Southern Magician" . . . added greatly to the entertainment of the audience.

Among the musical offerings for this event was the official *Inauguration March* by Edward Leinbach who, as composer and arranger, contributed several other pieces to the band's collection of music.[43] On several visits to the bandsmen while they were in the eastern part of the state, Edward would sometimes "sit in" and play cornet. Julius Leinbach, soldier-bandsman, paid the following tribute to his distinguished brother:

Here it would not be out of place for me to bear grateful and loving testimony to the deep and constant interest he took in our band from its first organization to the end of its existence. He had drilled us in our first efforts to master our instrument, composed and arranged a great deal of music for us, and in every way did what he could for our comfort and welfare all thru the wearying and trying years we spent in camp.

The concert tour following the inauguration was cut short by a yellow fever epidemic, then rampant among the troops in the eastern section of North Carolina. Nevertheless, three more concerts were

E-flat cornet part to *Colonel Hoke's March*, composed by Edward W. Leinbach, brother of Julius. (Image courtesy of the Moravian Music Foundation.)

given—two in Wilmington on September 10 and 11, and one in Goldsboro the following evening. Also, upon returning to camp at Petersburg, the musicians gave a couple of performances in the town's Phoenix Hall. These well-attended events were now even more popular, enhanced by the addition of Gus Reich and his bag of tricks! A small part of the money obtained from such appearances enabled the boys to maintain a slightly higher living standard than that of their fellow Rebs. More importantly, the majority of the

E-flat cornet part to *Colonel Vance's March*, probably arranged by Edward W. Leinbach for the Twenty-sixth Regimental Band. (Image courtesy of the Moravian Music Foundation.)

Letter from Dr. Peter E. Hines acknowledging receipt of a donation by the Twenty-sixth Regimental Band to the North Carolina hospitals in Petersburg. From the Julius A. Lineback Papers, Southern Historical Collection, Manuscripts Department, Wilson Library, University of North Carolina at Chapel Hill.

proceeds from concertizing was donated to hospitals and various relief funds, as recognized in a letter of appreciation from a hospital in Petersburg during the fall of 1862.

While at Petersburg, shortly before returning to North Carolina, the musicians obviously made a good impression on their new division commander, as Julius noted:

General Pettigrew had become very kindly disposed toward us and gave us the piano music of "The Rifle Regiment Quickstep," which he wanted us to have arranged and regard as his favorite piece.

During the time of our encampment near Petersburg, Colonel Burgwyn and Major Collins, our brigade quartermaster, repeatedly asked us to serenade their friends, both in the city and country, which we were very willing to do.

We usually had a pretty good time, light refreshments, and sometimes wine and good brandy were served.

Sickness continued to decrease the number of bandsmen present for duty, and several were frequently at home on leave during the late summer and fall of 1862. The increasing hardships endured in the marshy region of eastern North Carolina, marked especially by a scarcity of food and lack of clothing, were beginning to have a telling effect upon the stout lads who had left Salem just a few months earlier. On one of the forced marches, Leinbach recorded that "we had bought a large turkey, and our colored cook made us a midnight supper. We had a dish of sweet potatoes as astonished our stomachs, as accustomed as we had been for some time to rather poor and scarce fare."

One member whose health had been seriously impaired was Augustus Hauser, an original band enlistee. Word of his death reached the boys in camp on November 25. Hauser, at home on sick leave, was the only fatality suffered by the Twenty-sixth Band throughout its entire period of enlistment.

Within a few days, a fifth recruit cast his lot with the Salem Band. His enlistment was somewhat of an accident.

On November 30, Sam [Mickey] happened to meet Henry A. Siddall, from Salem, on his way to join the 55th N.C. regiment. As he was a musician and we needed another man in our band, he was persuaded to change his plans and join us, becoming our second B^b cornet [later B-flat tenor sax-horn] player.

Toward the end of the year, the Twenty-sixth was on duty either in southeastern Virginia or eastern North Carolina, and in December it was encamped in the Goldsboro-Kinston area. There, on December 19, the Eleventh North Carolina Regiment (formerly First Regiment, N.C. Volunteers) and band were assigned to Pettigrew's brigade.[44] Very likely the Salem bandsmen experienced mixed emotions when they learned of their new neighbors. They must have been only too glad to allot a measure of their playing duties to the band of the Eleventh but, at the same time, they probably were a bit jealous at the prospect of sharing the musical spotlight with another group. Even so, Mickey remarked that

About dusk the 11th N.C. Reg came down to where we were, and as they came by our Reg. there [sic] Band struck up, and played a very long piece. I was very glad that this Reg and Band had joined Pettigrews Brigade; as there was no other Reg. that had a Brass Band.

Leinbach, apparently confusing this band with the Thirty-third, stated that the

regiment had a band composed of men from our county, from Bethania and neighborhood. They had much of the same music as ourselves, composed by Mr. Neave of Salisbury, N.C., so that we could join forces and thus form a large band playing with fine effect.

In early January 1863, following another two-week furlough for the Salem Band, Mickey made another reference to the Eleventh Band.[45] He too apparently confused this band with the Thirty-third.

Saturday [January] the 24th some of us went to town to mail some letters, in the afternoon. J. Leinback [sic] and myself went to the 11th Regiment to see Prof. Neave, and asked him to come and teach us. If he would have come some of our officers were making up money, made up enough to teach us for 1 month without any trouble. We could not get him untill [sic] his time was out, and . . . he went home, was his excuse.

Neave, director of the Fourth Regimental Band, supplied music for the Thirty-third and no doubt other bands in the command; however, there is thus far no evidence of his doing so for the band of the Eleventh Regiment. The Twenty-sixth eventually engaged Neave to come and work with them.[46]

Any negative thoughts of competition were quickly dispelled, though, as the Salem musicians began planning for another brief respite from army routine. Just one day after the assignment of the Eleventh Regiment to Pettigrew's brigade, the boys began another two-week furlough.

On the 23rd, [we] left our camp for Goldsboro. While waiting for train at that place, the bodies of two lieutenants, who had been killed near Kinston, were transferred from one train to another, and we played several dirges meanwhile.

Leaving Goldsboro about 2 p.m., we arrived in High Point, about midnight. There was no stage connection with Salem at that hour, but it being a bright moonlight night, and we having had considerable experience in marching, we did not hesitate to walk to our friend Stewart's where we had breakfast prepared and found opportunity to send word again to Salem for the band wagon to meet us. Seated in that with our good friend Aug[ustus] Fogle, driving the four horses, we rode into town surprising our friends with music. Needless to say we spent a very happy Christmas at home, the time for our return to camp coming all too soon, on January 5, 1863.

The visit with family and friends during the Christmas season was in contrast to the first homecoming, marred by the death of Bill Hall's young son. But the recent passing of fellow bandsman Augustus Hauser again tempered feelings of joy. As before, several ailing members were left at home to recuperate while the remaining musicians returned to camp with some uncertainty as to their unit's location. While awaiting train transportation at Raleigh, Leinbach mentioned hearing

some conflicting rumors [as] to the location of our regiment. Having more baggage than we would be allowed to carry on a march besides our string instruments which we had brought with us, we decided to go to our old camp at Petersburg, where we would be sure of finding some one in charge, and from there start out to hunt [for] the regiment. . . . Col. Burgwyn had left instructions for us to follow up the regiment as soon as we should arrive. Storing our baggage with Booth and Summers in Petersburg we took train on January 8 at 7 p.m. Our latest information advocated our men at Garysburg near Weldon, and there we found them in camp. It was about 2 a.m., we had no shelter and the men were all asleep.

At the break of day, on snow-covered ground, the band made its official report to the regiment by blaring forth the strains of a Rebel favorite, *Get Out [of?] the Wilderness*. Strangely, this music "raised a shout of welcome all over the camp," quite an unexpected reaction at such an ungodly hour in the dead of winter! With the addition of Siddall, the band reported for duty with a full complement of twelve members, the maximum number reached during its service.

Shortly afterward the group returned to camp at Weldon—a move assessed by Julius as a "perfectly useless and objectless trick." Then the regiment moved southward again, following a somewhat circuitous route by way of Magnolia up to Goldsboro, the familiar stamping ground. Leinbach's account included a most unusual incident, mentioned also by Mickey, which occurred after reaching Goldsboro.

January 26, 1863, was the day fixed for the execution of a member of Company B for desertion. He had but four or five days notice of his impending fate, but expressed himself as being ready to meet his God. The brigade was formed on three sides of a hollow square, the prisoner being placed on the open side with the firing squad a short distance in front of him. This squad had been furnished with rifles loaded by us, half of them with ball cartridges, the other half with blank cartridges, none of them knowing how his gun was loaded. The assistant adjutant general stepped forward and read the sentence of the court martial to him, which condemned him to be shot to death. Then, to my intense relief [certainly to the one most concerned!], another paper was read, being his full pardon, and he was permitted to rejoin his company. He declared that he would never desert again nor did he, but was a good soldier and was killed bravely fighting at Gettysburg.

For most of the early months of 1863, the Twenty-sixth Regiment remained in the eastern section of North Carolina, enduring rain, mud, and hunger—rations were often reduced to cornmeal. At one point the band boys did manage a "feast" when their Negro cook, hired some months earlier, caught a possum.

Notwithstanding the prevailing hardships, the band remained musically active and provided the residents of Kinston and surrounding towns with a number of concerts. Although some stringed instruments were among the baggage the bandsmen brought back to camp from their Christmas vacation, there is no indication that they were used in any of the concerts. Leinbach mentioned on February 26 having brought these instruments from Petersburg where they had been stored. He noted that "we did our first practicing on them the next day." A statement by Mickey, placing their use at an earlier date, included additional information of interest:

Wednesday [ca. February 4] was the first night we had string music, and could not play but several pieces off hand. . . . Friday we had nice weather and practiced on our New piece *Washington Greys* [author's italics]; This was the first day we attempted to play it, and in the afternoon we practiced string[s]. Our first pieces we practiced of the string music were simple, and were arranged for 3 Violins[,] 2 Flutes, Cornet B flat [and] Violincello and Bass Tuba. [This is the last entry in Mickey's diary.]

The addition of strings would have added variety to the group's regular concert fare, as well as providing the same for some of the players; but the unsettled conditions of camp life, coupled with a siege of inclement weather, precluded adding strings to the performances. In fact, these delicate instruments appear to have been stored in Goldsboro and presumably remained there until after the war. Thus far, no record of their eventual fate has been discovered.

A welcome relief to the increasing stress of an itinerant existence came in Greenville on April 21—still another two-week furlough! No doubt fellow-members in the regiment were beginning to wonder whether too much favoritism was being shown to the windjammers.

On this visit to Salem the musicians arranged a heavy concert schedule, though several members, including Leinbach, were suffering from typhoid fever. Poor physical conditions notwithstanding, Julius wrote that there were performances and that they proved fairly profitable.

Saturday evening, April 25, the boys gave their first concert in the court house, and on Monday evening a second one. The proceeds of the two amounted to $206. On Wednesday evening we played for the scholars of the Salem Female Academy, the principal, Rev. Robert de Schweintz [sic], giving us seventy-five dollars.

I played with them at this concert but at its close went home while the others went to the hotel to play for a certain stranger who had taken a great fancy to the crowd. He gave them $20.

The musical activity continued on the return trip to camp, with concerts in Greensboro and Raleigh.

At Greensboro we all got into one wagon and made our "grand entree." Mr. Tarplay, superintendent of the government gun shops and Mr. Mortimer Vogler had made arrangements for our giving a concert and show in the courthouse which was filled with a $258 audience. We had intended giving but one performance but were importuned to repeat it. The next night we realized $195.

These soldier-musicians were making money, but the band's venture in Raleigh was somewhat less successful.

> We could not get the use of either the Blind Institute Hall nor Commons Hall for concert purposes and as the Town Hall was not any too respectable we had about decided not to perform at all but were finally persuaded to do so and had a fair audience, getting us $142.

Upon the group's arrival at Petersburg, again the campsite of the regiment, Julius was forced to return to Salem for further rest in his continuing ordeal with typhoid fever. After a few more days at home he, accompanied by Henry Siddall, another ailing member, left for camp to rejoin the rest of the band.[47] On Sunday evening, May 17, the two boys attempted to attend services at a Presbyterian church in Richmond. Because of the large crowd assembled for "Stonewall" Jackson's funeral, they visited an Episcopalian church instead.[48]

The following morning they reached the regiment, then encamped at Hanover Junction, just north of Richmond, and were greeted with the news that their brigade had been assigned to Maj. Gen. Henry (Harry) Heth's division, Lt. Gen. Ambrose Powell Hill's Third Corps, Army of Northern Virginia.[49] The camp was humming, and everything was in a state of readiness. The stage was set for that fateful move northward, a journey that was to lead the hope of the Confederacy to a heroic but disastrous July encounter among the rolling hills of southern Pennsylvania.

4 In Quest of a Victory

Greatly encouraged by the recent victory at Chancellorsville on
May 3, 1863, yet still lamenting the tragic loss of Jackson, the Army
of Northern Virginia, under the guiding hand of its master soldier,
prepared to press its recent success with a maximum effort to the
north.[1] Against vigorous and sometimes surreptitious opposition by
Lt. Gen. James ("Old Pete") Longstreet, commanding the First
Corps, Lee began planning in May for his move toward Maryland
and Pennsylvania.[2] Barring the unexpected, the plan was relatively
simple. His army would proceed by the most direct, accessible route
across the mountains westward into the Shenandoah Valley. Under
the protective cover of the Blue Ridge Mountains to his right, he
would then move directly into Pennsylvania, hook southeastward,
and fling his legions against the defenders of Washington. The
strategy might prove a decisive stroke for immediate peace and a
Southern triumph.[3] Every move and countermove during the month
of June was a buildup toward this objective.

For the Twenty-sixth Band, now located with the troops at
Hanover Junction just north of Richmond, the prelude to
Gettysburg began with a brigade review on June 1, 1863, exactly one
month to the day that would mark the short-lived but costly
Confederate victory at Gettysburg.[4] Sensing a significant happening
during the following days, Leinbach stated that

we had orders to prepare for inspection on the following morning by General
Heth's officer. Such an order was usually indicative of a move, and therefore
very unwelcome.

On the 3rd we were roused up early, with orders to be ready to march by
7 o'clock, our supposed destination being White House. We were ready on

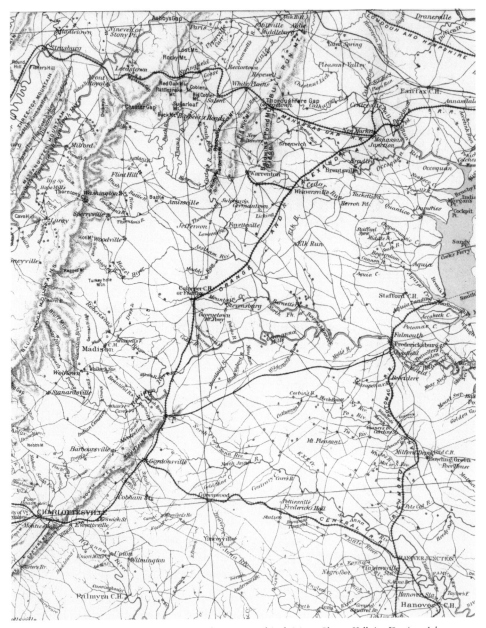

Northern Virginia. Detail of "General Topographical Map. Sheet II," in Davis, *Atlas to Accompany the Official Records*, Plate CXXXVII.

time and lay in waiting until towards noon, when the order was countermanded and the men directed to be ready for inspection which followed.

Finally, on June 6, following the revocation of more orders, most of the troops received instructions to move toward Fredericksburg, a distance of about thirty miles.[5] Because of inadequate transportation facilities on the overburdened Richmond, Fredericksburg and Potomac Railroad, many of the units, including the Twenty-sixth, were forced to delay their departure an extra day.

Sunday, June 7, dawned clear, the atmosphere much refreshed by a cooling rain the night before, and about 9:00 A.M. the restless troops boarded cars for what proved to be a final train ride for many a Confederate soldier; it was also the most commodious mode of transportation to be enjoyed by the majority of Lee's command for many months to come. As the heavily laden coaches creaked slowly over the North Anna River bridge, and the railhead of Hanover Junction gradually receded from view, spirits were high.

After a slow, bumpy ride, upon arriving at Hamilton's Crossing southeast of Fredericksburg, Heth's division of Hill's Third Corps was assigned to positions recently occupied by troops of Longstreet's First Corps and Ewell's Second Corps. The Twenty-sixth Regiment and band

reached Hamilton's Crossing about 3 p.m. The men were at once sent into the breastworks. The band of the 5th [55th] regiment and we were ordered to stay together with the wagons. We selected a place for our bivouac and then went forward to the brow of the hill to take a look at the scene, and a beautiful one it was. Far below us, extending for miles up and down within the range of our vision, lay the valley of the Rappahannock, several miles wide, lovely in its spring dress of green, with the river flowing peacefully thru it. The city of Fredericksburg lay in full view, and excited our pity for the place and its helpless occupants, when [we] saw how completely it was at the mercy of the enemy's guns on the opposite height.

We could easily see their encampments and the lines of their defenses. Soon after our arrival, some shells were thrown into, or very near, the city.

Bands usually set up camp near their regiments. On extended marches by larger units, they were frequently bivouacked in or near the staging areas of their respective brigades or divisions. This arrangement often invited a combining of musical resources for practice sessions and impromptu concerts, much to the enjoyment of musicians and troops alike. When the Twenty-sixth arrived at

Hamilton's Crossing, they discovered that their immediate neighbors were bandsmen of the Eleventh and Fifty-fifth North Carolina Regiments, as well as members of the Eleventh Mississippi band.[6] A musical get-together was proposed by the Salem boys, a suggestion promptly forbidden by their officers because of the proximity of the enemy and concern about his intentions. The rules of restraint were soon relaxed when it became evident that the Yanks were concerned with nothing "more hostile than music and cheering, or, on one or two occasions, such a bold display of pickets as to require a few shells at our hands."[7] Although such demonstrations indicated that Billy Yank was probably no more inclined to precipitate an engagement than were his Rebel protagonists, such boisterous action no doubt provoked a measure of uneasiness.

Ever since the troops arrived in the valley of the Rappahannock River near Fredericksburg, military action had been limited. Practically the only reminders of the grim business at hand—unknowing, of course, that a far more deadly ordeal lay in the not-too-distant future—were the occasional salvos of opposing artillery, mingled with the sporadic crack of desultory musketry. These sounds were punctuated frequently by perhaps the most disturbing element of all: the resounding crash of numerous brass bands of both armies.

It seemed as if every man in the Federal army opposite to us had a drum and was trying to make more noise with it than any one else could, while the bands did their best to increase the racket. What it all meant of course we could not tell. . . .

In the morning we found ourselves within two miles of the enemy, the picket lines plainly to be seen on the opposite hills.

Obviously determined not to be outdone, the Salem Band soon limbered up its own musical artillery and moved into a more advantageous position to engage the Federal musicians.[8] Although less than two miles from the enemy's breastworks, Salem's boys launched their initial musical barrage on the morning of June 9.

From an adjoining hill there was a splendid view of the valley. We had moved down the river some distance, so that Fredericksburg was far up to the left. At sundown we went to a battery close by, and commenced playing, when a citizen came to us and asked us not to play just there, as he feared we would draw the fire of the enemy's guns. To accommodate him, we changed our position some distance and finished our concert. . . . Gus Rich [Reich], our bass drummer, had gotten his drum heads wet, and not being careful in drying them, he burst them both.

One of many such concerts during the following days, these were no doubt duplicated by other southern bands in the area. From the abundant repertory of the Salem group alone, local citizenry and the soldiers were treated to music reflecting a variety of sentiment. There were such lugubrious favorites as *Dearest I Think of Thee, Do They Miss Me at Home, Irish Emigrants Lament, Who Will Care for Mother Now, Lorena,* and *Faded Flowers.* Proven crowd-pleasers included the rollicking airs of *Cheer Boys Cheer, Mollie Brown Quickstep, Here's Yer Mule Galop, Listen to the Mocking Bird, Bonnie Blue Flag,* and *Old North State* (the state anthem of North Carolina). Of course the familiar tune of *Dixie* never failed to generate excitement, especially with partisan crowds.[9]

While awaiting orders to move on, sometimes for several days, bandsmen welcomed the opportunities to perform for nearby communities. The impromptu concert or serenade became a favorite pastime in relieving the tedium of camp routine during prolonged rest periods. Value received for these appearances, even under

E-flat cornet parts to a medley of *Dixie* and *Bonnie Blue Flag*, and the *Twenty-sixth Regiment Quickstep*, the latter probably composed by Edward W. Leinbach. (Image courtesy of the Moravian Music Foundation.)

campaign conditions, frequently exceeded the bounds of gracious expressions of gratitude. Money was often forthcoming, particularly after formal concerts. Even those officers who were entertained with special performances made modest contributions to the musicians' coffers. Of probably more consequence were various eatables doled out from time to time by local townsfolk.

A few days before leaving Fredericksburg, and following the incident involving the wet drumheads, what appears to be one of several contemporaneous diary descriptions reads: "Wednesday [June 10]. Spent the day in practicing and enjoyed the splendid view. At night we serenaded an adjoining house, and were regaled with soured sweet pickle." Though savored then as a delicacy, within a month's time such a treat would have assumed the proportions of a substantial meal!

Once again Leinbach referred to Edward Neave, the Fourth Regiment's bandleader, and his contributions to the Twenty-sixth Band's library: "On Thursday we received some more music from Professor Neave, so that we had something to do practicing." Neave's friendship and influence also extended to other regimental bands, as will be seen.

One of many instances illustrating the informality existing between the Twenty-sixth musicians and their officers occurred on the evening of June 11, when Mickey and Meinung, accompanied by their colonel, visited a local residence to spend what Leinbach described as "a musical evening with piano and cornet." Meinung very likely did the honors at the keyboard while Mickey exhibited his skill as a cornetist. Nowhere are we informed of the colonel's musical talents, but young Harry Burgwyn's reputation as a "ladies' man" was common knowledge, as Julius commented, and he "lost no opportunity of making female acquaintances whenever it was possible."

For the most part, when not playing, the Salem Band was content to laze around, rest, and enjoy the scenery. Those who felt really ambitious devoted some time to individual practice on their instruments. Leinbach mentioned several instances of copying music for the band's books. All too soon, however, the time came to bid a reluctant farewell to this paradisiacal setting, to the picturesque valley in its verdant mantle of beauty so eminently characteristic of the Virginia countryside at that time of year.

Prior to leaving Fredericksburg, the troops received orders that no more baggage would be hauled, thus signaling an increased tempo of operations and a sure promise of livelier times ahead. Heretofore, the musicians had managed to keep a large portion of their belongings, enabling them to maintain a relatively decent life-style, no doubt to the envy of many fellow soldiers who enjoyed few such "amenities." The new regulations were unhappily received by the Twenty-sixth boys. They were hardly ready to relinquish their luxurious ways, if they could be so called, just yet. In this respect the Moravian bandsmen were aided by a friendly officer:

[June] 13th. Orders were issued today that in the future no baggage would be hauled not even that of the officers. Accordingly we sent our trunk to Richmond, with the officers' baggage. We still had my valise which served as a common receptacle for various articles belonging to the crowd, Sam's box of music and two carpet sacks and our mess chest. By connivance of our quartermaster [Capt. Joseph J. Young] we disobeyed orders by keeping these articles.

By the next morning it had been determined that the Federals under Maj. Gen. Joseph ("Fighting Joe") Hooker had withdrawn from their position on Stafford's Heights on the north side of the Rappahannock.[10] They had embarked on a course to keep abreast of Lee's movements, not a well-kept secret by any means.[11] Hill's Third Corps, having served its purpose as the rearguard watchdog, hastily moved to join forces with the commands of Ewell and Longstreet, whose legions, seemingly an endless gray horde, rolled as an inundating tide toward the northern reaches of the Shenandoah.[12] The route followed by Hill was essentially that taken by Ewell's corps.[13]

Hill's troops wasted little time getting under way, with "Dick" Anderson's First Division headed for Culpeper almost as soon as it had been determined that Hooker had left Stafford's Heights.[14] The following day, June 15, Heth's division took up the line of march, with the Twenty-sixth Regiment and band breaking camp about middle of the afternoon. At the same time, the leading elements of the Confederate war machine were swarming across the Potomac, headed for the Mason-Dixon Line and a wildly excited Pennsylvania citizenry.[15]

The end of the first day's march for Heth's division, begun in the late afternoon of the fifteenth, found the command encamped after dark on the outskirts of Chancellorsville. The band, passing through the village, arrived around ten o'clock that night, "very glad to lie down as we were very tired and sleepy." The following morning,

at 4 o'clock we were aroused and told to get ready to march. In a short time the regiment came up and we took our place at its head playing as we moved off. We marched until noon and were then ordered to cook two days extra rations. We had put our knapsacks in the wagons but as they were to go still farther we took them out for the night.

17th. Starting again at 4 o'clock, the boys pushed ahead in order to unload our knapsacks into the wagons again, but before we knew it we had passed our wagon in the long train that lined the road. . . . About 11 o'clock we marched thru Culpepper [sic] plain, and encamped a mile beyond.

The band, bivouacking with the wagons at almost every stop, pitched tents just beyond Culpeper Court House where, as Julius stated, "we sold our mess chest and gave away part of the contents." The decision to part with the chest was made only after further orders had been issued for the wagons to be searched thoroughly for baggage of any description. Luckily, Quartermaster Young, at considerable personal risk, continued to befriend the bandsmen and consented to haul at least their traveling bags.

The relative freedom with which the band operated throughout the line of march resulted in frequent separation from the command post, and very often the members found themselves far in advance of their unit. On approaches to towns, however, they were usually in position to play their regiment or brigade through the various communities. This was the case when, after a long hard march in extreme heat and drenching rains, the Salem Band headed up the sprightly Twenty-sixth as it proudly passed through Front Royal around ten o'clock on the morning of June 20. In grateful appreciation for this sample of Dixie's musical best, admiring young Virginia ladies were generous with their bouquets. As the band moved forward while playing, most of these gifts were quickly retrieved by the infantry immediately to their rear.

Losing no time, the troops made the Shenandoah River crossing about noon and, after a brief rest, pushed rapidly on to a point about two miles south of Berryville (approximately four miles below the West Virginia line), arriving there about 5:00 P.M. and going immediately into bivouac. The march that day had been another exacting ordeal. Having begun at 6:00 A.M.—the men had been ready to move since 3:00 A.M.—the trek had covered nearly thirty miles, much of it over difficult mountainous terrain. By now the consensus, according to Leinbach, was that Lee would cross into Maryland and divide his forces, "thus compelling the enemy to do the same, and then defeat him in detail."[16]

Obviously fatigued from his wearisome hike, Julius mildly complained that his "feet were becoming pretty sore." Nevertheless, the musicians appeared willing, if not actually eager, to provide entertainment for the men. The contiguous location of the band campsites again facilitated an arrangement of enjoyable concerts with friends in the Eleventh and Fifty-fifth North Carolina Regiments, together with the Eleventh Mississippi; "the bands played in succession until dark."

The Twenty-sixth's musicians never failed to express characteristic pride in the excellence of their group; at the same time, they also recognized the existence of other good bands in the Rebel command. Leinbach stated that

in our egotism we imagined that we could play better than any of the others. We were willing to acknowledge, however, that the 11th S.C. in Pender's division, composed mostly of professional musicians, was greatly our superior. That division had five bands, the 33rd N.C. amongst them.[17]

After the grueling march on June 20, the foot-weary soldiers welcomed the cancellation of marching orders for the next two days. This was particularly good news because the men had been alerted again at an early hour (4:00 A.M.) on the twenty-first, seemingly a routine wake-up call for breaking camp. With this momentary halt and unexpected time on their hands, the Rebs were rife with more than the usual number of campstool rumors. For example, there was the prevailing estimate concerning the strength of Lee's striking force: "100,000 infantry, 20,000 cavalry and 1,400 pieces of artillery."[18]

On the morning of June 23, after having their orders countermanded only once, the troops were much refreshed and stepped off at a lively clip shortly before daybreak. At least one early riser was on hand to greet them most enthusiastically:

As we were passing thru Berryville, a lady wearing the stars and bars came running up a side street shouting at the top of her voice, "Hurrah for the rebels." As she reached the street we were on she exclaimed, "I never was in such a fix in my life; whoop, I'm all out of breath." She was well cheered by the men.

From here the approach to the Potomac slowed considerably, Hill's corps having covered less than ten miles on this stretch before establishing evening camp just south of Charles Town. The following day the pace quickened. On the move again just after 4:00 A.M., the troops marched through the town where a number of ladies gathered to extend an early morning greeting to the passing parade. No time was lost, though, as the long gray line pressed rapidly forward, past Harpers Ferry, and arriving in the vicinity of Shepherdstown about noon. Within two miles of the Potomac and in full view of the Maryland Heights beyond, the greater part of Hill's corps established camp for the night.

It was just as well that a halt was called at this point; the swift march had been unusually trying, and the rigors of the relentless pace of the past few days had a particularly telling effect on Salem's musicians. The indisposed Mickey was forced to accept the comforts of the regimental ambulance, and Leinbach, too, was "not at all well." Exposure to continual rainfall and extreme heat, together with an insufficiency of food—hastily gulped bites while on the move—contributed significantly to the poor physical condition of the band and many of the troops by this time. Despite these adverse conditions, the men went to sleep with relative ease that evening. Even so, they must have had some unsettling thoughts of the next day's events, especially crossing into Maryland, where sentiment was mixed and palpable sympathy for the Confederate cause was uncertain.

Prior to breaking camp early the following morning, the band received special instructions from their colonel regarding their music. As a rule the musicians determined when, where, and what they would play; however, in this instance, the military brass made his special wishes known. Burgwyn informed the Twenty-sixth that, thereafter, when making camp, they were to play *The Campbells are Coming* and *The Girl I Left Behind Me*. Just why these particular tunes were specified is not clear, though the appropriateness of the latter as far as the young colonel was concerned has already been noted.

June 25 was no doubt a day long remembered by the citizens on both sides of the Potomac, at Shepherdstown and Williamsport, where the major portion of Hill's and Longstreet's troops made their respective crossings of the river.[19] This event, though fraught with potential danger, proved to be a comical sight nevertheless. In describing the movement of Longstreet's corps, one account stated:

In the afternoon we crossed the Potomac at Williamsport, Maryland. . . .
When the army started to ford the river the brigades filed off to the right and
left, and the men denuded themselves of their nether garments and shoes,
making a bundle of them, and carrying them and their cartridge-boxes upon
their shoulders. A number of carriages containing ladies, mostly young and
guileless, crossed the ford, coming from Maryland as our men were crossing
to the other side. The sight of thousands of "Confeds" in the water and in the
field, "sans culotte," must have been astounding and novel in the extreme,
and something the young ladies would not soon forget. Fifty thousand men
without their trousers on can't be passed in review every day of the week.[20]

Though fording the river at an earlier hour in the day, the Rebel
band from Salem had evidently provided any demure "flowers" of
Shepherdstown on the river's south side with a show equally as
interesting. The boys, according to Julius Leinbach, made the
crossing only after removing "shoes, socks, pants and drawers."

The bandsmen and many other Rebs were not entirely convinced
that Confederate sympathizers were to be found on the Maryland
side of the river. Leinbach, temporarily in charge of the band while
Mickey remained indisposed, unsuccessfully attempted to assert his
authority:

Just as I reached the Maryland side of the river, I stumbled and fell on my
knees, doing involuntary homage to the state. When we were again dressed,
one of our men asked us to play "*Maryland, My Maryland* [author's italics]."
Our leader being sick, I was next in authority and declined to do so, for
certain reasons of my own. A member of General Pettigrew's staff was close
by and heard me. He was seen to smile as he moved away and not long after
an order or request came from the general that we play that piece of music.

I did not decline again, and we continued to play other music while the
rest of the division was talking [walking?].

Such *gentle* persuasion usually got immediate results, as the boys
frequently honored musical requests not entirely consonant with
their own wishes.

They passed through Sharpsburg around noon and noticed many
remaining signs, a church in particular, of the bitter struggle that had
been waged in that vicinity on September 17, 1862.[21] In addition,
not surprisingly, it was observed that only two brave souls outwardly
expressed themselves as Rebel sympathizers.

Late in the afternoon the commands of Hill and Longstreet were
located in the vicinity of Hagerstown. Again, the day had been long

and the march severe; therefore, the troops wasted no time in establishing camp in their respective areas. While at this location the subject of plundering received special notice.

Strict orders had been issued by General Lee against depredations of any kind while in the enemy's country, especially the burning of rails, something the men were very apt to do whenever there were any within reach. Putting up our fly we found some straw nearby, and persuading ourselves that we were not depredating, as we would not consume it, we carried a lot into our tent and on it spent a comfortable night, altho it rained considerably during the night.[22]

The Twenty-sixth Regiment broke camp south of town later than usual (just after 7:30 A.M.) on June 26, following a night of constant rain. Julius stated that "our first morning in Maryland was a very disagreeable one, cold, rainy, and the roads muddy." These conditions notwithstanding, Salem's musicians appeared in rare form as they regaled some early risers of Hagerstown with a number of well-chosen tunes. The bandsmen now had become reasonably adept at playing on the march, thus allowing them to take in many of the local sights—especially the fair sex—as they played their way through the town. Special attention was given to a large number of ladies who were waving Confederate flags. Such demonstrations undoubtedly contributed greatly toward convincing many doubters that they might be among friends after all.

Prior to leaving Hagerstown, with the Pennsylvania line only about five miles to the north, orders had been issued that bands would henceforth refrain from playing through any enemy towns. At least two top commanders believed that the matter was theirs to determine. According to Maj. Gen. George Edward Pickett, Longstreet's favorite division commander, he had hardly crossed the Pennsylvania line when, at Greencastle, he had "his bands all . . . playing glorious, soul inspiring Southern airs: *The Bonny Blue Flag, My Maryland* [and] *Her Bright Smile Haunts Me Still* [author's italics]." In Chambersburg on June 27, a group of young ladies had one request: "Would you mind shooting off the bands a bit?"[23]

The following day, Brig. Gen. William ("Extra Billy") Smith's Third Brigade of Jubal Early's division of the Second Corps made its triumphal entry into York. Observing a group of local citizens advancing to surrender their town, Smith directed an aide, his son Fred, to

Go back and look up those tooting fellows . . . and tell them first to be sure their drums and horns are all right, and then to come up here to the front and march into town tooting "Yankee Doodle" in their very best style.

The band responded quickly, but first with *Dixie*, then *Yankee Doodle*.[24]

Similar instances would seem to indicate that little, if any, musical restrictions were imposed on or observed by bands of other commands as they moved through Maryland and into hostile Pennsylvania. For example, the soldiers of Maj. Gen. John B. Hood's Third Division of the First Corps enthusiastically crossed the Potomac into Maryland to the stirring sound of *Dixie*. General Hood's bands very likely continued to play their way at least through Maryland, as did the Twenty-sixth musicians. A reasonable assumption is that Hood would have allowed his men also to make a musical entrée into Pennsylvania, as implied by one writer.[25]

June 26 was the date on which the band of the Twenty-sixth Regiment first set foot on true Yankee soil! The troops crossed the Pennsylvania line shortly after 1:00 P.M., a little more than five hours after leaving Hagerstown. This was relatively rapid progress, considering the adverse weather conditions. About 4:00 P.M., they stopped "at a house where some of the men disobeyed orders by 'pressing chickens, vegetables, etc.' "

As the Twenty-sixth Band advanced into enemy territory, the members apparently were not sharing in the alimentary fortune enjoyed by a number of Lee's troops.[26] The band's larder had become depleted, and efforts to replenish it had met with little success. Could musical activities have seemed more important at a time when a food reconnaissance would have been more beneficial? Of more consequence was a reluctance to filch food along the route. Instead, there was a tendency to rely on the regimental commissary, not always at hand. Of course Southern diplomacy, generally considered a valid asset, contributed its fair share toward alleviating the acute problems of subsistence. This was demonstrated by Alex Meinung on the second day among the Pennsylvania Dutch, when he "got on the good side of an old lady by talking German with her and wheedled her out of some 'lat werg.' "

Added to increasing culinary problems was the loss of the band's Negro cook, who had been brought all the way from Carolina but had recently "left us and gone to the Yankees, as we supposed." The group was faced squarely with handling the matter of cuisine themselves, a task that involved considerably more than simple food preparation. Relating his turn as cook on the first night in Pennsylvania, Leinbach wrote:

It was 2 o'clock by the time I could lie down. It may seem strange that it should take so long to cook, but everything had to be prepared. Wood had to be cut and carried in and it was green, too, and did not burn well. Then one had to wait for the wagons to come in with the cooking "tools" and rations, and the latter had to be issued.

This burden was assuaged temporarily when a member of Company D from Wake County was detailed to serve as band cook for a few days, thereby leaving the musicians more time for what they, and probably the officers too, considered more appropriate duties. If ever there was a need for music to boost morale, the time was fast approaching.

Sunday, June 28, was significant for everyone concerned for two reasons. First, it marked the date on which Maj. Gen. George G. Meade assumed command of the Army of the Potomac, thereby becoming Lee's chief opponent for the forthcoming battle, the preparation of which was rapidly entering its final stages.[27] Second, the reports concerning Federal troop movements received by Lee that day forced the commander to commit his dispersed forces from a relatively quiescent state of inaction to one of celerity and intent.[28] Thus began the immediate convergence toward Gettysburg.

Having reached Fayetteville, Pennsylvania, without incident, the bandsmen and their fellow soldiers realized that all was not serene; excitement and expectation were beginning to build, according to a number of reports, some exaggerated, others outright false.

The men had strict orders not to leave camp without permission. Last night, however, some Missourians got into trouble with citizens in town, and Co. E of our [Twenty-sixth] regiment was sent to quiet the disturbance. General Early's corps left here last Thursday. McClellan was said to be at Harrisburg, with 150,000 men, largely militia, and Hooker was reported to have fallen back on Washington. Some furloughed men came into camp bringing papers of the 24th instant, containing a report of another victory at Vicksburg to the effect that General Grant had been defeated with a loss of 10,000 men. Of course, no one believed it and we only wondered how such extravagant tales got started. During the day our chaplain, Rev. Mr. [Abram N.] Wells, preached a very forceful and appropriate sermon on the text, "The harvest is passed, the

summer is ended and we are not saved." Jer. 8-20. This was the last sermon that
many men were to hear on earth. God grant that some souls were led to
consider and turn to Him who is ready to receive them, even in this eleventh
hour. In speaking about this sermon afterward in our tent some one remarked:
"Did you notice Col. Burgwyn during the preaching? He seemed to be deeply
impressed. I believe we are going to lose him on this trip." Sadly prophetic
words they were, fulfilled much sooner than any of us had the remotest idea.

A similar report, the original source of which is unknown,
appeared in a special section on the band in a history of the Twenty-
sixth Regiment:

On Sunday before Gettysburg, at Fayetteville, Pa., Chaplain Wells preached
before the Brigade. . . . It was an eloquent discourse and made a great
impression. After the services were over, and the band returned to its
quarters, the drummer (W. A. Reich) remarked: "Boys, I believe we are
going to lose our Colonel in the next fight. Did you notice his looks during
the sermon?" Captain Mickey replied: "Yes, I did; he looked right serious."
As appears in this history their Colonel was lost to them in the next fight.[29]

That evening the Twenty-sixth Band gave its last concert for
some time to come under what might be considered relatively
peaceful circumstances. As in the case of the sermon that morning,
the greatest significance of this gathering lay in the finality of the
occasion. Julius, continuing to show an interest in the fair sex, noted
that several ladies from town were on hand to hear this concert, "the
first Pennsylvania women to show us any recognition."
On the morning of June 29, the marching orders of Hill and
Longstreet, directing them to join Ewell's troops at Harrisburg, were
countermanded.[30] Instead, they were to concentrate their units in the
vicinity of Cashtown, approximately nine miles northwest of
Gettysburg.[31] Hill's corps moved out first, with Longstreet following
the next day. Ewell, still at Carlisle, was to join the other corps at
Cashtown or Gettysburg, as determined by the situation. On the
approach to Cashtown, and subsequently to Gettysburg, Heth's
division, led by Pettigrew's brigade, including the Twenty-sixth
Regiment and band, became the spearhead of the major portion of
Lee's army as it moved slowly, cautiously, southeastward.
(Reputedly, neither Lee nor Meade had envisioned Gettysburg as the
location of the forthcoming clash.) That evening Heth's division
bivouacked at Cashtown. This final period of concentration on
June 29 and 30, signaling action to come, was of immediate concern

to everyone. One of many lengthy reports by Leinbach, no doubt derived from brief, on-the-scene notes by various individuals, recorded the situation as events unfolded:

On Monday, 29. Expecting to start at daylight, we got up at 3 to prepare breakfast, but learned that our marching order had been countermanded. At 1 o'clock, however, we were on the move, passing by the ruins of Caledonia iron works.[32] Our rations were short, we could buy nothing along the road, and we were afraid to "press," even had there been an opportunity. The quartermaster and commissary departments pretty well cleaned up everything as they went. We only marched about six miles this day.[33] We were on elevated ground, and had a good view of the country in certain directions. Northwestwardly, the town of Gettysburg was plainly visible.[34] We were on the east side of the Blue Ridge, having crossed during the day. We still thought it was General Lee's plan to march on Baltimore. Our course, since entering Pennsylvania, had been eastwardly. The enemy's cavalry were reported to be in our rear, as most likely they were, but not scaring us very badly.

30th. There was some rain during the night. Orders were issued for the men to leave their knapsacks and those not able to make a forced march to remain in camp. This order was ominous of trouble, and Colonel Burgwyn gave us permission to remain in camp if we prefered [sic] doing so. We decided to remain. The men left at 6:30 a.m., going in the direction of Gettysburg.[35] Some of the officers had given us charge of their tents, and we moved them to the wagon camp near Cashtown, a quarter of a mile away. The enemy was reported to be in heavy force at Gettysburg. At 2 o'clock we heard that General Pettigrew, who had been making a reconoisance [sic] in force, had taken some prisoners, who said that Hooker had been reinforced by Meade.[36] It was evident that there were two very large hostile armies in close proximity, and that, under the circumstances, but one thing could be expected—a collision that would be terrible in results. Our troops, in coming in contact with a small portion of the enemy, had quite a little brush, but being under orders not to bring on a general engagement, fell back, followed by the enemy.[37] Artillery was moving forward constantly, while the rain was falling nearly all day. Before night the wagons went to the regiment and issued rations.

J. A. Transou joined us from home, having been on the road two weeks. Our brigade was in lead of the division, the Twenty-sixth Regiment having gone on picket for the night.

The eve of battle was at hand!

Of the many important battles fought during the Civil War, none has commanded more interest and attention than Gettysburg. It

Page from Julius Lineback's pocket diary for the period June 30–July 2, 1863. Lineback failed to change the printed "1861" as he did on other pages in the diary. From the Julius A. Lineback Papers, Southern Historical Collection.

stands as a classic that has been studied and restudied, told and retold, perhaps most of all, argued and re-argued. The many vexing questions concerning the number and disposition of troops; the tactics employed; strengths and weaknesses; achievements and failures of commanders and units; speculation as to what might have happened "if"—all have contributed to the luster that continues to surround this engagement more than 140 years later.

The Twenty-sixth Band was officially classified as noncombatant; yet, during those momentous days of July 1-3, 1863, its members were no less actively engaged than had they shouldered a rifle or unlimbered a caisson. In their dual roles as musicians-medics, serving with a regiment that was actively engaged for two of the three days and lost nearly 90 percent of its personnel, the bandsmen from Salem had their own story to tell, one that focused on the contributions of one group of musicians during this historic battle.

On the morning of July 1, the band withdrew to its assigned position with the hospital unit. Here the boys anxiously awaited the results of the first clash—the beginning of a cyclopean struggle, which after three seemingly endless days, reduced two puissant monsters of mass destruction to mere shells of their former selves.

The troops, leaving their knapsacks with the wagons, moved forward in the direction of Gettysburg about seven o'clock.[38] Brig. Gen. Joseph R. Davis's

Brigade followed with a battery of artillery. During the morning it was reported that our forces were expecting to advance on the enemy's position.

One year ago today the battle of Malvern Hill was fought, resulting in favor of our arms. We were filled with anxious thoughts, as we considered the possibilities of this day's encounter.

At 10 o'clock the battle began in earnest, raging unabatedly for two hours or more, becoming furious towards 12 o'clock. From an adjoining hill we could see the smoke of the infantry firing, while the roar of cannon was almost continuous. Hood's and Pender's divisions were pushing forward.[39] At 3:30 the firing ceased, except that some Yankee batteries continued shelling the woods. As it cleared off we again saw the town, and watched the puffs of smoke from the guns, followed by the report in sixteen seconds. Captured prisoners claimed that their forces numbered 250,000 men under General McClellan.[40] As reports from the fight began to come in, our hearts were saddened by the details, as the 26th and 11th regiments had been in the hottest part of it, and suffered severely. Our dear Col. Burgwyn was killed, Lieutenant Colonel Lane was very severely, if not mortally wounded, and

Major Jones quite badly hurt, as well as Adjutant Jordan, and nearly every captain in the regiment. Of course, it could not but be that many privates were stricken, but we did not learn, until later, how severe had been the loss. More than three-fourths of the men were either killed or wounded. Our colors had been shot down 14 times. Both Col. Burgwyn and Lieut. Col. Lane having received their wounds while carrying them. When Col. Burgwyn fell with the colors, the impact of the ball that struck him caused him to turn and he fell with the colors wrapped around him. Lane ran up, and seeing that his superior had been mortally wounded, spoke a few words to him, then took the colors himself and started forward.

Our brigade had been opposed by the celebrated "iron brigade" [of Brig. Gen. Solomon Meredith], which had boasted that it never yet had retreated in any fight. Our charge, however, was so impetuous that it was forced to give away. One man, Sergeant Charles H. McConnell, wanted one more shot before retiring, and seeing Col. Lane with the colors, rested his gun against a tree, took deliberate aim and fired, the ball striking Col. Lane in the back of the head and passing quite thru, just as he was looking back and calling his men to come on.

At this point, as Leinbach recalled the events of the battle, he inserted the following item of special interest:

About forty years after this Col. Lane attended a reunion of the Grand Army of the Potomac, at Gettysburg, and in an address there, told how he was shot. After the speaking a Union soldier came forward, and said, "I am the man that shot you." They shook hands and remained close friends until Col. Lane's death. When I was at Gettysburg, two years ago I saw and shook hands with this now Col. McConnell, and we spoke of the circumstance of his having shot Col. Lane. He also gave me one of his Iron brigade badges.

Continuing with his account of the first day's encounter, Julius stated: "As our wounded men came in, we helped the surgeons with them until 11 o'clock at night, when I was so thoroly [sic] tired I could do no more, and lay down for a little rest."[41]

On July 2 Pettigrew's badly mauled brigade remained in reserve in its assigned position on Seminary Ridge. For that pitiful remnant of the previous day's magnificent fighting force, it was a day of rest and recovery; for the members of the Twenty-sixth Band it was a period of unflagging service.

At 3 o'clock I got up and resumed the task of doing what I could for the men. While we had been thus engaged, we were sent for to come to the regiment and play for the men. Our brigade surgeon, Dr. [Llewellyn P.] Warren, sent Sam [Mickey] with a note to Col. [James K.] Marshall, who was in command of the brigade, Gen. Pettigrew having charge of the division, as Gen. Heath [Heth] had been slightly wounded, saying that the musicians could not well be spared as there were so many wounded men needing attention.[42]

To describe the delivery of the message to brigade headquarters by Mickey, Leinbach quoted from Sam's diary:

On reaching the brigade I gave the note to Col. Marshall, who approved it. While Capt. Grewer [sic] was with Col. Marshall, at his headquarters, I walked over on the hill where our men had met the Yankees the day before.[43] Pettigrew's brigade had charged thru two fields and a narrow strip of woods, down grade all the way, to a small branch [Willoughby Run], there they were in thirty steps of the enemy, who were said to have had three lines of men firing into our ranks. Our colors were shot down fourteen times. All the men of the color guard were shot down. Captain [William W.] McCreery, one of the general's staff, was said also to have fallen while carrying forward the colors of the 26th. After hard fighting the enemy was driven over the hill, Capt. Grewer carrying the colors thru. While there I saw many wounded Yankees, and about five hundred dead on the hill, and wondered how any of our men had escaped. On returning to the hospital, I found Col. Burgwyn's grave under a tree, in a large field, near a stone house, and Capt. [William] Wilson's and Capt. McCreery's graves near by. After returning to the hospital, having walked four or five miles, and being on my feet since 3 a.m., I felt like resting. I had rested but a few minutes when another order came from Col. Marshall, for the 26th and 11th [N.C.] bands to report to him and return to the hospital in the evening.

Continuing with his own account, Leinbach stated:

This was about six o'clock. Both bands played together for some time, heavy firing going on meanwhile, tho not in our immediate neighborhood. Our playing seemed to do the men good, for they cheered us lustily. We got back to the hospital sometime after dark, having come by way of the wagons to get as much cooked food as we could for the wounded men. We found many still needing our attention, while some had died during our absence.

We learned some time afterwards, from Northern papers, that our playing had been heard by the enemy, amid the noise of the cannon, and that they had supposed with wonder, that we were in the midst of the fight.[44]

July 3. We continued to wait on the wounded. Fortunately there was a good spring nearby, from which we could supply one of the most pressing wants of wounded men—water being their great need.

About 1 o'clock p.m. Dan [Crouse] and I went to the wagons for more rations. These were a couple of miles nearer the field of battle than the hospital. While on the way the firing of cannon was resumed and soon became fearfully furious. The very ground seemed to quiver under our feet from the awful concussion from the many guns, and the bursting of bombs. This was at the time that the celebrated charge was made by Pickett's and Pettigrew's commands, and was undoubtedly the heaviest and most terrific artillery firing that had ever been heard on the face of the earth, or perhaps that ever will be.[45] It had been estimated that for about half an hour, one hundred guns per minute were fired. It was a terrible time, and the slaughter of human beings was terrific beyond description. Every field officer in our brigade was either killed or wounded; every captain in our regiment, except one, and every lieutenant but three.

A very good skirmish line had been collected, and the gallant old 26th had sixty-seven privates and three officers present on the night of July 3, out of the eight hundred who went into battle on the morning of July 1.[46] Surely this regiment had done its full duty, had been baptized in blood, and could well be entitled to the appellation "The Bloody 26th." Towards evening the surgeons were ordered forward two miles and we went with them. The yard, road and field were full of men, some who had been wounded in the first day's fight, and received no attention. A good many had died here, and were still unburied. One man, that I particularly remember, was terrible to look at, having become bloated out of all human shape. We worked hard to give as much relief to the poor men as possible, until 1 o'clock at night when we were again thoroly [sic] worn out, and laid down for a little rest.

5 *Aftermath of Disaster: A Test of Endurance*

Repulsed, yes, defeated, no—this was the imposing thought as Johnny Reb retired to the stretches of Seminary Ridge on the evening of July 3. The day had been long, the experiences frightful, and the losses heavy; but all would be compensated on the morrow when Marse Robert would once again seize the initiative. Lee, however, had other plans. Even as his battered forces sought solace in the halcyon respite of sleep, the general was planning their return to Virginia.

Shortly after midnight Lee issued specific instructions to a cavalry officer, Brig. Gen. John D. Imboden, who was entrusted with escorting the large wagon train with its thousands of wounded during the retreat to the Potomac.[1] That the disabled soldiers were the chief concern of the Confederate commander at the moment is reflected in his charge to the cavalry leader:

We must now return to Virginia. As many of our poor wounded as possible must be taken home. I have sent for you, because your men and horses are fresh and in good condition, to guard and conduct our train back to Virginia. The duty will be arduous, responsible, and dangerous, for I am afraid you will be harassed by the enemy's cavalry. . . . Nearly all the transportation and the care of all the wounded will be intrusted to you. You will recross the mountain by the Chambersburg road, and then proceed to Williamsport by any route you deem best, and without a halt till you reach the river. Rest there long enough to feed your animals; then ford the river, and do not halt again till you reach Winchester, where I will again communicate with you.[2]

By midmorning on July 4, elements of the convoy began assembling on the road between Cashtown and Gettysburg. Adding to the existing confusion, a blinding rainstorm hit the marshalling area shortly after noon. It was not until around 4:00 P.M. that the first units of the vast train began their slow, plodding grind in the direction of Chambersburg along a road now almost axle-deep in mud.[3] The lashing storm continued unabated. The shouts and curses of the drivers to their recalcitrant, almost unmanageable teams were mingled with the heart-rending cries of the human cargo of wounded and dying in nearly every wagon. Still the interminable column pressed on through the night in its effort to escape much of the inevitable harassment by enemy cavalry. Daybreak of the fifth found the head of the train about twelve miles from Williamsport, the Potomac crossing point into Maryland.[4]

And where was the band? Leinbach began his report with the preparation for leaving Gettysburg:

Dr. Warren ordered us to get up a list of the wounded and pack as many as possible into the wagons captured by [J. E. B.] Stuart on a raid, and send them on to Winchester, and also advised us to go with them. . . . We did not feel quite safe in going to the rear without some authority for doing so, and I went forward to get a paper of some kind from Maj. Jones or Dr. Warren, but could not get to the Major and the doctor was too busy to give me any attention.[5] I went back to the wagons in a heavy rain. During a lull, E. Brietz, who had been wounded, went again to get a certificate from Dr. Warren, but he told us to go on as fast as we could.[6] When we got to our wagon yard, we found that they had already gone. The retreat had begun.

We started off in the rain and traveled until 9 or 10 o'clock [that night], a motley procession of wagons, ambulances, wounded men on foot, straggling soldiers and band boys, splashing along in the mud, weary, sad and discouraged.

Abe and I, with a couple of our men, were together, but separated from the rest of the crowd. Very tired, we lay down under a tree, too completely tired out to care very much whether the Yankees came and picked us up or not. Poor Abe had no shoes, and his feet were very tender. Heavier rain coming on during the night, we sat up with our backs against trees with our blankets over us, meditating on our forlorn condition until daylight.

Sunday, 5. Going half a mile further, we came to the 11th Regiment band, and all the rest of the boys, except Bill Hall, who was thought to be further ahead. We ate a little of our scant store of provisions and made another start, Joe Hall being in his stocking feet, some one having stolen his shoes. The wagon had been moving slowly all night, but we soon caught up to our position of yesterday in the train, our own brigade wagons being far in front.

Passed thru Greencastle, our objective point being Williamsport. Dan soon threw away his shoes as being worse than none, while mine were badly worn and rubbed my feet very sore. . . . It was [a] very fatiguing march, but we kept going, with frequent short rests. The roads were deep with the gritty mud that wore the feet of our barefoot boys badly, and getting into the shoes of those who possessed such articles was almost as bad for them.

This was the general pattern of retreat for nearly a month. In sharp contrast to the proud, eager group that had literally played its way to the brink of victory, the Twenty-sixth, now suffering the miseries of hunger and inadequate clothing, driven only by sheer determination, made its way slowly and painfully in the direction of home territory.

Impelled by the sharp pangs of hunger, the Moravian musicians committed their first acts of depredation (at least the first mentioned) in Pennsylvania—of all times, on a Sunday! On the outskirts of Greencastle, an interesting episode occurred on July 5.

We scarcely had anything to eat. Amongst us we had a few small pieces of silver money. We had poor success in buying or begging anything along the road. We came to one house where, for our money, a woman gave us some small slices of bread not nearly its value. This kind of "raised our dander," and some of the boys, going around the house, found the cellar door unlocked. That was all we wanted to know. While we were negotiating in front of the house, the rest went into the cellar and appropriated what we could find. Our stomachs and canteens relieved the milk crocks of their contents, a dish of cold meat was quickly transferred to haversacks, other portable edibles also, while Dan, the scamp, walked off with a ham-bone on which there was some meat, which he and I divided when we got behind the barn.

After dark I became separated from the others and got some distance ahead of them.[7] Later we learned that the enemy's cavalry had attacked our train in the morning, . . . capturing an ambulance and a number of men, amongst whom was our comrade, Bill Hall.

Leinbach reached Williamsport around 2:00 A.M. the next day. He stated:

I crossed the river on a ferry boat with the wagons. On the hill beyond, I concluded to stop and rest, as I could scarcely travel from fatigue. It was still raining, but in the dim light I found some fence rails, which I laid, one end on a stump, the other on the ground thus making an inclined cot, lying on which, and covering head and all with my oil cloth, I slept the sleep of the weary. After daylight I went back to the river, washed my feet, shoes and pants, which were all equally muddy, and re-crossed the river, having learned that our wagons, and probably the rest of our boys, had not crossed during the night. I managed to get a day's rations, and after a good deal of difficulty, found most of my comrades together, there being an immense concourse of wagons parked in the river bottom. Bill Hall was then supposed to be somewhere in front, and Abe and Joe Hall, barefooted, in the rear.[8] Wagons and wounded men on foot were ordered to cross as fast as possible, as the river was slowly rising from the heavy rains. Finding our commissary wagons after considerable hunting, we drew some flour, but had no meat of any kind.

Only a few troops were able to cross at that time, the Twenty-sixth musicians not among them. The bandsmen spent the next few days somewhat leisurely meandering back and forth along the north bank of the river. Delayed by the incessant rain and swollen river, the band and commissary wagons were finally able to locate their slower moving regiment, what was left of it, back with Heth's division near Hagerstown. Physical discomfort was relieved to some extent by the welcomed issuance of shoes and fresh beef; the more bibulous appetites were also indulged, as the commissary treated the group to mint juleps. Even those less inclined toward strong drink "were of the opinion that it was not bad to take."

The degree to which camp life reverted temporarily to a modicum of normalcy is reflected in a statement on Saturday, July 11:

Our men came in last night and bivouacked within three hundred yards of us. We went to them and found them in good spirits, eating breakfast. After we had eaten something, we played for them the first time since July 2nd, on the battlefield of Gettysburg. Soon orders were received for the brigade to go to Williamsport. We "played off" with the men and went a couple of miles when Maj. Jones ordered us back to the commissary wagons.

The respite was short-lived. Once again the bandsmen were faced with the major problem at hand, retreat without delay! The record for the next two days continued to reflect the aura of misery and depression that was the distinguishing mark of the entire return trip to Virginia.

Monday [July] 13. More rain. Wagons were ordered to cross the [Potomac] river by fording. We were told to get into them to help weigh them down. We all got over pretty well except Henry and Transou, whose wagons seeming to be in danger of going down stream, they got out and waded some distance to the bank. It had not rained while we were crossing, but began soon after. We went about three miles, and stopped for some time where we feasted on the finest of blackberries. A heavy shower drove us into a neighboring house for shelter. At 3 o'clock we were again on the move. Several of us got ahead of the troops, traveling until night in the rain, and stopping in a piece of woods. The rain increased in violence so we could not sleep or even lie down but squatted about under the trees like toads. About 11 o'clock Ed and Gus passed by, hunting shelter of some sort, and later Sam, Transou and Norton [unidentified] followed them. About 2 o'clock we squatters moved on too, the rain coming down in torrents. At last we found some of the others in a house where we all remained until daylight.

Tuesday. At 4 we started again, the rain having abated somewhat. After going about two miles, we came to a smith's shop, where we stopped to eat such breakfast as we could spare to ourselves. Dan joined us here, having spent part of the night in a hog pen. At 8 o'clock we reached Martinsville, where we bought bread and meat at a market house.[9] We had not seen or heard anything of our wagons or regiment since yesterday, but were too anxious to go on to wait for them, so, supplying ourselves with more food, we left Martinsville at 11 o'clock, having been told that there was no doubt about the fall of Vicksburg.[10] At 2 o'clock [that afternoon] we stopped at a vacant house by the road side and concluded to wait till we knew certainly how far the army would fall back. Sam, Dan, Henry, Transou and Abe started out in different directions to forage for provisions but had indifferent success. Pickett's division came up, and went into camp close by. The hard marching and exposure to rain, sleeping in wet clothes, and subsisting on an insufficiency of food, had been hard on our physical well-being, and we felt the effects of it. The wagons not coming up, we had to satisfy our stomachs with little food and big promises. Maj. Baker told us on the road that our wagons were about two hours behind.[11]

After receiving this report the band decided to continue its march for several more hours. Around 10:00 P.M. the group reached Bunker Hill (approximately ten miles south of Martinsburg), set up camp, and awaited the wagons that arrived sometime later. In talking with the men of other units, the bandsmen learned for the first time of Pettigrew's tragic encounter with the enemy at Falling Waters.[12]

On the morning of the fifteenth, Maj. John T. Jones assumed command of the brigade. One of his first official acts directed the musicians to perform at General Heth's headquarters; almost at the same time, there was an urgent request to report to General Lee. The latter directive, initially raising the flag of great concern, proved to be one of great relief, if not downright joy!

Maj. Jones sent us word to go to Gen. Heth's quarters and serenade him. We did so and he sent us out some brandy. Meanwhile General Lee sent a courier to our quarters with an order that we should report at his headquarters. Our regiment had been so terribly reduced in numbers, so nearly annihilated in fact, that we were not a little uneasy about our future condition, fearing the possibility of being put into the ranks. We obeyed the order therefore, with fear and trembling, feeling very much as a prisoner would who was about to receive his sentence. When we reported at Gen. Lee's quarters, however, he received us very kindly, said that he considered our band one of the best in his army, and hoped that we would do all that we could to cheer up the men, etc. Of course we were very greatly relieved by this expression of his kindly feeling toward us, and went back to our quarters with light hearts.

An excerpt from Sam Mickey's comments read:

On the retreat from Gettysburg to Bunker Hill, the band serenaded General Lee and other officers. After the serenade to General Lee, Colonel Taylor, his Adjutant General, came out of his tent and made a little talk. He thanked the band for the serenade, and said he didn't know how they would get along without bands; that they cheered up the men so much; that he noticed the style of our music was different from that of the other bands in the army.[13]

Bunker Hill was the campsite for several days, and for the first time since Gettysburg, the band was afforded the opportunity of directing more attention to musical pursuits, a welcome relief from army routine. As usual, visits with musicians in other units proved enjoyable and beneficial. For instance, Charlie Siegel of the Fourteenth South Carolina Band joined a practice session one day during this hot July.[14] Afterward, according to Julius, all adjourned to the Thirty-third North Carolina Band for a joint rehearsal.

Siegel's music, or at least his arrangements, seems to have been popular with the Salem bandsmen. Just prior to leaving Bunker Hill, Julius mentioned that Meinung and Mickey had spent considerable time copying tunes from the South Carolinian's repertory, paying thirty dollars per dozen selections. An examination of the Twenty-sixth's books reveals arrangements of at least the following:

Bonnie Eloise, Home Sweet Home, Schubert's Serenade, and [*In the?*]
Stilly Night. Further research will no doubt prove, as implied by
Leinbach, that there were others. Some interesting inscriptions
appear in two sets of books. First, the 2nd Tenor part of Book 4 has
a composition by Claudio Grafulla with the inscription, "Copied
from Chy. Siegel Jul. 19, 1863, Bunkerhill, Va." Second, Book 5,
containing the Schubert arrangement, has an interesting,
unexplainable note on the inside cover of Sam Mickey's E-flat
cornet part: "1st B♭ Cornet J. A. Lineback, #173 Schubert's
Serenade—Chas. Siegle, Rapidan, [Va.], 1864."

These periods of musical intercourse were facilitated greatly by
the comparative uniformity of repertory existing among neighboring
bands whose musical fare consisted of many numbers composed
and/or arranged by the same person—notably, in addition to Siegel,
Edward Leinbach, William H. Hartwell, and William H. Neave.
Although Julius mentioned Edward B. Neave a number of times, the
several compositions bearing the surname in the Twenty-sixth library
are inscribed, curiously, with the initials "W. H.," referring to
Edward's half brother.[15] The exchange of compositions between
companion bands—this was no doubt true of both Federals and
Confederates—provided a wellspring of repertorial variety and a
broader musical perspective for each group, not to mention a ready
means for expanding the different libraries.

Resuming the march on July 21, the troops pushed leisurely
southward into Virginia, through Winchester, Front Royal, across
the Blue Ridge, and finally arriving near Culpeper on Saturday, the
twenty-fifth. As the Federals' harassing pressure abated, the
Confederate convoy was allowed another week's rest from the rigors
of travel. The delay was particularly welcomed by the band, as a
number of its members were ill at the time. Recuperation was
evidently fast, though, for several trips were made to town in search
of supplies. Leinbach's quotation of contemporary prices is
particularly revealing: "Imitation coffee, at one dollar a package, ink,
one dollar for a bottle, sodacrackers, sixteen for a dollar, salt, fifty
cents for a half pint; and by hard begging a little flour at twenty-five
cents a pound."

Equally interesting are the bandsman's pithy remarks regarding his concern for certain problems of hygiene:

Soap was a necessary rarity, or rather, a rare necessity. I may as well mention here, once for all, that vermin were more abundant than anything else that could be mentioned. There was no such thing as getting clear of them. Officers and men were equally afflicted. One of our captains was compelled to sacrifice his beard, which was long and heavy, on account of the pests.

Having informed the folks at home of their miseries, the boys were promptly made aware of the profound sympathies of loved ones at home in a letter dated August 1. Replete with its effusive expressions of condolence, the letter arrived just prior to the band's departure from Culpeper on the second. In part it stated:

While we were glad and relieved to hear of your safety, it pained us to see that you were still subjected to hardships and privations, and these of such a character as we know nothing of in our experience. You poor boys are passing thru a fiery furnace. You, in your own persons, stand as the representatives of our country in all its sufferings. The counterpart of the ills which affect the body politic, may be found in your own individual cases. In a case of the moral diseases, which afflict society, we may consider your lousy condition as its representative. My bowels of compassion have been particularly excited by the account you gave of your pedal difficulties. A pair of number eight shoes, on a number five foot, and socks that are socks no more. I am not surprised that you are depressed.[16]

By then the majority of Lee's army had crossed the Rapidan River and were stretched out on either side of the Orange and Alexandria Railroad in the area surrounding Orange Court House. The command would be stationed in this general locality until mid-spring of 1864.

Discouraged by the hardships of the last three months and, at the same time, encouraged by their safe return to the friendly regions of Virginia, the Salem musicians optimistically contemplated an early visit home. Their request for a furlough, submitted the last week in August, was returned almost immediately by division commander Heth, who questioned the band's enlistment status, i.e., whether the group was, in Julius's words, "liable to conscription"—bringing this puzzled reaction:

If so . . . we ought to be regularly enlisted in some company and then, if thought advisable, we could be detailed as a band. Major Jones returned the paper with the endorsement that but few of us were liable to conscription but that our names had been reported to Colonel Mallett, conscription officer for North Carolina [and] we were . . . assigned to this regiment as a band. This was a startling piece of news to us.

The boys had regarded themselves as volunteers who served as the Twenty-sixth Regimental Band, but with a degree of independence, and bound to service more by moral obligation than by military regulation. Even though they appear to have then been officially designated as the regiment's band, no furlough was forthcoming![17] That this news was received with surprise, displeasure, and frustration is abundantly clear:

We had for some time been discussing various plans of changing our position as it had become somewhat unpleasant. . . . It was quite possible that some inkling of this had come to the ears of our regimental officers and they had adopted the above plan to hold us without having to pay us out of their own salaries.[18] Of course we were not only greatly surprised but deeply hurt and indignant that we should have been treated in this manner. We were fully aware, however, that we were helpless and must needs accept the situation with the best grace possible as any show of anger and rebellion would only tend to make our position still more unpleasant.

The tone of acquiescence by no means implied complete submission, or that the members were disposed to consider the issue closed. On the contrary, the surreptitious manner in which their interests had been disregarded and their status arbitrarily determined only intensified efforts toward effecting a transfer as soon as possible.[19] Leinbach, acting for the group, voiced their feelings more strongly a second time and revealed their intentions specifically in his notes for September 5:

The action of the officers of our regiment in having had us conscripted without our knowledge had angered us not a little and made us more determined to get away if we possibly could. We did not then, nor do I now know who was responsible and we could scarcely believe that either Colonel Burgwyn or Major Jones would have done such a thing, and Lieut. Col. Lane was at home severely wounded. All the same we had been conscripted or said to have been at least and we wanted to go somewhere else. A transfer to the convict [conscript] camp at Raleigh [Camp Holmes], seemed to be a desirable thing and as secretary of the band, I wrote to Colonel [Peter] Mallet [*sic*], in command there and also to Governor Vance, asking to have such a transfer made.[20]

For more than two months, thoughts of reassignment practically replaced hopes of a furlough, and Leinbach's diary indicated from time to time some progress in that regard. In the meantime, though, a war was being fought; the vicissitudes of conflict were at hand, and the Twenty-sixth musicians were confronted with more immediate problems of consequence.

Toward the latter part of September, Lee considered his forces sufficiently mended to launch an offensive against the weakened army of Meade, then extended north from the Rapidan to Culpeper Court House.[21] Having emerged from the recent Gettysburg Campaign with what has been described as their "material of command . . . close to exhaustion," the Confederates, now with a large complement of newly appointed general officers, were about to engage in what their commander deemed a necessary action.[22]

Orders were issued on September 7 for William W. Kirkland (now brigadier general) to assume command of the Pettigrew Brigade.[23] For the band of the Twenty-sixth, his relatively brief interim of leadership was one of uncertainty and annoyance, yet one of decided opportunity.[24] Whether directly as a result of Kirkland's bidding or of their own volition, the musicians, during the ensuing months, experienced one of the more musically active times of their military career.

Presaging any forthcoming tactical engagement of consequence was a formal review. The one staged on September 11, 1863, was quite a memorable event for the Salem Band. Aside from their own participation, by no means insignificant, the Twenty-sixth Moravians were afforded the opportunity of observing firsthand many of the finest bands of the Confederacy, as A. P. Hill's entire corps paraded for the first time under the watchful eye of Lee.[25] Obviously impressed by the magnificence of the occasion, Julius related that

twenty-five or thirty thousand men, were colected [*sic*] in one body all under the eye of one. We had to play for parts of several brigades, as the 21st band could not play. Still there were seventeen bands in the field which was some two miles from our camp. The troops were formed in three parallel lines four men deep. If in one it would have extended two miles or more. It took us fifty minutes to pass around and the corps, two hours to pass in review. It was certainly a grand sight. Here we heard the 16th Mississippi band for the first time. It was a pretty full one and they played well. Their review piece was "Dearest I think of thee," and we thought it the finest thing we had ever heard. Later we formed the acquaintance of their leader, Professor W. H. Hartwell, which resulted in an exchange of music and very pleasant associations and two years later in his spending a month with us as teacher.[26]

The evening's activities, though of protracted duration, were far less arduous and evidently more enjoyable than the morning exertions of trooping the line:

After supper we went to town to serenade General Kirkland, our new brigadier, but did not find him. Learning that they were probably at a house some three miles out in the country, we went there and found a ball in progress. Professor Ed. Neave and some of his associates were playing string music for the dancers. During the interval we played brass outside the house. It was 3 o'clock next morning when we got back to camp tired enough after our long and full day.

On Monday, September 14, the troops broke camp and were engaged the next few days in a series of maneuvers around Orange, designed to place Lee's forces in position for a projected offensive against Meade. During this time the bandsmen were musically active, but the most rewarding duty was copying more music for their library, rather than performing. Having made the acquaintance of Hartwell of the Sixteenth Mississippi, the boys wasted little time in obtaining some of his choice arrangements.[27]

By this time the musicians had captured the fancy of their new brigade commander. In addition to a regular schedule of rehearsals, camp concerts and parades, there were several impromptu "command" performances—at times bothersome—requested by General Kirkland. Following one of these, he presented the band with an aria from Verdi's *Il Trovatore* that he had had specially arranged in Richmond. Such friendly gestures were of course greatly appreciated, but there were times when the general's attentions were not too well received; in fact, he was thought to have gone a bit too far in one case, as noted in the following bit of drollery:

General Kirkland took a new freak into his head. He sent for Sam and told him he wanted one of us to blow calls for brigade drill. I was selected for the job. He had sent a copy of tactics in which the various calls were given, and I was to memorize a few but there were so many and I could not know what commands he would give, that I was much in the condition of the small boy going to school without knowing his lessons. I had this consolation however, that if I did not know the different calls, neither did the General, nor the men and so if I gave the wrong one, no one would be the wiser, so I put on a bold front as I walked up to headquarters at the appointed hour. I was put on a "fiery" steed and followed the General as he rode to the parade grounds. I could well imagine that the under officers and men were wondering what sort of circus performance was to come off. The general gave his command as for instance, "By Batallion, Right Wheel," which was repeated by the regimental and company officers. Then instead of his saying, "March," I was to give the prescribed call for that maneuver. Sometimes I remembered the correct call, mostly I knew no more than the veriest dunce in the ranks as to what tones I should play, but I blasted out something all the same and it answered the purpose. For two hours, this farce was kept up and then we rode back to camp, wiser men. I was never asked to repeat the performance.

There was a full dress parade on September 24, but only six musicians were present because of prevailing illness. Afterwards, the bandsmen received heartening news concerning their proposed transfer:

State of North Carolina
Executive Department
Raleigh, Sept. 21, 1863

Mr. J. A. Linebach:

Sir: I am directed by his excellency, Governor Vance, to inform you that Col. Mallett would be pleased to have the services of your band at Camp Holmes. You can correspond with him and ascertain terms and conditions upon which he will receive it. Yours very respectfully,

DAVID A. BARNES
Aid-de-Camp to the Governor

Although the letter was answered immediately, no reply had been received by the time Hill's corps began its move from the Rapidan toward Culpeper on October 9.

Along a circuitous route by way of Madison Court House (approximately twelve miles northwest of Orange), the Confederate troops struck the turnpike about six miles north of Culpeper on Sunday, October 11. Although often within full view of enemy detachments along the way, the band was requested to play a number of times. Orders to that effect were issued from General Heth on several occasions. On the morning of the fourteenth, as the army was approaching Bristoe Station, General Kirkland requested that the Twenty-sixth bandsmen head the brigade whenever it passed through any towns.[28] Did this signal a general shortage of musicians or was it recognition of the band's capability? Nevertheless, this latest directive by Kirkland obviously irked the musicians, who considered it another infringement on their rights; this prompted another expressed opinion by Julius:

He seemed determined to make as much of a brigade band of us as possible. He really had no right to take us away from the regiment to which we belonged, but of course neither our regimental officers nor we could afford to make any objections if we wanted to, which we did not.[29]

After a brief but disastrous encounter at Bristoe Station, Lee's army fell back across the Rappahannock (October 17–19) and camped in the vicinity of Brandy Station for nearly three weeks. During this time musical activities were at a minimum; the band boys spent the major portion of their time ministering to physical rather than aesthetic needs. The shortage of food became more critical. For example, parched white oak acorns served as a coffee substitute. Adding to the sad state of affairs, scanty, threadbare cotton clothing offered little protection against the cold, damp fall nights.[30] On October 21, Leinbach, writing for the band, stated:

I wrote to my brother James at Raleigh asking him to see Colonel Mallett in our interest. We were heartily tired of this kind of life and wanted to get away from this army very badly.

Sam Hall [of the "Sharpshooter" Band] came to see us . . . [to] get some music and I copied for him. Higgins of the 27th band was also copying. Our class of music was very popular with the men and appreciated by other bands.

There obviously was some satisfaction in being so appreciated by other musicians and the soldiers; however, the general hardship of army life and uncertainty of their status, particularly as it related to General Kirkland, had the Salem bandsmen still thinking of a transfer. Feelings of disaffection and frustration, and perhaps outright envy, intensified when several friends in the Twenty-first Band paid the Twenty-sixth a visit and expressed hope of an early trip to Salem. Leinbach was spurred to make another inquiry about the transfer.

28th. Wrote again to brother James asking him to see Colonel Mallett and let us know at once how matters stand and what the prospect is of our being transferred, as we are fixed in our idea to either go to Raleigh or join the 21st as a brigade band.[31]

There was then a brief respite from shifting campsites and light skirmishes, and the band was afforded time for attending to less taxing matters—music! On October 29, "Sam went to Culpeper to mend instruments while I continued my occupation of writing music, this time for the 4th band." (E. B. Neave was also drawing on Salem's repertory.) The following day Julius received a letter from his brother James:

Colonel Mallett was very desirous to have us but does not know how to get us away from our present position. From his evident conscientiousness we formed [a] very favorable opinion of him and became hesitated to send up a formal application for a transfer as we were fully convinced that neither General Kirkman [Kirkland] nor general Heath [Heth] would approve it. Another letter was sent to Colonel Mallett, telling him how matters stood here and asking him to try thru the secretary of war to have us transferred. Colonel Jones was to have given his written consent to be enclosed in this letter but did not get it ready.

Meanwhile, the musicians were on hand for duty, a decided point in their favor as the epidemic of desertion fever was spreading dramatically among the Confederate soldiery of the Virginia command. Recent military defeats, and deprivation of food, clothing, and pay were mainly responsible for the steady disappearance of Johnny Reb and the alarmingly shrinking rosters of his units at morning roll call.[32] In attempting to combat the widespread defection among his forces, Lee finally admitted that moderate measures of punition were wholly ineffective. Reluctantly, he would have the death sentence imposed on all captured deserters.[33] Officers not only seem to have complied faithfully with this austere order, but they also made sure that the seriousness of the offense and resultant consequence were impressed upon the minds of those under their command. The narrative provides another vivid, firsthand illustration:

Sunday, November 1st. This day had been set for the execution of a deserter from the 44th regiment. Several of the 44th had been shot during the last few weeks, but I had managed not to be a witness of any, but we were ordered to be with the regiment at this one.

The brigade was marched to the field of execution in slow time and formed in three sides of a hollow square, the condemned man being placed in the middle of the fourth, beside his coffin and already dug grave. The firing squad of twelve men stood a short distance from him under command of one officer. If ever my heart went out in sorrow and sympathy for a man it was then, as the poor prisoner stood there, blindfolded, his hands tied behind him, having spoken his last word to any human being, looked his last upon God's beautiful earth and having the consciousness that in a very few minutes he would be face to face with his Maker. It was my first time to look upon such a scene and I prayed that it might be my last.

After the sentence of the court martial and the order of the commanding general that he be shot to death had been read by the adjutant general of the brigade, the officer of the guard commanded, "Attention, make ready, take aim, fire." The volley was almost instantaneous. Six of the muskets had been loaded with ball cartridges and six with blank cartridges and given to the men who were to do the firing so that no one could know whether he had shot a ball into his late comrade or not.

The impact of the balls seemed to raise the man off his feet and he fell backward and was dead almost instantly. The troops then marched past the prostrate form and back to camp in quick time.

Unfortunately, this soldier's fate was sealed from the outset, unlike that of the deserter whose life was spared during the Carolina Campaign of 1862, only to be killed at Gettysburg.

Though the musicians had no thoughts of deserting, the desire to alleviate their wretched existence by legitimate measures was as strong as ever. If progress in this direction was slow, it was at least encouraging, because Leinbach was then corresponding personally with a sympathetic Colonel Mallett in Raleigh. His heartening response to Julius's latest inquiry appears in the accompanying facsimile of a letter written on October 29 and received on November 2. The bandsmen impatiently awaited a favorable word from their officers.

Letter from Col. Peter Mallett to J. A. Lineback, concerning the proposed transfer of the Moravian band to the state conscript camp at Raleigh. From the Julius A. Lineback Papers, Southern Historical Collection.

Resuming the move southward from the Rappahannock on November 8, the troops, by a forced march, reached their old campsite at Orange before daylight the following morning. The first flurries of snow had begun to fall during the last few days, and as it appeared almost certain that Lee's winter camp was to be established in this locale, the boys began to construct a more durable, permanent (or so they hoped) habitation out of birch timber and stone.[34] The hut was completed within a few days—"a very snug and comfortable domicile, the best . . . since . . . Petersburg [fall of 1862]." There was obviously cause for celebration on the evening of the twelfth. The musicians sat down to "a vegetable supper of turnips, etc.," supplemented with a few sweet potatoes that had been purchased by Leinbach for five dollars. The concert for the regiment that night was by far one of the best in some time!

No new information had been received relative to the transfer, and all band members appeared resigned to their present situation; at the same time, however, they were becoming more content with existing conditions. Contributing undoubtedly to this degree of satisfaction were the comforts of snug living quarters, as well as supplies recently arrived from Richmond. An iron pot and two quilts comprised the band's share. Of more importance was a decidedly improved financial status. A number of concerts for officers netted sizeable sums, and disbursements of *back* pay—an almost inconceivable spin of good fortune—were forthcoming on several occasions.[35] Mere expressions of generosity? Not altogether. That the fetor of design was strongly detected is revealed in Leinbach's terse comment: "Have . . . [the officers] gotten some hint of our attempted change of position, I wonder?"

In spite of the appalling number of desertions, the depleted ranks of Lee's army during the fall of 1863 were slowly being strengthened by returning convalescents, particularly those wounded at Gettysburg, as well as by recruits and conscripts. The band also experienced a decided boost in personnel. Dan Crouse, the baritone player, returned from the Lynchburg hospital on October 23. Then on November 18, the boys added a much-needed second alto player, Charles Transou. He came along just in time to fill the vacancy created by the capture of Bill Hall on the retreat from Gettysburg. This newest member was the nephew of an original band member, Julius Transou, and the second one recruited somewhat by accident. Charlie originally intended to join the North Carolinians of the Fifty-second Regiment, but not the band. He is reported to have known "something of music"—not too strong an endorsement—but it was sufficient reason for the Twenty-sixth to seek his services because they badly needed a replacement. Quickly supplying him with an instrument and some music, the Salem veterans lost little time in attuning this newest addition to their *modus vivendi*. With the addition of Transou, the band consisted of eleven members.

Transou's instrument may well have been the E-flat Alto found on the battlefield of Malvern Hill in July 1862. Providing sheet music for the instrument posed a more difficult problem, of the solution to which Leinbach had this to say: "I wrote to my brother Edward, for new copies of the 2nd alto part, from the scores he had arranged for us." (Only one score of the Twenty-sixth band music has thus far been located.) The request no doubt brought a quick response; also, there were other sources in nearby companion bands. In one instance, toward the end of November, Julius mentioned going to the Fifty-fifth Band "to copy some music for Charlie." Another time he singled out the Twenty-seventh Band as one of the Twenty-sixth's sources for music.

In late November, just when it appeared that life had resumed a degree of normalcy, as nearly as possible under existing conditions, reports were received concerning suspicious actions by Meade's forces to the east. Fearing a major Federal push toward Richmond, Lee set his army in motion once again.[36] Ewell's Second Corps, temporarily under the command of Maj. Gen. Jubal A. Early, began moving toward Fredericksburg on November 26.[37] The next day Hill's Third Corps, spearheaded by Kirkland's brigade (detached from Heth's division, which occupied the second position in the corps' order of march), followed via the old Orange Plank Road toward Verdiersville. That afternoon elements of the Second Corps made initial contact with the enemy near Locust Grove, approximately twenty miles northeast of Orange on the Orange-Fredericksburg Turnpike. After an extended period of relatively heavy fighting, Early withdrew his forces about three miles, to the west side of Mine Run.[38] They were joined subsequently by Hill's troops, and for a time it appeared that a major engagement was at hand.

All musicians in the bands of Heth's division were grouped together behind the front line and merged with the hospital personnel, standard operating procedure before any major engagement. Ambulances were ready to move at a moment's notice, and operating tables were set up quickly in fearful anticipation. The expected clash failed to materialize, however, and the next few days witnessed only light skirmishing that resulted in few casualties among Heth's forces. The entire experience was, in fact, described as "decidedly monotonous" for the band. A few practice sessions helped to relieve the unanticipated ennui, and, once again, a considerable amount of time was enjoyably passed in copying music.[39]

On December 2, just prior to a proposed attack by Lee, the Union forces withdrew across the Rapidan.[40] Having achieved no positive result from the encounter, and not desirous of pursuing Meade at that time, the Southerners began their return to Orange the following day. Thus ended what is referred to as the Mine Run operations.

This brief interlude had been most trying for the band and other personnel of the Twenty-sixth, occurring when the remnants of this once-proud and magnificent body—now a mere skeleton of its former self—were slowly being restored in spirit and strength. The abysmal condition of the regiment is best described by Col. John Randolph Lane, then commanding the unit, who had rejoined his troops around the middle of November.[41]

I found the regiment so low in spirits and few in number that the day I reached camp, was, I believe, the saddest day to me of all the war. I realized then as not before, the deaths of my Colonel, Harry Burgwyn, of our General Pettigrew, and so many other officers and friends in the regiment.

Regretting so much to see the gallant old regiment go down, notwithstanding the fact that I was entirely unable for active service, I reported myself for duty. . . . I went to work with all the will I could possibly bring to bear to recruit, drill and equip my regiment and restore it to something like its former numbers and efficiency.

I was informed by General Kirkland that if consolidation of regiments were effected, that the Twenty-sixth Regiment was named as one to be consolidated. I used every influence at my command to avert the threatened consolidation, and through the noble concert of action of the officers of the regiment, I had the proud satisfaction of seeing the efforts crowned with success.

Such was the harmony, energy and regimental pride of the officers and men, and so well did they work together to promote its interests, enlivened by such soul-inspiring music as only Captain Mickey's band could furnish, that by the first of May, 1864, the regiment numbered 760 strong; and so well was it drilled that General Heth pronounced it to be one of the "best drilled regiments in the Army of Northern Virginia."[42]

Spurred by this encomium and with their very existence at stake, the Twenty-sixth musicians steeled themselves to a rigorous schedule of drill and discipline. For the next few months, the band operated both within and without this framework of preparation.

Throughout the remainder of December, the boys occupied themselves primarily with improving their living conditions. To ward off the bitter blasts of a Virginia winter, two huts were hastily constructed—one occupied by Leinbach, Crouse, Siddall, and J. A. Transou; the other, more spacious, shared by Mickey, Meinung, Gibson, Peterson, Joe Hall, Reich, and Charlie Transou. In adopting a communal system of management, "household duties" were delegated to various members of the band and rotated periodically. At that particular time Leinbach's group served as bakers.

The musicians' resourceful nature was especially apparent in matters of food getting. To supplement the limited quota of issued rations, various edibles were often purchased in town.[43] Those mentioned specifically included salt, flour, bacon, and crackers, each selling for one dollar per pound. On one occasion "butter and an o'possum" constituted a decided treat; on another, oysters were obtained for five dollars a quart! Thus the greater part of earnings received by virtue of the boys' musical talents were then spent in this way, whereas previously generous amounts were donated to hospitals and relief causes.

Nothing, however, compared to those bounteous contributions from home. Several boxes that arrived on December 13 contained "eatables, clothing, etc. [and] a good deal of music, amongst the latter being a march and waltz composed for us by our good friend, Miss A. A. Van Vleck."[44] That such fortunes of opulence smiled all too infrequently was underscored rather humorously by Leinbach many years later in a speech before the Wachovia Historical Society in Winston-Salem:

December 10th was a special <u>fast</u> day—we had had a good deal of experience of "fast" days—whether it was considered in the sense of abstaining from food (because we had nothing to eat) or of fast marching, either before or behind the enemy—and had not perceived that either kind conduced very much to spirituality.

With the approach of Christmas, the boys wished even more strongly for their transfer, the prospects diminishing with each passing day. At least a surprise furlough, hopefully, would enable them to reach Salem in time for the holiday season. Instead, much to their regret, they were forced to abandon their agreeable surroundings and move to a new location about four miles south of Orange on December 22. Undaunted by this unexpected turn of events, the musicians again demonstrated their ingenuity in matters of "architecture and design."

23rd. During the night and early morning, there was a light fall of snow. We four bakers intended putting up another house.

Before beginning on our cabin, we offered to help the others build their large one first, as that would be needed for general gatherings, practicing, etc. But as they had not fully decided as yet whether to build such a one or several smaller ones, we made a beginning on ours. We cut, split and carried up nearly all of the logs for the house the first day.

24th. We finished the body of the house and commenced the fireplace. Stones were scarce so we made a dirt fireplace in the following manner. Split out pretty thick pieces of pine wood into slabs and drove them into the ground as we wanted the inside of our fireplace to be. Then a foot or more outside, we set another row and filled in between them with mud, packing it tightly. By the time the inside bulwark was burned out, the clay had hardened into a solid brick back, which lasted all winter.

Even in the midst of this urgent display of industry, culinary traditions of the season were not to be denied. The fancies of appetite were undoubtedly a primary concern. The boys indulged their meager finances to the amount of thirty-two dollars, twenty dollars alone for four quarts of oysters; and the contents of recently arrived boxes from home were supplemented with other delicacies purchased in Orange, all of which contributed to the plenteous fare of the band's evening meal.

Not to be ignored, of course, were the long-standing bonds of Moravian custom, so effective against the afflictions of apostasy induced by army life for many Rebs. Of particular significance was the observance of the deeply inspiring love feast and Christmas Eve vigil, the warmth of which imparted the true spirit of Christmas.[45] This special day was primarily one of labor, though it appears that a degree of fun and festivity relieved the toils of construction at times:

December 25th. Christmas morning. Some of the boys went to town to celebrate. I [Leinbach] would have liked much to go too, but we were anxious to get our cabin done as the weather was threatening. We covered it and daubed the walls but the want of an axe interfered much with our work.

The boys found all the stores closed in town by order of General Lee, so that they were greatly disappointed in their trip. There was some brandy running around loose, however, and we had some funny scenes which had best not be described.

There was a dance too at a neighboring house [in] which we did not participate.[46]

Within the next few days, both band huts were completed, a project that evidently attracted considerable attention. Quite unexpectedly, on December 30, none other than General Heth paid the musicians a visit for the purpose of inspecting their new quarters. He took a special interest in the larger structure that was to serve as a rehearsal hall.

Continuing to follow the dictates of tradition, the bandsmen remained awake later than usual on the evening of the thirty-first. At the stroke of midnight, the sound of their instruments was heard throughout the camp to announce the dawn of a new year with the traditional *Nun danket alle Gott* (*Now Thank We All Our God*).[47] As the solemn strains of the Johann Crüger chorale broke the chill and stillness of the night, no doubt many Rebs wondered if the year 1864 would indeed fulfill expectations and hopes for better times ahead, more propitious for expressions of gratitude.

Inclement weather had forced the cancellation of several dress parades during the last few weeks; however, in spite of hardships and weakened physical conditions, the band was relatively active, rehearsing and complying with numerous requests for serenades at various officers' quarters.[48] General Hill and his wife were among those so honored on one occasion.

Almost resigned to the fact that no transfer was forthcoming, Leinbach again submitted a request for furloughs. Hopes were high that they would be approved this time, as it was learned on January 16 that the Thirty-third North Carolina Band had just departed for their homes in and near Bethania. Several anxious days were passed while waiting. Finally, on the evening of the twenty-eighth, following a serenade for brigade quartermaster George P. Collins and his wife, Mrs. Collins thanked the boys for their music and presented each with his long-awaited leave.

On January 30 the group gathered at the Orange train station where they met members of the Twenty-seventh North Carolina Band, on their way to Greensboro.[49] By mid-morning an elated Salem Band was headed for Richmond, then on to Salem for perhaps the most joyous furlough of its army enlistment.

Around 7:00 P.M., after a nine-hour train ride from Orange, the bandsmen arrived in Richmond. Overnight accommodations were obtained at the Spottswood Hotel. (It is remarkable how the boys managed to bunk in various hotels and other special places during their service!) Early the following morning, having enjoyed their best night's rest and first decent meal in months, the group boarded the early train for Raleigh, arriving at the capital late that afternoon. At the station a chance meeting with their old friend Governor Vance set the stage for a memorable diversion toward the end of the furlough. At the governor's request, the bandsmen agreed to accompany him on a proposed speaking engagement at Wilkesboro in the western part of the state.[50] There was one condition: Vance would obtain an extension of their leave. He agreed and promised to advise the musicians within a week or so when and where to meet his party.

Continuing their trip by train, the bandsmen arrived around 9:00 P.M. in High Point, where they were met by friends and relatives from Salem, who accompanied their soldier boys home.[51] About 5:00 the next morning, Captain Mickey and his group let their presence be known to the sleepy Moravian community, with a parade through town to the resounding tones of brass instruments.

The Salem stay lasted nearly three weeks, during which the usual round of visits, locally and to outlying villages, occupied a major portion of the leave. Only one concert, at Salem Female Academy, was mentioned as having been given during the furlough. A reasonable assumption is that the then-famous Twenty-sixth Regimental Band afforded the residents more music! In summing up this visit that, incidentally, proved to be the band's last furlough, Leinbach simply stated: "Of our stay at home, it is not necessary to say more than it was very happily spent."

Word was received from Vance to join him in Wilkesboro on February 21. In a carriage and two wagons, the bandsmen and several interested local citizens began their journey on the morning of the twentieth. After spending a pleasant night with friends at Yadkinville (approximately twenty-five miles from Salem), the party moved on the next day and reached Wilkesboro late in the afternoon. The heraldic arrival of this jocund crew of musicians, playing their musical best, must have created no small degree of excitement among the residents of the sequestered mountain hamlet. Proceeding directly to Trainor's Hotel, headquarters of the Vance party, the boys met the governor, had supper, and presented a short concert to what Leinbach described as an "admiring crowd."

The Wilkesboro trip, though brief, was lively, interesting, and kept the band busy for most of the time.

Feb. 22. About eleven o'clock we went to the court house and played up the crowd. At twelve the Governor commenced speaking and continued for nearly two hours. It was estimated there were from twelve to fifteen hundred persons present. Of course the Governor's talk was strongly in advocacy of the war but it was evident that the feeling of his audience was not entirely in sympathy with him and it was an open question whether he had accomplished much good.

The people of Wilkes county were somewhat independent in their ideas and did not take kindly to anything that interfered with their freedom of thought and action. They had no negroes to fight for and did not believe in being shot at for the sake of somebody else.

We saw something new under the sun, for us, in Wilkesboro, to-wit, viz: women going into the grog shop to drink whiskey with the men.

After the speaking was over, Sam went with Captain H. Horton to his home to see his cousin, Mrs. Horton, now [nee?] Miss Mary Jane Vogler, to return next morning. The rest of us made preparation to give a concert and show in the courthouse at night, which proved quite a success, yielding us nearly $350 at $2 a ticket.

    Feb. 25. Before leaving town we gave a short open-air concert in front of the hotel. Our return trip was without incident.

Upon returning to Salem on February 25, they found, much to their delight, the following letter:

State of North Carolina
Executive Department
Raleigh, N.C., Feb 17, 1864.

    Pass the Band of the 26th North Carolina Troops, eleven persons until the 27th instant. By permission of General Kirkland.

(Signed) Z. B. Vance

The time at home had passed all too quickly, and the return to camp obviously lacked the thrill of anticipation felt on leaving camp for home.

On Tuesday, March 1st, we again bade our dear people goodbye and started back to the army and hard times. We had overstayed our time several days, but had no anxiety about getting into trouble.

    Our number had been increased [by] one, Will ["Billy"] Lemly having joined us [as a snare drummer]. We proposed giving a concert in Raleigh, and had asked Mr. T. F. Crist to go with us that far to help as door-keeper and then bring our "home clothes" back to Salem.

The pangs of nostalgia felt in having to leave the homefolks were no doubt relieved to some extent by succeeding events. Citing bad weather on their departure, Julius gave a descriptive account of the beginning of the return trip to camp:

It was a cold, rainy, disagreeable evening. . . . There were other passengers, so that the stage was well loaded. Several others with myself were riding on the deck seat above the driver. When within a few miles of High Point, the wheels on one side ran into a ditch and over went the stage and the nineteen occupants. I was so nearly asleep that I knew nothing of the fall until I found myself lying in the fence corner. One man was quite seriously hurt, having fallen against the fence. None of our boys were injured fortunately, nor any of our instruments. The horses had run off, so our driver and Mr. John

Clements, one of the owners of the stage line, went to a neighboring house and got a wagon to take us to town. We missed our train, of course, and spent the night at the hotel, nor could we get a train until 2 p.m. the next day, which landed us at Raleigh at eleven o'clock [on March 2]. We thus lost an evening for our concert.

On the train we had a jolly time, J. Clements making himself entertaining in a clownish way. A newly-married couple afforded us a good deal of amusement also.

Governor Vance had secured a hall at the blind Institute for us in which we gave a concert the next night, apparently much to his enjoyment as well as that of the entire audience, our receipts amounting to $480. We were in need of decent clothing, and on the Governor's order were enabled to buy material for uniform suits of the State Quarter Master.

[March] 4—Sending our surplus clothing, etc., home by Mr. [T. F.] Crist, we took train for Weldon [at] 7 p.m. In transferring our boxes at this place, in some unaccountable manner, one of them was lost. Most likely it was stolen by some soldier. It was a serious loss to us. On to Richmond that night, and on to Orange on Sunday [March 6], our boxes following us the next day. That night we had a supper of good things, and invited our Col., Major and Doctor to eat with us.

The musician boys from Salem had been away from camp since January 30, and now, upon returning to Orange, they obviously wondered what had taken place in their absence. More importantly, what about their future? With these thoughts in mind, they nevertheless had much to do and set about giving immediate attention to physical comfort, as well as all things musical. Indeed, there were sufficient demands to keep them busy!

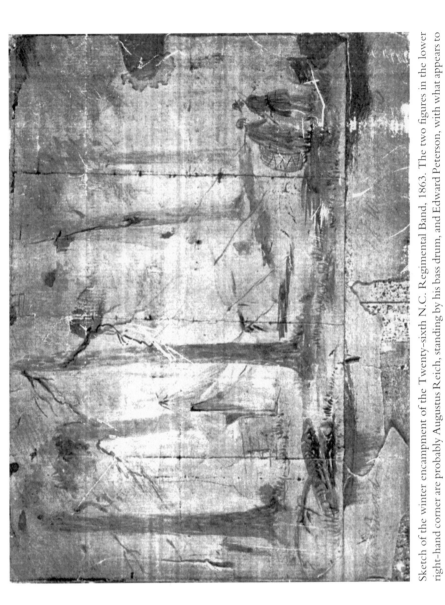

Sketch of the winter encampment of the Twenty-sixth N.C. Regimental Band, 1863. The two figures in the lower right-hand corner are probably Augustus Reich, standing by his bass drum, and Edward Peterson, with what appears to be a trombone over his right shoulder. (Image courtesy of the Moravian Music Foundation.)

6 *Lengthening Shadows of Defeat:*
A Long Road Home

Upon returning to camp from the lengthy furlough at Salem and subsequent political trip to Wilkesboro with Governor Vance, the band discovered that the regiment was now serving picket duty along the Rapidan. The members proceeded directly to the temporary encampment near the river. By mid–March, however, they were back at their main camp below Orange and remained there, happily ensconced, for nearly two months.

Throughout the narrative, Leinbach expressed his feelings for the beauty of the natural surroundings. In this instance he inserted this description, taken from a letter to his family, dated March 15, 1864:

I wish you could be here a short time to enjoy some of the glorious scenery around us. From the camp we left yesterday, we had a splendid view of the country. We were on the last of the river hills and below us lay the valley of the Rapidan (or Rapidarian) and Robertson rivers, which join a short distance below us. And beyond are the mountains in all their grandeur, every separate ridge and valley plainly to be seen. Scattered here and there are patches of cleared land, whilst the green pines intermingled with the more sombre colored oaks, together with the shadow of the clouds moving over the mountains, make the whole a most beautiful scene.[1]

Sounding a musical note of special interest two days later, he wrote:

We had been speaking of engaging the services of Prof. W[illiam] H. Hartwell of [Carnot] Posey's [Mississippi] Brigade to give us a course of instruction. The band that he has instructed plays so well that we know he can improve our playing. Sam went to see him but did not succeed in making arrangements with him.

If time passed without military incident during this period, life was by no means dull for the troops. One of the more engaging pastimes during these winter months was that of snowballing. The extent to which this popular sport might provoke serious consequences was suggested by the encounter that took place between the brigades of Cooke and Kirkland.

> March 23rd. At noon yesterday it began to snow and this morning it lay a foot deep upon the ground.
> The men of Cook's [sic] and Kirkland's brigades had been talking of having a snow battle whenever a suitable opportunity should occur, and this seemed to be just the time. All parties being ready[,] our men were marched to an open field one half mile from camp and formed in line of battle. After some time Cook's men came and took position opposite. After some preliminaries the fight began. Snow balls flew thick and fast, the men on both sides becoming excited. Charges and countercharges were made in the attempt to capture prisoners and each others' colors. Col. [William] McRae [Fifteenth North Carolina], who commanded Cook's men, was pulled from his horse and perhaps too roughly handled. It was hard to say which side had the advantage, and after a two hours struggle it was agreed to call it a drawn battle.[2]

To the musicians with their schedule of concerts and serenades, as much as the business of war would allow, went much of the credit for relieving the tedium resulting from extended periods of inaction. Thus occupied, the bandsmen found little time to experience monotony. Some of the men in the regiment, when not otherwise engaged, and routine camp duties permitting, avoided boredom and derived enjoyment by attending some of the Twenty-sixth's band rehearsals.

Recognizing their musical shortcomings, the Salem boys devoted considerable time to improving individual and group skills. In this respect, March 1864 was a particularly active month. One significant happening was, as noted earlier, to seek the assistance and tutelage of William Hartwell, whose Sixteenth Mississippi Band had singularly impressed the Moravian bandsmen. Though this first attempt was unsuccessful, arrangements were made months later whereby the distinguished musician contributed his services to the North Carolinians. In the meantime, he passed along some of his music.

This relatively long period of inaction also provided ample opportunity for writing more letters to those at home. The following, written in early April, described a special kind of diversion, as well as concern over the possibility of another campaign in the near future:

Yesterday [April 11] we went to see a grand tournament. We had never witnessed anything of the kind and were very much entertained. It was gotten up by the army officers and an immense concourse of people were present, the ladies being out in full force.

Along the course were placed some twenty-five yards apart, first a wooden head on a post, then was suspended a two-inch ring, next a wooden head on a low post, 8 inches from the ground, and lastly a similar one on a six foot post. Horsemen at full gallop were to cut off the first head, catch the ring on their sword, cut off the low head and impale the high one. Prizes were offered of course, some forty officers entered the list, each of whom rode five times, so that the affair lasted for several hours. Some men were quite expert, while others afforded the spectators much amusement by their awkwardness. A crowning of a Queen of Love and Beauty and a dance followed at night, which of course we did not attend.

We were made unpleasantly aware that the spring campaign was expected to open soon. Orders for the sending of surplus baggage to Richmond had been issued. There are camp rumors that this army is to be reinforced by a strong body of cavalry and infantry. That we will have a severe campaign, there can be no doubt. God grant that it may be a successful one for us.

My breakfast this morning consisted of corn bread and coffee. The feast is over and we will be most likely on short rations most of the time hereafter. How near starvation our condition may become before the summer is ended remains to be seen and felt.

Some of the recruits that came in during the winter have become so much frightened by preparatory orders that thirteen deserted from our regiment last night. Poor fellows, they had much better remained. There would have been some chance of their going through the campaign safely. If they were caught now, their fate is sealed.

Even as army life left its damaging mark upon the physical condition of the musicians, it was equally hard on their instruments.[3] To replace these with a complete set of silver horns had been the bandsmen's wish for some time, but the irremediable problem of financing such a purchase should have settled the matter without further ado. Generally, any money received from recent concerts had been quickly spent on food, much of which Leinbach described as "indigestible trash." Following the group's return from furlough, however, the subject was considered again, and this time someone was ready with a solution—an application to their friend Zeb Vance. Their former colonel seemed to favor his band boys, so why not appeal to his obliging nature in this instance? Within a few days there would very likely be the opportunity of broaching the subject in person, as the governor, currently touring the North Carolina troops of Lee's command, was scheduled to speak to the brigades of Cooke and Kirkland on March 29.[4] Inclement weather forced the cancellation of his visit to the bandsmen's area, so they resorted to correspondence in their quest for help. That the power of suggestion rather than a direct appeal for a monetary gift might be the best approach was expressed by Leinbach:

Gov. Vance has been exporting cotton and importing supplies for the army, and so we have written to him about our project. In reply we received the following letter:

STATE OF NORTH CAROLINA
Executive Dept.
Raleigh, N.C., April 13, 1864

Mr. J. A. Lineback:

Sir:—His Excellency, Gov. Vance, has received yours asking if you can export cotton enough to purchase a set of instruments for your band. He directs me to say he will ship the cotton for that purpose if you will furnish it, provided the steamers continue to run.

> Yours very respectfully,
> DAVID A. BARNES
> Aide-de-Camp for the Governor

Imagine the band's surprise when Vance failed to take the hint! In Julius's words, "it is practically unnecessary to say that we could not and did not furnish the cotton, and therefore did not get the coveted set of silver instruments." With this statement the issue was no doubt closed; the subject was dropped, or at least Leinbach omitted mentioning it again.

Rumors of an impending spring campaign had been circulating through camp during the last few weeks, and with vivid memories of past experiences in the field, several of the bandsmen were understandably seeking assignments elsewhere. Without initiating any such move, Alex Meinung appeared to have the means for his deliverance. While engaged in his favorite pastime of sketching camp scenes, he attracted the attention of an unnamed officer who recommended him for assignment in the Topographical Office at Richmond. Much to Alex's disappointment, the proposed transfer was rejected.[5] Once again, the hand of unappreciated authority interposed to preserve the integrity of the Salem Band.

Toward the last of April, as if by magic, the sleeping hills and valleys of the Virginia countryside appeared to awaken overnight. Against a sylvan background of bursting buds and blossoming dogwood lay a greening landscape, ornately tinted by the season's first flowers and shrubs.[6]

Touched by the freshness of an early spring, the Army of Northern Virginia also came to life. Orders were issued to ship all surplus baggage to Richmond. Realizing the necessity for traveling light, the bandsmen reluctantly quartered their tent flies so that they could be transported individually, thus allowing each member some measure of protection should the group become separated, which experience had proved to be inevitable under such conditions. The usual directive to preserve and prepare extra rations for travel was simply regarded as a joke. Any curtailment or storing of edibles would have reduced the boys' subsistence almost to a complete state of imagination. A caustic reminder of the band's food status is that the "regular bill of fare consists of corn bread and bacon [in limited amount] with an occasional change to bacon and corn bread." Wild onions from nearby fields, fried in bacon gravy, were an added treat!

The medical department of Hill's corps underwent a minute inspection on April 30, with the band "playing during the time." This was a well-known omen of impending action and dispelled any doubt as to the imminence of a tactical engagement. Something was afoot. But what had evoked this state of urgency that so rudely disrupted the relatively peaceful flow of life in the Confederate camp?

On March 9, Maj. Gen. Ulysses Simpson Grant had been promoted to lieutenant general in the United States Army; three days later, he was placed in command of all the Union forces. Within two weeks he established headquarters at Culpeper Court House with Meade's Army of the Potomac and shortly thereafter formulated his plan for the total defeat of the Confederacy.[7] In keeping with his assignment to coordinate the movements of all Federal troops, Grant devised a master plan of concerted action to begin the latter part of April. The immediate move of Meade's army on Richmond was the foremost concern of Lee's soldiers.

By May 2, after days of speculation, Lee had correctly assumed that Grant intended pressing immediately against the Confederate right flank with a march to the south.[8] On the morning of the fourth, the Confederate commander's belief was confirmed by a mass Federal movement in the direction of Germanna and Ely's Fords.[9] Correspondingly, Lee's forces were set in motion that same day about noon.[10] As the Confederates made camp that evening, the Army of the Potomac made its way across the Rapidan.

Both armies were moving early the next morning. The Federals, having completed their crossing of the river, proceeded southward along the Germanna Plank Road, practically at right angles to the eastbound forces of Lee. The inevitable occurred shortly before noon. The leading elements of Ewell's corps made initial contact with the enemy about two miles from Wilderness Tavern, at the intersection of the Germanna Plank Road and the Orange-Fredericksburg Turnpike. By mid-afternoon of May 5, the Battle of the Wilderness was well under way.[11] This signaled the opening of the series of hard-fought operations known as the Wilderness Campaign.[12]

Taking their position with the hospital unit for the next few days, the bandsmen were again busily engaged in the unpleasant duty of ministering to the wounded and dying, of which there were many! During the early hours of battle the shouts of command, the din of artillery fire and musketry, as well as the screams of wounded and dying were all too familiar reminders of the grim task ahead. Among the early casualties was Lt. Col. John T. Jones, who had for many months acted as regimental commander of the Twenty-sixth during the absence of Colonel Lane. The musicians had grown to love and respect this capable officer and, in Julius's words, "considered him the best friend we had in the regiment." Realizing that Jones had suffered mortal wounds, Mickey and Reich remained with him through the night of May 6. The next day, following his death around 10:00 A.M., the boys sadly prepared the body for burial in Orange the next morning.[13]

For nearly three days the battle swayed back and forth with neither side gaining a material advantage. On May 7 Grant withdrew towards Spotsylvania Court House. Throwing his forces against Lee's entrenched troops shortly after daybreak on a foggy morning five days later, he climaxed the fierce struggle by capturing the greater portion of the Confederate center.[14]

From this point the scene of action shifted slowly southeastward, as Grant edged closer to Richmond by means of a series of flanking maneuvers. The Confederates always countered, however, with moves of their own. On May 21, Ewell, followed closely by Longstreet, then Hill, moved southward along Telegraph Road.[15] The following evening Lee's troops encamped on the south bank of the North Anna River.

Following the engagement at Spotsylvania Court House, the Confederates were under constant pressure to keep moving. This forced the field hospital and bandsmen to maintain a position uncomfortably near the combat units. Frequently, the breastworks were clearly visible, and Leinbach reported many instances when the enemy bands were distinctly audible above the incessant firing of opposing picket lines.

On numerous occasions the Twenty-sixth musicians were ordered from the relative safety of their hospital posts to furnish music for the frontline troops. Earlier, on May 14 near Guinea Station, after General Kirkland had ordered all bands of the brigade to the breastworks, Mickey was forced to borrow an E-flat cornet from a member of the Forty-fourth North Carolina Band because his instrument had been stolen the night before. Several days later, after a sojourn to the front for another concert, Ed Peterson and Gus Reich, having become lost while returning to the hospital, spent half the night in locating their camp, though it lay only a couple of miles away from the spot where they had performed.

By May 23 the boys had emerged from the Wilderness and were located near the South Anna River. There, for the first time in several days, they relieved themselves of an accumulation of dust and grime. Presumably the issue from the commissary wagons had been particularly bountiful, because a good breakfast was mentioned. Disconcerting news was passed down about the same time: orders to cook three days' rations. Fortunately, food was available this time. The provisions were welcome, of course, but the extra preparation could mean only one thing—push on, more action to come.

The following afternoon the hospital was established at Winston's Farm near Taylorsville, located just north of the South Anna on the Richmond, Fredericksburg and Potomac Railroad. Another letter written by Leinbach from this station indicated that at least the musicians were optimistic concerning the present series of operations:

Field Hospital near Taylorsville, Va.
May 26th 1864.
     Seated under my little fly, tailor fashion, I will try to reply to your last letter. The other boys are variously engaged in sleeping, cooking, eating, etc. . . . Tho Grant is nearer than he was three weeks ago, he is only so geographically and is no nearer having this army whipped than when the first gun was fired. Nay, not so near, for he has lost much more heavily in these fights than we have . . . and his troops, at least so we are told, are discouraged whilst ours are in better spirits as each day shows our advantage. Our line of battle now runs nearly east and west just above Taylorsville. We have been in this position several days and Grant shows no disposition to attack. I imagine his object is to flank us and get closer to Richmond before he does any more fighting, but he would find General Lee a match for him in maneuvering.

Beginning the morning after writing this letter, Julius recorded a series of events in diary format, but there is no indication whether these are extracts from letters that he had written to Salem or from another source.

     27th.—At 2 o'clock a.m. we had orders to get ready to move. We left the hospital camp at 8 o'clock and reached Ashland at 12, having had a very hot and trying march. Here we lay until 6, when we were ordered to join the men on another road some miles away.

28th.—We started again at 3 o'clock crossed the railroad and at 6 stopped for breakfast. A short distance further on we again stopped, while other troops passed us. Borrrowing a "Dutch Oven" at a house close by, we baked some bread[,] paying for its use in music. At noon we went on down the railroad some distance. The wagons not coming up, we ran short of rations.

Sunday, 29th.—The wagons arrived and [we] soon went to cooking. Serenaded some ladies at General Heath's [Heth's] quarters and were paid with milk and eggs which we considered a legal tender. Moving a mile further, troops were thrown into line of battle, whilst we went to the ambulance camp for the night.

30th.—Fearing that our men would get into trouble with the enemy, we prepared our hospital, that is put up operating tables, but fortunately they were not needed at that time.

31st.—All bands were ordered to their regiments to remain there until an engagement should occur. We quartered ourselves under a large tree by the roadside and played for the men while fighting was going on to our right. About sundown we went to General Kirkland's quarters to play but did not do so on account of heavy skirmishing not far off. On getting back to the regiment, which was in support of a battery, we mounted the breastworks and played but without drums.

Continuing the line of march on the following morning, the troops veered sharply southeastward and proceeded in the direction of Bethesda Church, just northeast of Richmond, to head off the Federals who, on the same day, were moving southward toward the Pamunkey River at Hanovertown, about fourteen miles from the capital. The ensuing engagement was the fierce struggle known as Cold Harbor.[16]

By 8:00 A.M. on June 3, Grant had failed to carry Lee's heavily entrenched lines, thus ending the present assault against Richmond. On the evening of the twelfth, Grant called off the attack in this sector and withdrew his forces across the Chickahominy, reaching the James River southeast of the city on the following night.

During and after Cold Harbor, the hospital served by the band was located at several points in the vicinity of Mechanicsville and Gaines's Mill, practically on the outskirts of Richmond. In referring to the establishment of hospitals at the various places, Julius indicated that it was largely a matter of setting up the operating tables. There was little fighting for several days following the intense encounter on June 3, so the musicians made frequent visits to various units at the front. On the eighth, while visiting the troops of Kershaw's and Hoke's brigades, the Salem boys had the opportunity of hearing the fine bands of the Fifteenth and Twenty-fifth South Carolina Regiments.[17] Commenting on the excellence of the latter, Julius stated, not surprisingly, that the organization "is composed of Germans who have been playing together for thirteen years. They played a good deal of operatic music."

On the afternoon of June 14, when it seemed likely that Petersburg, not Richmond, would probably be the next field of action, the Confederate forces were deployed accordingly.[18] Moving southward from its position northeast of Richmond, Hill's corps was located eventually in familiar territory near Malvern Hill, between the Chickahominy and James Rivers. Leinbach related that the task of preparing food on the march was by no means an easy or enviable one:

14th.—Moving a mile further, we rested all day, receiving orders to march in the morning. The enemy is said to have left the north side of the Chickahominy. Preparatory to the marching, I was up all night in "the kitchen" cooking and baking bread. It may seem strange to my readers (should I ever have any) that it should take all night to cook the little that we received. But when it is remembered that all night meant in our case from perhaps 10 o'clock until 4[,] and during that time we had to wait for our rations to be issued, cut and carry up wood, green of course, get a bed of coals and our utensils hot, make up our dough, after carrying water, sometimes from long distances, etc., it can well be imagined we had no time to waste.

15th.—I was quite sick after my night's work. Our marching orders were countermanded and troops threw up breastworks instead. . . . We made our hospital arrangements on Frazier's Farm, near the Charles City road.

Lee's movements were reassuring to the citizens and defenders of Petersburg who, understandably, believed that their town was seriously endangered.[19] On the seventeenth, Hill's corps was ordered to Chaffin's Bluff on the north bank of the James River, about fourteen miles north of Petersburg. There was confusion among some of the Confederate command in trying to determine the enemy's next move, because much of Grant's force seemed to have disappeared. Instructions were issued accordingly: prepare for a move in either direction—Richmond or Petersburg—as the situation may require.[20] By early the next morning, the decision had been made:

At 4:30 a.m. we started toward Drewry's Bluff [approximately thirteen miles due north of Petersburg on the south bank of the James]. The fortifications at this point were pretty extensive. It being the main defense on the James River against the advance of gunboats up the river to Richmond. It was very hot and dusty. At 10:30 we crossed the James River on [a] pontoon bridge, above which was moored a war vessel "Patrick Henry." We marched on toward Petersburg, going very fast, the stretch across the river bottom seeming almost like going thru a furnace. There was much straggling by the men, "of whom I was which." Five or six miles from Petersburg the troops took train, debarking again a mile from the city. The hospital was located a mile from the railroad and turnpike on the north side of Petersburg.

It was a glad day indeed for the town's citizenry, when Hill's corps marched through the streets on the afternoon of June 18.[21]

The adverse effect of the march on the musicians, together with some first impressions of their new theater of operations, was reported in the first of several letters written from this station to Salem:

Hospital, one mile from Petersburg,
June 22, 1864

My last was written from York River Railroad. Next evening, the 13th, we left that place, marching a good part of the night, and took a very early start again the next morning, but only went a very short distance, coming upon some of the enemy at White Oak Swamp. That night I again cooked all night, and next morning became very sick, unable to hold up my head. Fortunately we did not move as we had expected. For several days I was far from well, riding in an ambulance when we did move. Meanwhile, we had gotten to Malvern Hill. The fortifications were not occupied by any of our troops. The enemy's gunboats were within shelling distance, down the river. I recognized many familiar landmarks, the place where I had gotten my knapsack in '62, etc.

On Friday evening we took the back track for a few miles and then next morning went toward Drewry's Bluff and on to Petersburg. That was a march to be remembered. It was exceedingly hot and dusty, the men marching very fast, there apparently being great need for them in this vicinity. I was not well yet, and therefore could not keep up with the rapidly moving troops, and so I "fell out." Presently Dan came creeping along and we two soon lay down, companions in misery and slept until everything had passed. We then took our time, resting long and at frequent intervals. Gus also came up to us, and at noon on Sunday we got to the hospital, scarcely able to crawl.

Since then I have been improving. Yesterday Sam and I went to Petersburg and called on some of our friends and got a capital dinner, with a lot of vegetables to take back to camp "free, gratis and for nothing." This morning I exchanged some corn meal for a cup of milk and some biscuits and if I only had money could fare very well. But all of us are financially busted and the pies and cakes, bread and vegetables that are offered daily, tempt us in vain. Cold corn bread as a regular diet is not very good, and I gladly swap rations whenever I have anything to spare.

But about the situation. Grant does not seem disposed to charge our works just yet. There is some shelling going on, some bombs falling in the city, but not doing much damage so far. The enemy is busy mounting heavy siege guns that will no doubt be heard from later.

Most of the citizens have left the eastern, more exposed part of the city. The whole place can be reached by bombs, but that would be a barbarous piece of work, that Grant will surely not stoop to. Why he didn't take the city some time ago, when it was admitted he had it in his power, can only be explained by what is reported, that he mistook the city water works for a heavy battery. Just at this minute I hear the brigade is moving and must stop.

That same day, the brigade was ordered south of the city.[22] The musicians occupied a quasi-combatant role in this maneuver, though armed only with their instruments. They were detached from hospital duty and "ordered to play on the extreme right of the brigade; the object was to give the enemy the impression that our line extended much farther in that direction."[23] Unfortunately, there is no indication as to what extent, if any, the Yanks were intimidated by this ruse.

For the remainder of the summer and early fall of 1864, the opposing forces in the Richmond-Petersburg sector were engaged in frequent, sometimes heavy fighting.[24] Though achieving a modicum of success in these engagements, the Confederate defenders were, nevertheless, becoming ever more exhausted, physically and mentally.

Plagued by seemingly endless adversity that summer, the Salem musicians steadfastly continued to function with their customary spirit and resolve, at least most of the time.[25] When physically able, they gave a good account of themselves, either playing for troops at the front or at the hospital, depending upon the demands of the situation. An exacting schedule of regular musical activities included an abundance of impromptu performances for officers, and playing for regiments other than their own. A large number of dress parades and guard mounts added to the burden.[26] Kitchen skills were increasingly on trial, as the boys were repeatedly detailed to cook for the regiment. On the evening of July 1, they baked corn bread for the troops—250 pones by 1:00 A.M. the following day!

A few days later, thoughts turned to pay, and it was noted on Saturday, July 9, that

the men are being paid two months wages. As we do not belong to any company in the regiment, we need a pay-roll of our own and not having it, can draw no pay from the government at present and will have to wait awhile.

The following day another bit of bad news was received: Orders had been promulgated that no more sugar and coffee would be issued to noncombatants. This would have been a "great deprivation if we had been getting these articles in any amount. As it is it makes 'no difference.' " Thoughts returned to more pressing matters:

The division moved down the railroad about dark to guard trains coming up from Stony Creek. A surgeon and two men from each band accompany them. Henry and I accompany them.

Five of Cook's [sic] captured a Yankee with papers that gave us the first information of [General] Early being in Maryland. Trains on the south side of the road pass in and out only at night and then as quietly as possible.

Monday, 11.—The band was again called on to cook for the men. About sundown one of our batteries close by us did some heavy cannonading, possibly a blind.

12.—The regiment returns to camp. Sam and I go to Major Walleck's [Maj. Charles S. Wallach] to get payrolls for our crowd but do not succeed.

Finally, "we at length get pay-rolls [sic] and Captain Young pays us our pitifully small wages. We have been going to the regiment [from the hospital location] to play every evening." We are left to wonder if the subject of the bandsmen's need for their own payroll in order to be compensated had been discussed before; if not, why? Until this latest "flap" was finally resolved by getting a payroll of their own—no mention of how this was achieved—had the boys not received any money for several months? It seems strange that once the musicians were officially designated as the regimental band in August 1863, though rated as noncombatant, they would not have been qualified for pay like the other troops in the regiment.

With the bandsmen having much-needed money in their pockets, most of which would no doubt be used to enhance stringent diets, the band's feelings were assuaged greatly as they renewed their duties with the troops. As guards for various wagon trains, a duty recently imposed, the bandsmen were afforded yet another opportunity for service and to prove their versatility. For the first time, helping to maintain ambulance service on the constantly shifting battleground was mentioned in Leinbach's account. The ever-present stress of hospital duty appears, though, to have taken precedence. The extent to which Leinbach had come to regard himself as particularly adroit in this distasteful charge is revealed in his vivid description, inserted as "Note" in the narrative:

By this time we had had considerable experience in giving first aid to the wounded and I for one got myself to believe that I could amputate a man's leg as well as some of the doctors; having so often helped in the several processes of applying tourniquet, cutting and slipping back the skin for a flap to cover the end of the stump, then cutting the flesh, tieing the arteries, sawing and trimming the bone and closing the wound. . . . [T]here were no antiseptics used. Such a thing as blood poisoning was not thought of, it had not been invented. Gangrene seemed to be the only later danger that was feared. Chloroform was of course administered in cases of severe operations. During the time of unconsciousness, most of them lay perfectly quiet; some however, would sing, some few perhaps swear while others would pray. One man in particular, I remember, prayed at the top of his voice during the whole time that his leg was being taken off as I never heard one pray before nor since. The limbs that were amputated were usually buried by us unless some of the ambulance corps were ordered to do it.

Toward the latter part of June, a letter was received indicating that the home folks were also experiencing hard times: "Writing paper, 75¢ to $1 per sheet; handsaw files, $10.00; salt fish, $2.00 [per] pound; cherries, 75¢ per quart; corn $10.00 per bushel." Leinbach countered on July 24 with a rather descriptive account of some of the present hardships being endured by loved ones in service:

Have just eaten heartily of a first rate dinner, composed of a potato stew gotten up in good old Dutch style with dumplings. We are much like snakes, swallow a week's supply of food when we have it, then starve for awhile. Where we are located at this time, we can get almost anything we want in the eating line if we have money to pay for it. In the morning, market carts pass by on their way to town and later in the day women come out with pies, cakes and other edibles that coax the dollars out of our pockets at a fearful rate.

What have I to complain of just now is that I will soon be reduced to the condition of the little "niggers" one often sees, who can boast of a very scanty supply of clothing unless our quartermaster soon returns from Raleigh with a supply. I have a shirt and one pair of drawers in pretty good condition. And the other garments I possess are only in part. From the top of my head to the soles of my feet—well, Solomon in all his glory was not arrayed like I am. My hat is one that I had discarded long ago; my coat or jacket has long since ceased to make any pretensions to respectability; the ends of the sleeves have been faced with material of a different color and are drawn and tuckered into a pretty fair representative of a sucker's mouth. My pants,—it is not worth while to say where they have given out. Sox heelless and toeless and shoes one having sole and body tied together with strings and the other badly run down and busted. Such is my picture at present. I hope sometime to present a more respectable appearance.

At one point he despairingly inquired: "What is more uncertain than a soldier's life and movements?" Ostensibly, this uncertainty assumed added significance for the Twenty-sixth musicians following their arrival at Petersburg. The constant shifting of their unit's base of operations; the frequent impromptu dashes to avoid the enemy; the severity of travel conditions on many marches, separated from the other band members; and the hurried relocation of the field hospital—all added up to the stringent nature of the boys' plight and, indeed, threatened their very survival!

There were times, nevertheless, when even the austerity of travel and constant danger faded during brief periods of relaxation and pleasure. One evening the band went serenading with General Heth as he visited friends at "a rather pretentious residence" on the outskirts of Petersburg. As an abundance of food and drink was usually in the offing on these occasions, the boys were always ready to oblige, even at a moment's notice. Another time, after having witnessed a review of General Kirkland's new brigade, the group

Charlie Transou's "Minié Ball Book." This band book was apparently pierced by an enemy ball while the band was camped near Petersburg in early August 1864. As Julius Lineback recorded: "During the night we could hear the balls singing over our heads but considered ourselves quite safe behind the bluff. However, one night as Charlie was about to lie down, using a booksack as a pillow, he heard a thud and on examination found that a minié ball had struck the book sack, striking one of his books." (Image courtesy of the Moravian Music Foundation.)

attended a Petersburg concert given by their fellow musician friends Hartwell, Charlie Siegel, and others.[27] An added treat was the privilege of spending the night "on the floor in the public room of

Jarrett's Hotel." Of course their occasional visits to the troops, often uncomfortably close to enemy lines, usually afforded the Moravian musicians an opportunity to hear and critique the bands of their adversary—no doubt a most enjoyable pastime.

By the middle of September, a number of the band's instruments were in serious need of repair, that is, if the troops were to continue enjoying the musical services of the talented Twenty-sixth. Evidently making his point with sufficient emphasis, Mickey accordingly secured a two-day leave *in the interest of regimental morale.*

Shortly after Sam's return from Petersburg with the newly repaired horns, Mickey's own instrument, which had been stolen the preceding May, was recovered from a Negro who was passing through the camps with a sale on his mind. Happily (and understandably), the cornet was recovered without the peddler receiving the desired recompense. Maybe the tide of fortune had at last begun to turn in favor of the Salem Band—instruments in decent playing condition once more and the recovery of their leader's fine cornet. Well, perhaps, but for the moment it seemed the time for writing another letter to Salem, updating present conditions:

Petersburg, Va., Oct. 6, 1864.

Altho I still date from the city, we are still some miles from the place of my last letter. The miserable Yankees have had us running hither and thither and have succeeded in gaining considerable ground on us by strategy, but not by fighting between the Weldon and Southside roads. . . .

Some days ago there was a pretty general impression that preparations were being made to evacuate Petersburg. But I do not think there was any ground there for [concern].

Following this letter, several items (resembling diary entries) in the account indicated another move was imminent; yet there was still time to focus on some music making:

7th.—Had our bacon stolen last night.

8th.—Orders to pack up and be ready to move. The men went into the trenches and sharpshooters were sent out while we went to the cook yard. There was no fighting.

10th.—We changed our position again. There was some skirmishing.

11th.—Several of us went with the 27th band, serenading in Petersburg. The Yankee bands and drums were very noisy all night.

18th.—The 27th band and ours serenaded General McRae.

25th.—Sam went to the 14th South Carolina band to play with them at of [a?] cavalry review. On his way back next day he very narrowly escaped being captured.

November witnessed the battle of the opposing giants calming down to a series of minor clashes, as the armies prepared to entrench for the winter.[28] Ironically, the day Sherman began his famous March to the Sea (November 15, 1864), the troops in the Twenty-sixth Band's area laid out their ground for winter quarters. Within a few days the musicians had once again provided themselves with huts similar to those constructed at their Orange Court House encampment. They were hardly settled when Hartwell paid the boys a visit, and arrangements were satisfactorily concluded for his long-awaited professional help. Not until December 22, though, did the band receive its first instruction from the Mississippian.

Following the usual routine, life settled down somewhat for the first time in months. If monotonous for many of the Rebs, the Salemites, once again, experienced few dull moments. There was

guard mount, breakfast, practicing, dress parade, dinner—we usually had two meals a day, still left much time to [be] disposed of. Writing letters, getting up wood, etc., visiting other commands, playing games, principally whist, never any gambling, sometimes sleeping, such were some of our pastimes. Sometimes Gus would get up an impromptu entertainment with some of his simpler slight [*sic*] of hand tricks, singing comic songs and making nonsincical [*sic*] speeches and he would always have a good audience of dead heads. Everything in the way of reading matter was at a premium. Shakespeare, Godolphin, Los Mizerables [*sic*] (we called ourselves Lee's miserables), were standard. The men were always in good humor and ready for fun of any kind.

Added attractions included the occasional appearance of civilian eccentrics who, if not made the butt of good-natured jokes, proved a source of entertainment for the Rebs in a variety of other ways. Such was the case when, on November 17, a surprise visit was paid the Twenty-sixth by

a crank of a man, Davis, by name . . . making speeches about an invention he had made which he called "Rare Avis," a bird that was to ascend and make observations of the enemy's movements, drop bombs into their camp and all sorts of things.

With the approach of another Christmas, thoughts turned again toward the possibility of obtaining a furlough. Any notions entertained in this respect were quickly dispelled by Brig. Gen. William McRae, who had commanded the brigade since Kirkland was disabled by a wound received at Cold Harbor.[29] Disapproval of a leave at this time undoubtedly set the stage for one of the more dismal holiday seasons of the band's enlistment. The musicians and the combat troops were dismayed by daily reports of Confederate reverses in other theaters, and physically weakened by the ever decreasing ration supply and the severity of the weather.[30] The troops had been without meat for some time, and daily weather reports indicated rain, snow, and/or sleet. At the same time, the bandsmen were burdened by increased demands for their musical services.[31] The combined effect of all of these factors contributed to a state of utter disillusionment experienced by the Twenty-sixth musicians during the *joyous* Yuletide. As if to add salt to wounded spirits, they sadly watched their friends of the Twenty-seventh Band depart on December 31 for Greensboro, the central assembling point for men of that regiment, or at least the band.[32] Though more poignant at this time, the voice of gloom and despair had laconically been sounded in a Leinbach letter of early October: "Time will show what the end will be and I care not much how soon it comes."

By mid-February 1865, the lengthening shadows of defeat had indubitably extended across the withering armies of the Confederacy, the major portion of which, for all practical purposes, were located in Virginia and the Carolinas. News of the fall of Fort Fisher on January 15 was a devastating blow to the gaunt, thin line of troops at Petersburg.[33] Lee's attack on the Federal forces at Hatcher's Run on February 5-6 proved both costly and unsuccessful; and with Sherman's advance through North Carolina, which reached Goldsboro by March 23, the Confederate's principal route of supply, the Weldon Railroad, was seriously threatened.

Rumors of an armistice had persisted since the first of the year; however, for the many who would have preferred ending the conflict then, Grant on March 4 had spiked any hopes of a negotiated peace.[34] There was no alternative but to fight it out until the bitter end.

On March 26, following a desperate, unsuccessful attempt by a Confederate force under Maj. Gen. John B. Gordon to take the Yankee-held Fort Stedman just east of Petersburg, Lee decided to remove his army to the south and join Gen. Joseph E. Johnston's troops in North Carolina.[35] Anticipating such a move for several days, Grant had ordered the destruction of the vital Richmond and Danville and South Side Railroads, an action that would force the Confederates from their entrenchments.[36] This series of operations precipitated the engagements at Dinwiddie Court House and White Oak Road on March 31, and the Battle of Five Forks on April 1.[37] Occurring in the general vicinity of the Twenty-sixth Regiment, the ensuing sequence of events affected the immediate fortunes of the Moravian musicians.

The night of March 31 was spent in the breastworks with a portion of the regiment.[38] The following day, about 3:00 A.M., the bandsmen were rudely awakened by a wounded picket loudly proclaiming that an enemy charge in that sector was imminent and that the musicians had best remove themselves to their accustomed position in the rear. Uttering the familiar expression, "realizing that discretion was the better part of valor," Leinbach and the rest of the boys hastily retired to their cabins, gathered up their few belongings, and moved back even further to the general headquarters area. Having satisfied themselves that there was no immediate danger, they prepared breakfast, then proceeded to catch up on lost sleep. But Billy Yank was really persistent this time.

Dan and I had just gotten down to the foot of a tree, when "pat" a minnie [*sic*] ball struck it just above our heads. I jumped up and said: "Boys, let's get away from here." Just then some one said: "The Yankees are coming," and sure enough a long blue line, sparkling with flashes of musketry was moving rapidly toward us and our men in pitifully small numbers in full retreat.

We needed no one to tell us what to do. I then and there was hurrying to and fro. Snatching up our baggage, we left, and stood not on the order of our going. . . . Over fences, across fields, deep in soft ground, from the rains, we made our way as best we could. To lighten our loads, some of us discarded what we thought we could best spare. I emptied my little sack of corn meal and savings of weeks. One of the boys, of a somewhat peculiar disposition had accumulated souvenirs and treasures of various kinds which he had in pouches slung around him. As he was floundering along, encumbered by his many possessions, he exclaimed: "Oh Lord, what shall I do." Another one with more vehemence than reverence volunteered the advice that he should "throw away some of them damned bags." As we passed wagon yards, drivers were hurriedly harnessing their teams and driving off furiously.

After we had gone a few miles and seemed to have gotten away from everybody else, we came to a house where the good lady gave us some bread and meat, for which we returned our acknowledgements by playing "Lorina," [sic] thereby ending our musical career as the 26th North Carolina Regimental Band.[39] Altho we knew it not at the time. Someone told us we had better stop playing as the Yankees would hear us and would certainly try to capture us.

We were between the road and the river. . . .[40] Despairing of [not] being able to cross the river, we followed it up stream until we were thoroly [sic] tired and worn out and took up bivouac in the woods.

Next morning [April 2] we started again and went some distance until we came to a bluff, covered with pretty thick growth, which we thought would make a pretty good hiding place for us until the Yankee army had passed by, when we hoped to be able to cross the road and make our way toward Weldon, and either rejoin our command or strike out for home.[41]

Under the protective cover of a hill the confused group remained for a couple of days, pondering their fate. Though practically in the path of a steady stream of Federal troops, the boys did risk several trips to a nearby house for food.[42] Finally, the benevolent farm woman serving the Rebs, fearing measures of reprisal from the Yankees—her actions had been reported by neighbors—refused to supply the bandsmen any longer. They must move on, though still undecided as to what course of action should be followed. The situation became more critical.

[To] remain where we were we could not. We had nothing to eat; Yankees had said that they were going to have us dead or alive. We believed that the cause of the Confederacy was in such desperate straits that should we even succeed in reaching our regiment, there was great likelihood that we would be put in the ranks and while that would have been bad enough earlier in the war, now when all hope for the success of the South seemed to be utterly gone, we were not willing to become marks for Yankee bullets. We therefore determined to leave our retreat, cross the road if we could and if not give ourselves up as prisoners of war. Striking a little by road we followed it

E-flat cornet parts to *Lorena* and *Bright Smiles*, by J. P. Webster. According to Julius Lineback, *Lorena* was the last piece played by the Twenty-sixth Regimental Band. (Image courtesy of the Moravian Music Foundation.)

until it took us into the main road and right into a squad of the enemy. We walked up to them and were taken in charge. Our instruments were taken from us and that seemed to be the bitterest experience of all. I had learned to love my B$^\flat$ cornet more than all the rest of my few possessions and to see it go into the hands of another and know that I would never see it again, was a very hard thing to endure. Sam had saved his silver E$^\flat$ by putting it in his haversack and taking Henry's B$^\flat$ [saxhorn], the latter having Transou's alto horn at the time, its owner being at home. The saddest reflection I had, and have, is that

(*Above*) Samuel T. Mickey's E-flat cornet and case. (*Right*) Detail of engraved name beneath the maker's mark. (*Below*) E-flat bass (saxhorn) played by Julius Lineback and Joe Hall early in the war, but left at Salem in 1862 in favor of a better horn found on the battlefield of Malvern Hill. Both instruments are now in the Collection of the Wachovia Historical Society. (Images courtesy of Old Salem, Inc.)

if I had done as Sam did, I could have saved my horn as well, as we were never searched at any time.

It was late in the afternoon of April 5, 1865, that we "joined the Yankee army" with which we marched on until night. Our guards shared their rations with us, and we had a better supper than we had enjoyed in a long time.

Along with other prisoners, the remnants of the band reached Petersburg, scene of happier times past, on the day of Lee's surrender at Appomattox. No one there, however, was aware of the series of events then taking place sixty miles to the west. The following morning, April 10, news was received of the army's capitulation.

At that time, one of many twists of fortune that steered the Twenty-sixth's course throughout the war intervened to decide its immediate and final fate, a decided turn for the worse. According to Leinbach, if the group had been in jail or a prison compound when news was received of Lee's surrender, they very likely would have been subject to immediate parole. As it was, after lengthy deliberation among their captors, it was decided that the prisoners should be transferred to the Federal prison at Point Lookout, Maryland. (None of the band members were then aware of their ultimate destination though.)

Julius waxed sentimental in expressing the air of gloom, dejection, and uncertainty as they were marched toward the outskirts of Petersburg:

Then we realized more fully than we had done that we were prisoners indeed, and that each step we were forced to take was away from home and all that we held most dear. When would we be permitted again to see our loved ones, or even to communicate with them and relieve the anxiety they would naturally feel for our safety and welfare? Where were we going and what treatment would be accorded us? Sad and gloomy indeed were our thoughts.

Farewell home and friends, farewell Southern Confederacy, farewell 26th North Carolina regiment, farewell 26th North Carolina Regimental Band. No more would we play for guard mount and dress parade. Never again shall your familiar airs cheer and be cheered by the men, who for three years were wont to call you, "our band."

There is no more any 26th North Carolina regiment. It had passed into history, and such a history as any organization might well be proud.

Go on then, you men who but a few days ago were proud to call yourselves the 26th North Carolina Band,—go on, driven by [as?] cattle to your future abode in the "bull pen," there to herd with other men as good or better than you, but more filthy only because they have been longer in that place of abondation [*sic*].

At that point Leinbach snapped out of his state of pathos. He continued with remarks concerning the fate that had befallen Ed Peterson and Gus Reich. When they

reached the main road, they soon came in contact with a squad of Yankees, who quickly took them in charge. Ed had to give up his slide trombone, while one of the men took Gus's bass drum and beating it called out: "Keep step with the music." Rain coming on, they all took refuge in a box car, the floor of which was thickly covered with flour of which some was taken to a neighboring house for the lady there to bake into bread, for doing which she was given a silver tankard, that had evidently been stolen from some other house. When they all left the car, our boys were told to go where they pleased. Somehow the two got separated from each other. Gus eventually getting to the regiment, where he was greeted with a shout: "The band has come," to which he had to reply, "This is all there is left of it." He was paroled with the band and worked his way home. Ed fell in with Joe [Hall] and the two kept together, Joe giving away his big bass horn, rather than carry it, and both reached home a few days after Gus.

Having marched to City Point, approximately ten miles northeast of Petersburg on the James River, the prisoners in Leinbach's group were placed aboard a small craft about 11:00 A.M. on April 12. After a miserable voyage in this open, over-crowded vessel, its human cargo soaked by persistent showers, the captive band boys debarked at Point Lookout on April 14. The ensuing period of affliction and anguish was a condition best described by one so closely touched:

We were examined, registered and everything of value taken from us. Then we were put into small inclosures in which were some 2,500 or 3,000 men and given a large bell tent for our quarters. In a few days we were transferred to a larger pen, surrounded by a highboard fence at the top of which negro guards, with loaded muskets, marched back and forth. Guarded by "niggers." Could anything be more humiliating?

We had not been thus incarcerated many days, when President Lincoln was assassinated. That tragedy made our condition somewhat critical. The whole country was wrought up and our negro guards especially so and we were warned by officers who came thru the camp not to give any signs of rejoicing or gathering in groups as the negroes were very vindictive and would be glad enough of an excuse to shoot someone. After a few days, however, the tension wore off. The pen was crowded with poor wretches, many of whom had been there for a long time. We were dropped off here and there and assigned lodging with others, wherever room could be found. Here we soon learned what poverty, misery, helplessness and dependence meant. Dirt and filth made our tent or whatever shelter we might have, almost unendurable. We had scarcely any opportunity to wash either our persons or clothing; privacy was impossible and our condition was as near that of brutes as could well be imagined, the difference probably being in favor of the latter. There were a number of wells in the inclosure, only two or three of which yielded water that could be used for drinking while that from the others was hardly fit for any other purpose and we were closely restricted in the quantity of water we used. Here we, with thousands of other miserable creatures, dragged out a miserable existence, many poor fellows giving up their unequal fight for life every day.

Those of the band who had kept together up to this time, and were now in this slough of despondency were the following: Sam Mickey, Abe Gibson, Henry Siddall, Charlie Transou, Will ["Billy"] Lemly, Dan Crouse, and J. A. Lineback.

Our food consisted of a piece of bread in the morning and a piece of meat and a pint of soup at 1 o'clock. Sometimes decaying codfish would take the place of the meat. Whatever the noon rations might be, it was arranged on both sides of a long table in a large hall. We were mustered into double ranks and marched into the cook-house, one file going on one side of the table and one on the other, the first man stopping at the end and taking his place there, the next one passing on to his and so on. It sometimes happened that at one place there would be a small piece of meat or a bone and at the next a nice chunk of solid meat. In such a case, an exchange was sure to be made if possible.

On this poor and scanty fare we managed to exist, but were in a chronic state of hunger. Every morning sanitary policing was done and a place on the detail that do this disgusting work was eagerly sought for the sake of a double ration. Some set traps at the cook-house for rats to add to their bill of fare.

In this abominable hole we lay for nearly three months. . . . Every army of the Southern Confederacy, "so called," had been disbanded and the brave southern soldiers had gone to their homes to begin life again, while we were still held in confinement for what reason we did not know. I had sent one letter home and had received one from there, so I knew that my people were aware of my whereabouts. At last in the latter part of June, there began to be hopeful talk of our being paroled. When the day really arrived for our paroling to begin, all prisoners whose names began with "A" were ordered to assemble opposite the office, then they were called in one by one and given their parole papers. Of course, we began to calculate how long it might be until our respective turns might come, but all our calculations were knocked out when after several letters of the alphabet had been gone thru, the call was made for names beginning at the end of the alphabet. After the regular number for the day had gone out, boys were called and those from the most distant states were sent out first. Billy presented himself as a boy, but when he had to say that North Carolina was his home, the officer in charge, Colonel [Allen G.] Brady, who was on horseback, said: "You can't go. Your home is too near." Billy caught him by the leg and begged so hard that finally the colonel said: "Well, go on." So our youngest member was the first to get away.

My turn came at last on June 28th. What a sensation of relief to get out of that wretched place, never to go back again. In the office I was measured and weighed. My parole and discharge was made out, the former of which I signed in duplicate, and after I had taken the oath the articles that had been taken from me when I entered the prison were returned to me except my oil cloth which having been United States property was retained. There was a small sum standing to my credit which was paid to me. I was a free man once more!

I think that I was the last of the boys to get out of the pen. Sam was just one day ahead of me and he let my people know that I was coming. I did not know any of those who were released with me, but what did I care? I was going home; home and nothing else mattered. . . . [At High Point] I found an acquaintance from Winston, N. W. Nading, who had been on the same train and we two soon started on foot for Salem. Some miles out we met my brother James in a buggy, coming to meet me with a nice lunch, which we two, dirty, half-starved ex-Confederates quickly disposed of. We reached Salem soon after noon on Sunday, July 2, 1865.[43]

After three long years, to be home at last! This was the paramount thought of each bandsman, returning to nurse the physical, mental, and moral wounds inflicted by the adversities of conflict. From the acme of triumph to the nadir of defeat—this has been their story, colorful and moving. Significantly, the personnel of the Twenty-sixth Regimental Band stemmed from the milieu of a devout people whose musical traditions stand in the front rank of America's cultural history. The band is only one aspect, but a most significant one, of that heritage. The Twenty-sixth's wartime service is a tribute to the suffering and hardship endured by musicians of the Northern and Southern armies alike. The Moravian Twenty-sixth Regimental Band from Salem was indeed the "Pride of Tarheelia." On this closing note the curtain descends.

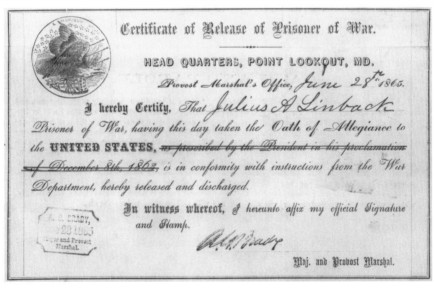

Oath of allegiance of Julius A. Lineback and his certificate of release as a prisoner of war, June 28, 1865. From the Julius A. Lineback Papers, Southern Historical Collection.

Epilogue

The Salem Band entered Confederate service in March 1862 as a group in search of a "regimental home," unlike most bands in North Carolina, if not the entire South, who derived their membership from musicians originally enlisted in companies. By a turn of fate, Salem's boys soon became the musical representative of the Twenty-sixth Regiment, one of the most distinguished bodies of musicians in Lee's Army of Northern Virginia.

Ten companies that would comprise the regiment, recruited from the western Piedmont and mountains, assembled at the camp of instruction at Camp Crabtree in Raleigh on August 27, 1861, to form the Twenty-sixth North Carolina State Troops (Infantry), originally for twelve-months duty. In keeping with custom, the regiment elected its own commander: Capt. Zebulon Baird Vance (1830-1894), Company F, the "Rough and Ready Guards," of the Fourteenth North Carolina State Troops. Prior to entering the service, Vance, a Whig congressman from Asheville, was already a renowned politician in the Old North State. Upon assuming command of the Twenty-sixth, he was promoted to colonel.

An excellent second-in-command was Maj. Henry "Harry" King Burgwyn Jr. (1841-1863), commandant of the camp of instruction. Burgwyn, who had graduated from the Virginia Military Institute in May, was described by a fellow officer as "a youth of authority, beautiful and handsome; the flash of his eye and the quickness of his movements betokened his bravery."[1]

Unfortunately, this brilliant officer, among many budding leaders, was killed at Gettysburg. The Twenty-sixth Regiment, actively engaged on July 1 and 3 in the regiment's first major encounter, was decimated. More trouble lay ahead as it fought its way through the fierce engagements of Bristoe Station, the Wilderness, Spotsylvania Court House, Cold Harbor—the list continued until the final days before Appomattox.

The regiment counted among its leaders, in addition to Colonels Vance and Burgwyn, some of the brightest men to wear the Confederate gray. Serving on Vance's initial staff was the former captain of Company G, John Randolph Lane (1835-1908). Having risen through the ranks, Lane was promoted to lieutenant colonel when Burgwyn succeeded Vance. Severely wounded at Gettysburg,

Main Street in Salem, looking north, 1866. Photo attributed to Henry A. Lineback. (Image courtesy of Old Salem, Inc.)

Lane later distinguished himself after he returned to head the Twenty-
sixth Regiment for the duration.

Bearing testimony to the Twenty-sixth's service and sacrifice
throughout the war, especially at Gettysburg, are the large number of
casualties sustained by enlisted personnel, as well as officers. So great
were the losses, the regiment could only count about 130 parolees
who made it to the bitter end! It is therefore remarkable that the
"Band Boys," often right up front, had been able to remain united,
though separated many times, throughout their enlistment.

Of course there is no way of knowing just how long it took the
members to recover—though never fully—from the horrors of the
previous three years. As in the case of most war veterans, there was a
certain amount of distressful residue that weighed heavily on the
quality of life for years thereafter, more intense for some than others.
This was undoubtedly true with Salem's bandsmen, but many battle
scars eventually disappeared, and the musicians again became actively
involved in the community's postwar musical life.

The years following the return of Julius Leinbach, a relatively
young man of thirty-one years, sparked many thoughts in the mind
of this veteran. One, probably of immediate concern, was the future
of "his" band: Would it fade into the background with the passage of
time, or would it survive during these early years of readjustment?
Would it flourish in the hands of succeeding generations?

Some insight into Leinbach's own thoughts and feelings appears in
a few paragraphs appended to the conclusion of his narrative. The
first of these, reflecting a modicum of inactivity and a degree of
disillusionment, recalled the postbellum years.

> And now what of the 26th band? Where was it? As such, it was no more.
> The boys were here, but only two of our instruments had been saved, Sam's
> and Alex's. We borrowed horns and joining a remnant of the 21st band and
> some younger boys, played together at times and even furnished music for
> commencement occasions at various schools and colleges, playing some of
> our wartime pieces, but it was not the same band any more.

Meinung's tenor saxhorn is missing among the period
instruments, some of which date from the eighteenth century, in the
Moravian collection at Salem. This is quite unusual in that the
Moravians are noted for having preserved so much of their culture.
One day, hopefully, it will surface in someone's attic or basement.
Because the E-flat bass horn played by Joe Hall was in Salem—it had

been replaced by an abandoned Yankee instrument after the Battle of Malvern Hill in 1862—a total of three of the original instruments were on hand with which to start anew after the war.

That the members borrowed some instruments from the "21st band," as Leinbach noted above, raises another of many unanswered questions: why have none of these horns been discovered—there are apparently no records of them either—over the years? At least none reside among the museum pieces in Salem. After all, the musicians of this group, whether identified as the Twenty-first Band or that of the Sharpshooters, came from the Salem community. The fate of their instruments remains a mystery.

That the band played on is reflected in the many notices the group received in the postwar local newspaper, in which two performances were brought to public attention within a few years after the boys had returned home.

The young gentlemen composing the Salem Brass Band, assisted by Professor ("Gus") Rich, will give a concert on Tuesday evening next, May 24, at Butner Hall, for the purpose of obtaining funds to improve the condition of the band.

Our people have a pride in sustaining this band, and therefore, we know they will give it a rousing

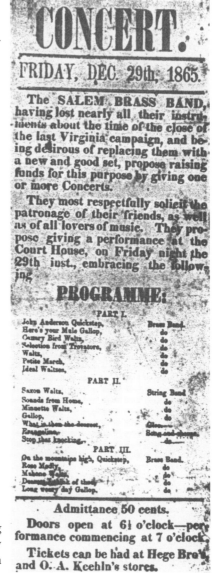

Newspaper advertisement for fund-raising concert of the Salem Brass Band to be held at the Forsyth County Courthouse on December 29, 1865. From the Collection of the Wachovia Historical Society. (Image courtesy of the Moravian Music Foundation.)

"benefit." Music is a "gift of the gods," and its mission in this vale of tears is pure, refined and elevating. Whoever loves it has an angle [angel?] ever in the heart, to speak soothing thoughts and spread around sweet influences. As the great dramatist has said:

"—Orpheus' lute is strung with poet's sinews,
Whose golden touch can soften steel and stone,
Make tigers tame, and huge leviathans
Fors[a]ke unsounded deeps to dance on sand."[2]

A more descriptive follow-up by an unidentified reporter appeared a week later in the *Press*:

The Salem Brass Band gave one of its recherche entertainments at Butner Hall on Tuesday evening last. The audience was large, select and appreciative. Waltzes (wicked things those waltzes—ask Mrs. Grundy)[,] marches, shottisches, quicksteps and gallops, et cetera, till the end of the chapter, relieved at intervals by the amusing feats of Prof. Guss Rich, the prestidigitateur, (if he can pronounce that, it will be another feat.) We thank the gentlemen of the Band for the usual compliments, but found it inconvenient to attend[,] having other things to look after. It is "piping times" with us, as well with them[,] only the pipes we play on are somewhat different from theirs. Though absent, however, the music floated over to us, mellowed by the space it passed, and we were almost as much pleased as if we had been right there.

The success of the Band on Tuesday evening was so gratifying, that they have determined to give another entertainment this (Friday) evening, at the same place, with an entire change of programme.[3]

Nearly forty years after returning home, Julius received what must have been a most gratifying note from Colonel Lane, who had shared the musicians' suffering, as well as some of the lighter moments, of the war years. In August 1903, he wrote:

We did not only have a good regiment but we did have the very best band in all of General Lee's great and grand army. General Lee said so on the first of May, 1864, the night before we started out to meet General Grant at the Wilderness. Your band did its full and whole duty.

The above words are included as a small note in the final pages of Leinbach's handwritten history. The closing paragraph of this document reads:

Since beginning the foregoing, another one of the boys has crossed over [November 28, 1903]. Dan [Crouse], dear old Dan, to whom I was drawn during and since the war, nearer than to any other, and to whose clear

The J. E. Mickey Tin Shop in Salem, ca. 1895, with its historic "Coffee Pot," in which a Yankee soldier reportedly hid to evade capture. Standing in the doorway of the shop are Sam Mickey (*left*) and his brother, J. E. Mickey (*right*). (Image courtesy of Old Salem, Inc.)

memory I am indebted for so much of this imperfect history, has left us, and joined that great silent majority, silent for us, but loud in praise and thanksgiving to God for his great salvation. And that Dan is one of the redeemed I am confidently assured.

[Signed] J. A. Lineback

Salem, N.C.
July 27th 1904.

Writing a little over a decade later, Julius humbly added this final note to his series of newspaper articles:

I have been asked, repeatedly, how many of the 26th band are still living. There are five, viz: —Julius A. Transou, of Pfafftown, N.C., Henry A. Siddall, of Sumter, S.C. and Wm. Aug. Reich, Wm. A. Lemly, and Julius A. Lineback, of Winston-Salem, N.C.

In closing this series of extracts, I desire to thank the many friends who have so kindly expressed their interest in them. Their words helped to alleviate the fears I have felt at times that I might be imposing something on the readers of the *Sentinel* [author's italics] that they did not want.

I fully appreciate the crudity and imperfection of my story and can only repeat what I said when beginning it, that it was never intended or expected to come under the eyes of the public.

J. A. LINEBACK

Winston-Salem, N.C. April 3, 1915

That the band hardly lost a step in civilian life continued to be revealed in its subsequent history. Leinbach and his companions would be pleased to know—perhaps they do—that the Twenty-sixth Band survived for several years under its pre-war designation, the Salem Brass Band. In keeping with the national trend, this "town band" became larger and added woodwind instruments over the years to become the Salem Band. From this group, toward the middle of the twentieth century, a "reconstituted" Twenty-sixth Regimental Band—in full dress and with some of the original instruments—emerged to perform from the original band books on special occasions. First led by the late Austin P. Burke Jr., then by Sam Fort, these latter-day "Civil War musicians" added just a touch of spice and history to many formal concerts of Moravian music. Although there is no longer a "period" Twenty-sixth Regimental Band, plans call for a revival of this cherished musical unit, hopefully in the near future. In the meantime, the Salem Band remains active

Julius A. Lineback, early twentieth century. (Image courtesy of the Archives of the Moravian Church.)

under the directorship of Jeff Whitsett. It rehearses regularly in the old band hall and can be heard periodically in open-air concerts on Salem Square.

In addition to its significance as a local historical institution, the Twenty-sixth Band commands increasing interest nationwide in its music and its history. Other "resurrected bands" from the era are attending various Civil War reenactments, and playing and recording music copied from the original Civil War band books. Undeniably, the record of the Twenty-sixth Regimental Band occupies a distinctive place in the history of American band music.

Selected Companion Bands of the Twenty-sixth

Through shared music, musical experiences, social contact, and the ordeal of army life in general, a degree of camaraderie was established between the boys of the Twenty-sixth and musicians of other regiments—a closeness that can well be appreciated by service personnel of any period. Some of the bandsmen listed in the following sections were men whose contact with the Salemites was more than just by chance. The ancillary material that follows has been included as a matter of general interest, as a follow-up to special references in the text, and as a point of departure for further research in this particular area of American band history. It also serves to verify—and to amplify in some instances—some of the statements, assumptions, and conclusions of the author, as well as those appearing in some other published accounts.

The two principal sources used in preparing this section include microfilm copies and photocopies of original muster/payrolls, and *North Carolina Troops, 1861-1865: A Roster* (both references are cited fully in the bibliography).

Basic information extracted from the original rolls appears in abbreviated or modified form. Names, when they could be determined, replaced initials appearing on the official rolls. When several rolls for the same band cover different time periods, the one(s) included below are arbitrary selections by the author. In addition to the basic roster essentials, brief statements are included for each regiment and band. A special point of interest is that company rosters of musicians usually include a statement indicating a transfer to the band on a given date, *even when no band actually existed at the time.* It appears almost certain that this was simply an administrative matter to comply with existing procedures.

Fourth Regiment, North Carolina Troops, Infantry

Organized from ten companies at Camp Hill, near Garysburg in Northampton County in May 1861, the regiment was mustered into Confederate service on June 28, 1861. It spent the remainder of the summer primarily on post duty around Manassas, Virginia. Although the record of the Fourth Regimental Band is outside the purview of the Twenty-sixth's wartime history, a few extended comments of related interest with Salem's neighbors seem to be in order.

Most band enlistments for this regiment—those for which dates have been determined—occurred shortly after the time of the initial regimental muster. The majority appears to have been from Rowan and Iredell Counties as members of the "Rowan Rifles." (Records reveal that at least one member was enlisted from as far away as Craven County, near the coast!) In keeping with what appears to have been common practice with many regiments, but in contrast to the Twenty-sixth Band, which entered service as a group, the "Band" listed with the field and staff of the Fourth Regiment drew members from nearly all of the companies.

Prior to the war, a fledgling group of Salisbury musicians, purported to have been trained and led by a German named Hermann, gave its first concert as the Salisbury Brass Band "at the old courthouse in 1852." Two years later it joined forces "with the famous Salem band at the Masonic picnic, then held at The Shoals (Cooleemee) in Davie County." Entering the picture during this period was Edward B. Neave (1841-1927), an E-flat cornet player of note, and one whose connection with the Twenty-sixth band has been mentioned throughout the Leinbach story. More than a year after the outbreak of hostilities, and about a year following his future band members into service, Neave joined the "Rowan Rifles," Company K, Fourth Infantry. Attaining the rank of sergeant, he became the director of the local group of "company musicians" who eventually became the large Fourth Regimental Band listed below. The roster is from *North Carolina Troops,* 4:12-113; historical tidbits are from George Raynor, "The Brothers Neave: Professional Musicians," in *Piedmont Passages* (Salisbury, N.C.: *Salisbury Post,* 1991), 5:48-60. For further information on the Neaves, see Appendix B.

Band	Enlisted	To Band
Neave, Edward B., sergeant, chief musician	6/23/62	2/11/63
Austin, Green B.	6/4/61	2/11/63
Barber, John Y.	6/3/61	9/1/61
Brawley, William R. I.	6/7/61	2/11/63
Gillespie, Thomas P.	6/9/61	9/15/61
Goodman, John T.	6/7/61	2/11/63
Gorman, William R.	Not given	2/11/63
Harbin, William T. J.	4/20/61	9/?/61
Heyer, Charles	7/4/61	9–10/61
Jackson, George W.	6/28/61	1/11/63
Moose, William A.	?	9–10/61
Patrick, James M. (drum major)	6/3/61	4/2/64–7/13/64
Patterson, Robert English	?	2/11/63
Raymer, Jacob Nathaniel	?	2/11/63
Shuford, George	4/25/61	10/61–2/62
Steele, James Columbus	?	9/4/61
Stinson, Edgar B.	?	9–10/61–2/62
Trumbo, James R. (drum major)	4/15/61	ca. 4/1/63
Weant, Mathew J.	5/30/61	2/11/63

Eleventh Regiment, North Carolina Volunteers; Twenty-first Regiment, North Carolina Troops, Infantry; First Battalion, North Carolina Sharpshooters

The status of the regiment and band through their various stages has been discussed in chapter 3; therefore, only brief statements, with some new information, are included in this section.

The single extant muster/payroll of the Eleventh Regiment (copy in the author's possession) is identified as "MUSTER ROLL of the FIELD, STAFF, and BAND of the Eleventh Regiment of N.C. volunteers from the 24th day of May 1861 to the 31st day of August 1861." An appended note reads: "This record has been filed with rolls of 21st Regt. N.C. Infantry (State Troops)." When the

regiment was organized in Danville, Virginia, on June 18, 1861, the
seven musicians appear to have *already* been assigned to the band and
entered on the roll under the heading "Rank." A recently published
roster shows all members as having been "transferred to the band"
from Company E between July and September, with two exceptions:
James Reich and Calvin Wren had served Company D as fifer and
drummer, respectively. Thus the original band of the Eleventh
Regiment, North Carolina Volunteers, consisted of the following
musicians:

Band	Enlisted	To Band
Brendle, John P.	7/3/61	ca. 8/14/61
★ Carmichael, William F.	5/24/61	7/3/61
★★Crouse, Daniel B.	5/24/61	7/14/61
Eberhardt, L. D.	5/24/61	ca. 9/1/61
Hall, Samuel G.	5/24/61	8/14/61
Murchison, David B.	5/24/61	7/3/61
Reich, James	5/24/61	?
Wren, Calvin	5/22/61	8/10/61

★Carmichael later became chief musician of the larger, special group of North Carolina
Sharpshooters as shown below.
★★All signed for payment except Crouse, who later served with the Twenty-sixth Band for
the duration.

Through several shifts in reorganization, the band also served the
Twenty-first Regiment temporarily, though records thus far reveal
no regimental band per se. By the spring of 1862, the band's status
appears to have become stabilized with the First Battalion, North
Carolina Sharpshooters. The names of an enlarged membership,
increased over time from the original seven comprising the Eleventh
Regiment, North Carolina Volunteers, were designated as "Band"
with the field and staff of the First Battalion, North Carolina
Sharpshooters. The names also appear on the roster of Company A of
this special detachment and so remained until the war's end.

First Battalion, North Carolina Sharpshooters

Band	Enlisted	To Band
Carmichael, William F., chief musician	5/24/61	4/26/62
Brendle, John P.	7/3/61	4/26/62
Brietz, Samuel	11/1/63	11/1/63
Butner, Lewis E.	1/1/63	4/26/62
★Carmichael, L. F.	?	4/26/62
Eberhardt, L. D.	5/24/61	4/26/62
Hall, Samuel G.	5/24/61	4/26/62
Hill, William C.	6/1/63	6/1/63
Keesler, Samuel G.	?	1/4/63
Murchison, David B.	5/24/61	4/26/62
Parkes, Robert T.	5/24/61	4/26/62
Reich, James A.	5/24/61	4/26/62
Siewers, Nathaniel Shober	11/1/63	11/1/63
Winkler, Christopher	11/1/63	11/1/63

★Nowhere is there any record of his being a musician.

Twenty-seventh Regiment, North Carolina Troops, Infantry

The regiment, after much shifting of companies, was organized initially in eastern North Carolina, primarily in the New Bern area, as a twelve-month body on September 28, 1861. In accordance with a general reorganization of all regiments, the term of enlistment was subsequently extended to three years or for the duration. Yet unexplained is Leinbach's having identified the Twenty-seventh Band as being from Greensboro. None of the bandsmen appear to have been specifically from Greensboro; however, the homes of Higgins, Lipscomb, and Sloan are given as Guilford County.

Band	Enlisted	To Band
Aldridge, Bennett Franklin	4/17/61	9–10/64
Briley, James A.	4/20/61	11/62–10/64
Burroughs, William H. H.	6/18/61	11/63
Dickson, Samuel A.	4/20/61	9/62
Faircloth, Matthew	6/12/61	11/62–10/64
Higgins, Edward B.	4/1/61	ca. 8/62
Jones, Richard E.	4/15/61	9/10/62
Kinsey, John I.	6/17/61	11/62–10/64
Lipscomb, Samuel M.	4/20/61	ca. 8/62
Manker, Guilford	4/20/61	9–10/64
Sloan, Thomas J.	4/20/61	8/62
Spence, James A.	4/27/61	5/6/62
Suggs, John H.	4/17/61	9/62
Turner, Samuel D.	9/6/61	9/10/62

Thirty-third Regiment, North Carolina Troops, Infantry

The nine-company regiment, having first been authorized as a two-company body of state troops on September 20, 1861, was transferred to Confederate service with a redesignation of the original company letters on January 9, 1862. With the addition of one more company the following month, the unit was complete. The official muster roll for December 31, 1861–February 28, 1862, shows the following musicians with the field and staff. Most, if not all, of the bandsmen were Moravians and had enlisted in Pfafftown on the outskirts of Salem. A recently published record indicates that they were originally in Company I when transferred to the band in early 1862 on the dates given below.

Band	Enlisted	To Band
Anderson, William W.	8/1/61	2/1/62
Butner, William N.	8/15/61	2/1/62
Conrad, James H.	7/15/61	8–10/62
Dull, Edwin C.	7/20/61	ca. 2/1/62
Fulk, Charles H.	8/10/61	ca. 2/1/62
Hartman, Lewis A.	7/18/61	ca. 2/1/62
Lehman, Peyton T.	7/1/61	ca. 2/1/62
Stauber, Julius F.	8/3/61	ca. 2/1/62
Stroupe, Levin J.	7/22/61	ca. 2/1/62

Fortunately, the thirteen extant rolls of the regiment give a fairly complete picture of the band's growth and personnel changes through the early part of 1865. The peak enrollment of fifteen members appears to have been reached in the fall of 1863, while the regiment was at Brandy Station, Virginia.

In time the number was reduced to fourteen. The majority of the "Band" with the field and staff were drawn from Company I— muster rolls usually omit this information—sometime between early February 1862 and the fall of 1863. The original muster/payroll shows that most of these enlistees were from the general area of Salem, with two from Fayetteville and one from Gates County in northeastern North Carolina. The following list was taken from the muster roll of field, staff, and band for August 31–October 31, 1863. An examination of the list of transferees to the band on this roll reveals a degree of uncertainty and fluidity, precluding a precise statement as to the group's membership during the period. More information may be found in the published account, *North Carolina Troops*, 9:221-232.

Band	Enlisted	To Band
Dull, Edwin C., chief musician	7/20/61	ca. 2/1/62
Butner, William N.	8/10/61	ca. 2/1/62
Crator, Reuben J.	3/?/62	5–10/62
Harris, Allison B.	9/9/61	ca. 9/1/63
Hartman, Lewis A.	7/21/61	2/1/62
Jones, Robert M.	7/31/61	9–10/63
Kimbrough, John Anderson	3/1/62	5/1/62
Lehman, Oliver J.	7/5/63	ca. 2/15–28/63 (?)
Miller, Gideon Leander	8/15/62	7–10/62
Miller, Virgil P.	3/1/62	3–10/62
Parker, Wiley E.	2/10/62	9–10/63
Reynolds, Jesse	8/27/61	3–10/63
★Stroupe, Levin J.	7/20/62	2/1/62 (?)
Williard, John A.	7/20/62	4–10/62
Williford, William F.	2/11/62	2–4/62

There is no explanation for the enlist-to-band errors in the cases of Oliver Lehman and Levin Stroupe (reported in the published record as having deserted). Of the original members, William Anderson died of wounds on August 15, 1862; taken prisoner that year were James Conrad (July 10) and Julius Stauber (August 19). The muster roll of December 31, 1862–February 28, 1863, indicates that Conrad had been released from captivity and returned to the band. The same record also shows Williard and Williford as no longer with the band; however, their names reappear on the roll of August 31–October 31, 1863. There is no explanation for either their absence or return.

Parolees with the regiment at Appomattox included Butner, Crator, Dull, Hartman, P. T. Lehman, Miller, and Parker. See Clark, *North Carolina Regiments*, 5:543. Film copies of muster rolls were supplemented with information from *North Carolina Troops*, 9:121-122, 180, 216, 221-227, 231-232.

Eleventh Regiment, North Carolina Troops, Infantry

The Eleventh Regiment, an eleven-company war unit, succeeded the First ("Bethel") Regiment of North Carolina Volunteers, which was mustered in for only six-months service (May 13–November 14, 1861). The successor regiment was formed upon the reorganization of troops at Camp Mangum on March 31, 1862.

The regiment was in Pettigrew's brigade of Heth's division with the Twenty-sixth North Carolina in the center of the line at Gettysburg on July 3, 1863. This band, though not necessarily all of the members, and the Twenty-sixth were reputedly heard playing during the late afternoon of July 2. Significantly, none of the members listed below, according to the personnel designated as the "Band," had been "transferred to the regimental band" at the time of Gettysburg. (Certain personnel information, such as enlistments, is carried forward from roster to roster.) We are left with the question of just who constituted the Eleventh Band on the second day of the battle. One likely possibility is that these company musicians came together to form a group then and at other times. Even so, with most of these musicians available since 1862, it does seem strange that formal recognition as a musical unit was such a long time coming!

Microfilm copies of the three extant muster rolls of this regiment—August 31–October 31, 1864; October 31–December 31, 1864; and December 31, 1864–February 21, 1865—show the same band personnel. The first of these was compiled at Petersburg, Va., on October 31, 1864. A recent source is *North Carolina Troops*, 5:8-9.

Band	Enlisted	To Band
Todd, Elisha, chief musician	1/23/62	9/10/64
Cline, William A.	9/?/62	2/65
Coon, Adolphus S.	61/62	2/65
Crowell (?), Elias M.	6/1/62	ca. 10/64
Davis, James T.	2/1/62	ca. 10/64
Goodson, John L.	3/1/62	9/10/64
Hicks, Joseph S.	2/15/62	9/10/64
McConnell, James H.	8/1/61	9/10/64
Martin, William E.	4/25/62	9/10/64
Morrison, William T.	11/1/62	9/10/64
Motz, Charles	5/3/62	9/10/64
Seagle, Moss	5/8/62	9/10/64
Todd, Nehemiah J.	11/24/63	9/10/64
Wingate, Charles C.	2/1/62	9/10/64

Forty-seventh Regiment, North Carolina Troops, Infantry

This regiment was organized at Camp Mangum near Raleigh on March 24, 1862, enrolled for state duty on April 11, and transferred to Confederate service in May as a three-year regiment or for the duration of the war. Whether or not the regiment had a band awaits further research. The only information we have in this respect is a published record of personnel in *North Carolina Troops*, 11:247. Listed with the field and staff of the regiment under the heading, "MUSICIANS," are the following:

BRAGG, W. P., Musician
Previously served as Musician (Drummer) in Company C of this regiment. Transferred to the Field and Staff on or about November 1, 1864. Reduced to ranks and transferred back to Company C on an unspecified date.

JOYNER, MARCELLUS E., Musician
Previously served as Musician in Company G of this regiment. Transferred to the regimental band in May–October, 1864. Last

reported in the records of the Field and Staff on December 1, 1864. (North Carolina pension records indicate that he survived the war.)

SMITH, WILLIAM D., Chief Musician
Previously served as Musician (Drummer) in Company C of this regiment. Promoted to Chief Musician and transferred to the Field and Staff in May–October, 1864. Last reported in the records of the Field and Staff on December 27, 1864. (North Carolina pension records indicate that he survived the war.)

Although there is the mention of a regimental band in the comments on Joyner, these entries nevertheless appear to lend some credence to the earlier statement that the regiment had no band, or at least one able to function, at the time its colonel requested the service of the Twenty-sixth in the fall of 1863.

Fifty-second Regiment, North Carolina Troops, Infantry

Also organized at Camp Mangum with ten companies one month after the Forty-seventh Regiment (April 28), the Fifty-second appears to have had only four musicians, as indicated by the published rosters of companies B, C, and F. Although listed as "Band" with the field and staff and explicitly identified as such, the following four musicians would hardly have comprised the regimental band. The persistent question, here and elsewhere, remains unanswered: to what group of instrumentalists does the expression, "transferred to the regimental band," apply? That the colonel of this regiment was also in need of a band and had to call on the boys of the Twenty-sixth seems likely.

DECAMP, CHARLES, Chief Musician
Enlistment date reported as August 25, 1862; however, he was not listed in the records of this company [C] until July–August, 1864, when he was reported absent wounded. Place and date wounded not reported. Appointed Chief Musician (Drum Major) in September–October, 1864, and transferred to the regimental band. *North Carolina Troops*, 12:441.

PIERCE, JOHN H. C., Musician
   Previously served as Private in Company C, 26th Regiment, N.C. Troops. Enlisted in this company [F] at Franklin, Virginia, November 15, 1862, for the war as a substitute. Mustered in as Musician. Reported present or accounted for on surviving company muster rolls through May, 1864. Hospitalized at Richmond, Virginia, June 25, 1864, with chronic diarrhea. Furloughed for forty days on August 4, 1864. Transferred to the regimental band prior to November 1, 1864. *North Carolina Troops*, 12:476.

SHAW, WILEY H., Musician
   Born in Randolph County where he resided as a farmer prior to enlisting in Randolph County at age 18, April 8, 1862. Mustered in as Private. Appointed Musician (Drummer) in May–June, 1864. Reported present or accounted for on company [B] muster rolls through June, 1864. Transferred to the regimental band in July–October, 1864. *North Carolina Troops*, 12:437.

WARREN, ROBERT F., Chief Musician
   Born in Wilkes County where he resided as a farmer prior to enlisting in Wilkes County at age 18, March 14, 1862. Mustered in as Private. Appointed Musician (Drummer) prior to July 1, 1862. Appointed Chief Musician in July, 1862–August, 1862. Transferred to the regimental band on an unspecified date (probably in July–October, 1864). *North Carolina Troops*, 12:479.

Fifty-fifth Regiment, North Carolina Troops, Infantry

   Ten companies came together to form the unit on May 16, 1862, one of several North Carolina regiments organized at Camp Mangum.
   A seventeen-piece band, drawn from several companies, is listed with the field and staff of the regiment. Brief information for each member indicates that all were "transferred to the regimental band" between July and October, 1864. Unfortunately, insufficient evidence precludes determining the existence of a band prior to the transfer of personnel as indicated on the roster below. Enlistment

dates for each band member are to be found in their respective company rosters in *North Carolina Troops*, 13:432-433, 440-483.

Band	Enlisted	To Band
★Jacke, Charles Emil, chief musician	3/20/62	7–10/64
Adcock, Henry C.	3/1/62	7–10/64
Beam, M. Rufus	3/29/62	7–10/64
Bernard, Francis N.	7/8/62	7–10/64
Bernard, John Paul	7/8/62	7–10/64
Cleland, William H.	1/1/63	7–10/64
Ellington, Jacob C.	5/16/62	7–10/64
Falls, George Lewis	2/13/63	7–10/64
Geauffretean, Eugene	1/1/63	7–10/64
Horne, William Henry	4/30/62	7–10/64
Pearson, Jacob C.	4/29/62	7–10/64
Rowland, William Henry	5/1/62	7–10/64
Shelly, William H.	ca. 9/62	7–10/64
Summerell, Burton P.	4/2/62	7–10/64
Turnage, Henry Calhoun	4/15/62	7–10/64
Tyson, Archibald Alfred	9/9/62	7–10/64

★Listed as having deserted! Company E roster includes no statement about desertion; however, Jacke (a sergeant) is listed as being on detached service in June 1862.

Fourteenth Regiment, South Carolina Volunteers, Infantry

Although the regiment is indicated as having been a volunteer unit, the term of enlistment is given as "war." As in the case of the North Carolina bands, there appear to be no published records with company rosters showing dates of transfer to the band, if such had been the case, and no attempt was made to locate and search the original company personnel for this information. (The "To Band" column appearing on the North Carolina registers has been replaced by the respective places of enlistment for each member.) We are left to speculate as to whether this group and that of the Twenty-fifth band below enlisted as bodies or were formed from company musicians. An interesting aside is that the list of personnel for both of these regiments appears with the surname last. (Common practice with all South Carolina regiments?) Names for the Twenty-fifth were not arranged in alphabetical order.

The following personnel information was derived from a photostatic copy of the "Band and N[on] C[om] staff of the Regiment of South Carolina Vols, . . . from the 1st day of May 1863, when last mustered, to the 30th day of June 1863." A notation on the second page states "Near Gettysburg, Pa., June 30th, 1863." This document and the one following of the Twenty-fifth Band were obtained from the South Carolina Department of Archives and History.

Band	Enlisted	Place
Charles L. Siegel, chief musician	11/?/61	Charleston
John Alexander	8/10/61	Darlington
L. H. Bryan	8/10/61	Edgefield
W. D. Bryan	8/10/61	Edgefield
Thomas A. Cater	9/3/61	Camp Butler
H. A. Clark	8/12/61	Edgefield
L. A. Clark	6/12/62	Edgefield
C. B. Crouch	9/19/61?	Edgefield
W. T. Fairbain	8/19/61?	Laurens
H. T. Green	8/25/?	Edgefield
Lott Jennings	7/20/62	Edgefield
William Lott	3/18/62	Edgefield
L. O. Lovelace	6/15/62	Edgefield
E. M. Martin	8/12/61	Edgefield
R. Nicholas	4/20/61	Edgefield
S. A. Oliver	8/6/61	Laurens
S. E. Owen	8/12/61	Laurens
C. P. Parker	8/12/61	Abeville [sic]
T. Y. Taylor	8/12/61	Laurens

Payment for two months: Chief Musician Siegel, $42.00; all musicians, $24.00.

Twenty-fifth Regiment, South Carolina Volunteers, Infantry

As in the case of the Fourteenth Regiment, the Twenty-fifth was a volunteer group with the term of enlistment indicated as "war." Only two muster rolls appear to be extant: field, staff, and band, November 1–December 31, 1862; and field, staff, and band, July 1–August 31, 1863. The roster for July–August, 1863, has been selected for inclusion because it covers the Gettysburg period; however, the same list of bandsmen appears on both rolls with one exception: the name of Benjamin Hernandez on the earlier roll is absent from the later group. Unlike the muster roll for the Fourteenth Band, there is no separate payroll for the Twenty-fifth.

Band	Enlisted	Place
R. Mueller, chief musician	2/24/62	Charleston
W. Galway, chief bugler	2/24/62	Charleston
[?] E. Berry	2/24/62	Charleston
William Canar [?]	3/15/62	Orangeburg
A. Dufft	2/24/62	Charleston
John Haas	2/24/62	Charleston
C. Mittschen	2/24/62	Charleston
F. W. Ortman [?]	2/24/62	Charleston
Henry Ortman [?]	2/24/62	Charleston
Julius Ortman [?]	2/24/62	Charleston
Philip Saltus	10/5/62	James Island

Selected Personnel

NEAVE, Edward Baxter (1841–1927). Born in Arbroath, Scotland, he came to the United States with his family at approximately the age of sixteen and is reported to have received a "practical education" in the public schools of Cincinnati, Ohio. He moved from there to Salisbury, N.C. (Rowan County), presumably just prior to the war. Strangely, a brief biographical sketch in R. D. W. Connor's five-volume history of North Carolina supplies the only date we have on the man: May 30, 1861, when he enlisted in the "Rowan Rifles," which was later assigned as Company K to the Fourth Regiment, North Carolina Troops. Like his half brother William, he was a talented musician, and was made leader of the Fourth Regimental Band. A brave and courageous soldier, he continued with his command until the surrender at Appomattox.

Even the above enlistment date conflicts with the one entered on the compiled roster of Company K, which reads:

NEAVE, EDWARD B., Private
Resided in Rowan County and enlisted on December 23, 1862, for the war. Present or accounted for until appointed Chief Musician (Sergeant) on February 11, 1863, and transferred to the regimental band.

The time element becomes further complicated—interesting, to say the least—when recalling the first mention of Edward Neave by Sam Mickey in connection with the Twenty-sixth Band: "Saturday [January] the 24th [1863]. . . . J. Leinback [sic] and myself went . . . to see Prof. Neave, and asked him to come and teach us." If we accept the transfer date of Neave from Company K of the Fourth Regiment to the band in early February, as indicated on the company roster, we are left with an interesting question: was his status that of a private the previous month, when the Salem boys approached him? (For further information, see Appendix A.) Be that as it may, contact with him was eventually made, to the Salem Band's benefit, after the regimental band was an active unit.

From the relatively small amount of biographical information we have on Edward Neave, as compared with that about his older half brother William, we learn that he returned after the war to Salisbury, where he became a prominent businessman and community leader. There is thus far no indication to what extent his many activities included music, although he was reputedly an excellent player on the E-flat cornet, the instrument reported to be in the Rowan County Museum (see sources below).

NEAVE, William H. (1820–1902). William also moved with his family to this country from Scotland. Prior to settling in Salisbury, he reportedly visited the town as leader of a small circus band in 1860 and inquired if the local band needed any music arrangements. He evidently made a favorable impression with a number of townsfolk, so impressed that "local bandsmen requested that he remain here, but pleading his [circus] contract," he returned, presumably, to Cincinnati. A short time later he came back to Salisbury after having met and married Josephine Lange, a classically trained German musician who was teaching in Statesville at what would become Mitchell College. This union, it has been stated, probably "influenced him to settle down to one place, Salisbury."

William Neave, by all accounts, was an excellent musician, very likely overshadowing young Edward. William was reportedly a fine trombonist who, as one well versed in all instruments, is believed to have had something to do with leading the budding Salisbury Brass Band. He reputedly took the band to Virginia to accompany the Sixth North Carolina Regiment at the battle of First Manassas (Bull Run) in July 1861. The band had been hired by the regimental colonel at the fee of fifty dollars a day! William, widely known as a staunch Unionist (as were many Johnny Rebs in North Carolina), had been so impressed with the open, friendly nature of his southern friends that he enlisted in the Confederacy as a bandsman, reportedly with the Eleventh Regiment, and later "became the bandmaster for the Army of Northern Virginia." Records supporting this statement of service—in fact a record of any band service—await discovery, especially the part regarding Lee's army having a bandmaster.

The aforementioned biographical sketch of Edward states that William, at the outbreak of the war, "was commissioned band master in the Confederate Army." A search of various records has thus far failed to reveal any active service connection with a band. On the other hand, his apparent association with the Twenty-sixth musicians is revealed by the inscription, "W. H. Neave," on a number of pieces in the Moravians' band books.

A number of interesting facts about William H. Neave are reported in a highly informative article by George Raynor on famous Rowan County families during the nineteenth century. One suggests that William was a rather carefree, irrepressible individual. While in Tarboro, out of contact with his regiment in April 1863, he wrote to a friend in Salisbury that he was stranded and in dire financial straits while searching for his regiment. Living a sort of hand-to-mouth existence, he made the acquaintance of a local, black barber-musician, who persuaded William to join his five-piece band—twenty-five dollars, plus room and board for a week! In his words: "I never lived better before the war. And they attend to all my wants as if I was a lord. . . . I do not know where the 11th Regt. is but hear that it is going toward Kinston."

Although Leinbach and Mickey never mentioned him, William supplied music to the Twenty-sixth, and possibly other bands too. His arrangements may have been passed on by his bandleader half brother. This might account for Edward's name being singled out several times in the Twenty-sixth's history. Until his identification with a Confederate band is verified, William Neave's Civil War service record must remain somewhat a mystery. After the war William and Josephine conducted a music school in Salisbury, with the wife continuing the school after her husband's death in 1902, until her own in 1927.

Sources: "Edward Baxter Neave," in R. D. W. Connor et al., *History of North Carolina*, 5 vols. (Chicago and New York: Lewis Publishing Company, 1919), 5:69; *North Carolina Troops*, 4:12-13, 110-111; James S. Brawley (Salisbury, N.C.), correspondence with the author, fall 1961; George Raynor, "The Brothers Neave: Professional Musicians," *Piedmont Passages*, 6 vols. (Salisbury, N.C.: *Salisbury Post*, 1990-1991), 5:48-60.

Music Written/Arranged bearing the name "Neave" in the Twenty-sixth Band Books

Medley: *Aura Lee, Mary of Argyle, I've No Mother* [dated February 2, 1865]

Medley: *I Dream of Thee By the Campfire, Lonely Watch, Officer's Funeral* Quickstep: *Cast That Shadow from Thy Brow*

Quickstep: *Forget and Forgive*

Carolina Polka

Here's Your Mule Galop

Katy Darling

Melange Waltz

Waltz Olga

"March" from the opera *Belisario*

HARTWELL, William Henry (1827–1914). The primary cause of death as indicated on the death certificate was pneumonia, with the contributory factor of senility. The official grave registration states that Hartwell was born in Adams County, Miss.; however, contradictory information on the death certificate indicates his place of birth as the State of Maine, as was that of his parents.

The official Confederate Military Records in the Department of Archives and History, Jackson, Miss., list Hartwell on the roll of Company I of the Sixteenth Regiment Infantry, Mississippi Volunteers (twelve months) of Carnot Posey's brigade. (Change to enrollment for the duration is not indicated.) The twenty extant rolls are for the period June 1, 1861–December 1864. The roll for Company I, June 1 to August 31, 1861, indicates Hartwell was enlisted at Lynchburg, Va., as a "Musician" on August 1. Remarks entered on the next roll (September and October 1861, same station) state "Reduced to the ranks October 25th 1861. Pay due him as Musician, 1 Mo. 25da, & as Private 5 days." The following record for November–December, strangely, shows the enlistment at Corinth, Miss., on June 1, and detailed "on extra duty as Musician." There is no apparent explanation for a part of the next roll (same period) showing the date of enlistment again as August 1—*but back at Lynchburg.* For the first time, significantly, remarks include "Detailed as Band Master, 28 Nov 61[?]." Remaining rolls for later dates list Hartwell as "Chief Musician" of the regiment. A significant remark for May–June, 1864, states "dropped from rolls [as] Chief Musician— Regt. Transferred to Rolls staff & Band."

Personal data, including Hartwell's musical talent and love of music, appears in a rather lengthy obituary in *The City Itemizer*, Water Valley (Yalobusha County), Miss., March 12, 1914. Under the heading "Death of Professor Hartwell," we are informed that he was a Civil War veteran and a well-respected resident of Water Valley for twenty-four years. One paragraph reads:

He was passionately fond of music, which was his realm. His life had been devoted to it. He was a composer of note, and had contributed much to this delightful field. He had been actively engaged in musical effort from his young manhood, until age [almost eighty-seven] rendered it impossible for him to prose . . . the work further.

Although it was common in those times to address many accomplished musicians respectfully as "Professor," the title in this case appears to have been apropos. According to correspondence with the author in connection with the first edition of this book, Hartwell reportedly served a period as "Professor of Music" at Madison College, Sharon, Miss., although the obituary fails to mention music as a profession, or even Hartwell as director of the Sixteenth Mississippi Band. Recent attempts to obtain more information on this musician and at least a roster of his band have proved fruitless.

Music Written/Arranged by W. H. Hartwell in the Twenty-sixth Band Books

Rock Me to Sleep, Mother★
Invitation à la Dance★
Canary Bird Waltz
Rappahannock Polka
Dream of Home Waltzes
Double Quickstep
Mazourka★

Screech Owl Galop
Southern Victorial March
Dearest I Think of Thee (Grand March)

★Designated specifically as having been arranged by Hartwell. Some of the remaining pieces may well be originals. Only one of his compositions appears to have been published: *Confederates Grand March* in Harwell, *Confederate Music*, 68. Published (piano) by Blackmar & Bro., Augusta, Ga., ca. 1862. An earlier edition was issued by Blackmar & Bro. of New Orleans, ca. 1861. This piece may be one of two (with modified title) in the Twenty-sixth band books: *Grand Confederate March Quickstep* (Book 4), and *Confederate March* (Book 2), both listed in Leinbach-McCorkle, "Repertory of the 26th Regiment Band."

REICH ("Rich"), William Augustus (1833–1917). Born in Salem, N.C., "Gus" or "Guss," as he was popularly called, was the son of Nancy (née Geiger) and Jacob Reich. A tinsmith by trade, Gus joined the Twenty-sixth Band as its second recruit (bass drummer) while the regiment was encamped at Dunn's Hill near Petersburg, Va., in July 1862. Thus far, no determination has been made that Gus served as drummer for the band prior to the war. Reich was one of those irrepressible individuals who added color and spice to the group's performances during and following the war.

Reich was a person of many talents, and musician appears not to have been in the fore. His ability as a tinsmith was, however, widely recognized. One of his major accomplishments was the construction of a coffin for the Siamese twins, Chang and Eng Bunker, while Gus and his wife resided temporarily at Mt. Airy, N.C. (1871–1873). Using thirty-four sheets of tin and receiving twenty dollars for the job, the proud smith remarked that "it was a sight to see the people come to my house to see me make the coffin. It was the greatest job I ever done." This ubiquitous individual appeared to have "been into everything!" His seemingly boundless energy and interest even extended to the area of invention. In February 1879, he received a patent from the Scientific American Agency for an Eggbeater and Butter Churn unit.

Next to his chosen trade, fame for Gus came in an entirely different field of endeavor as a sleight-of-hand artist. Although recognized as a magician prior to and during the war, Reich

Gus Reich's tin shop in Salem, ca. 1900. From the Collection of the Wachovia Historical Society. (Image courtesy of Old Salem, Inc.)

reputedly dubbed himself with the sobriquet by which he came to be known: "Wizard of the Blue Ridge." Inspired by the majestic Blue Ridge Mountains while he and his wife were residing in Mt. Airy, this engaging individual exclaimed, "Mary, . . . I am the wizard of the Blue Ridge." The suggestion that Reich was also something of a "sketch" artist who, along with Alex Meinung, made contributions to the Salem Band camp life, remains unverified.

As a magician, Gus was usually in demand whenever the band appeared in concert—during the war and for several years thereafter. Following his death, Reich's widow donated his interesting collection of paraphernalia to the Wachovia Museum of Old Salem.

Two major sources: (1) "Research on William Augustus Reich (1833-1917)," comp. Mathilde Dumond, Museum of Early Southern Decorative Arts (MESDA), Old Salem, Inc., 1987; and (2) research material of Gary Hunt, Durham, N.C., also on file at MESDA.

Three "Prospective" Drummers: An Enigma

The Leinbach story of the Salem Band's Civil War service is replete with interesting details, some of which raise a number of unanswered questions. Probably the most intriguing of these centers on statements by Sam Mickey relating to his early quest for a capable drummer to serve the Twenty-sixth. The search proved unfruitful; however, it did bring to attention the names of three musicians unmentioned in previous writings on the Twenty-sixth Regimental Band: Hackney, Long, and Boyd. That Mickey included these names in the band's history is interesting and strange in view of their absence from Leinbach's account. Their connection with the Salem Band becomes more of a mystery in light of information in their respective service records.

One of five extant muster rolls of the Twenty-sixth lists a "Joseph D. Hackney" of Chatham County who enlisted in 1861 and was a member of the band during the last few months of the war. (Official Muster Rolls: August 31, 1864–October 31, 1864; October 31–December 31, 1864.) One source indicates that he had been a Baptist preacher (Clark, *North Carolina Regiments*, 2:398).

Advertisement for postwar concert by the Twenty-sixth North Carolina Regimental Band, featuring the "magical mystifications" of Guss Rich, the Southern Magician. From the Julius A. Lineback Papers, Southern Historical Collection.

North Carolina Troops provides the following information about the three musicians:

Band (Field and Staff)

HACKNEY, JOSEPH D., Drum Major

Previously served as Drum Major of Company E of this regiment. Transferred to the regimental band in September–October, 1864. Present or accounted for through February 1865. *North Carolina Troops*, 7:465–466.

Company I

LONG, J. M., Drum Major

Resided in Caldwell County and enlisted at Camp Carolina at age 23, August 31, 1861. Mustered in as Musician (Drummer) and was promoted to Drum Major prior to November 1, 1861. Present or accounted for until he died in hospital at Goldsboro on or about June 23, 1862, of disease. *North Carolina Troops*, 7:582.

Company K

BOYD, CALVIN R., Musician

Resided in Anson or Montgomery Counties and enlisted in Anson County at age 30, July 1, 1861. Mustered in as Musician. Present or accounted for until he died on September 8, 1862. Place of death not reported. *North Carolina Troops*, 7:590.

Alexander C. Meinung, ca. 1865. (Image courtesy of Old Salem, Inc.)

Field Sketches by Alexander Meinung

Alexander Meinung was one of several members of the Twenty-sixth Regimental Band who possessed a special talent other than music—in his case, an exceptional use of the pen. Nowhere is this more evident than in his wartime sketches recording various field scenes during the band's military service. His artistic talent, as already noted, caught the eye of an officer who wanted the bandsman transferred to the topographical office in Richmond, a move that was almost immediately disapproved.

Inserted throughout Leinbach's handwritten narrative are approximately thirty field sketches by Meinung, whose remarkable ability to capture the moment is revealed in his drawings depicting various episodes in the army life of the Twenty-sixth Band. Most are from the year 1863. Twenty-seven of these are included in this section. Descriptive comments for twenty-four of the sketches were written by Leinbach, identified by the author from samples of Leinbach's writing in the notebook narrative. In a number of places in the notebook and carried over to his comments about the sketches are examples of Julius's custom of underlining passages with wavy, snake-like lines. Two of the sketches have no identifying comment. One of these shows a bugler on a horse, a sketch no doubt prompted by the comical scene of Leinbach, for the first and only time, serving as bugler for General Kirkland!

The remaining descriptions or "captions" are in the same hand. These may conceivably have been written by Meinung, although this tentative identification remains to be verified. The writing style is definitely not that of Alex as shown in the back of his band book.

The sketch on page 201 appeared twice in Leinbach's notebook. The sharper image is included in this collection, and its brief caption is supplemented by a more detailed description taken from the other, less clear image: "Pontoon bridge on Shennandoah [sic] Riv. Va. Retreat from Gettisburg [sic] July 23d 1863. Near Front Royal Va."

Some of Leinbach's descriptions carry page numbers ("p. __,"), indicating the location of the particular sketch in the handwritten

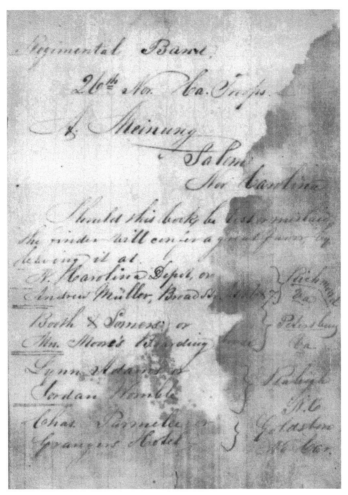

This page from Alexander Meinung's band book illustrates his refined penmanship. (Image courtesy of the Moravian Music Foundation.)

notebook; however, several fail to coincide. This would seem to indicate that Julius made some changes in the text without carrying these over to the sketch locators.

Where locations and dates are lacking, approximations by the author in brackets are based on statements in Leinbach's text, the physical settings, and general conditions at the time.

"Winter Quarters at Camp French [Va.] 1862."

"December 1862. Rail Road Bridge near Goldsboro."

"December 1862. Our 'Comfortable' Quarters."

"1862. Variously Occupied and Unoccupied."

"January 1863. Our Camp at Night."

"January 1863. Night on a March. No Tents."

"Febry. 1863. Crossing a Swamp."

"Retreat from Washington, N. Car., April 16th, 1863."

"Pontoon bridge on Shennandoah [*sic*] Riv. Va. Retreat from Gettisburg [*sic*] July 23d. 1863. Near Front Royal Va."

"Sabbath. Divine Service in Camp. Aug. 1863."

"Baker at Work."

"On the March. Watering at both Ends."

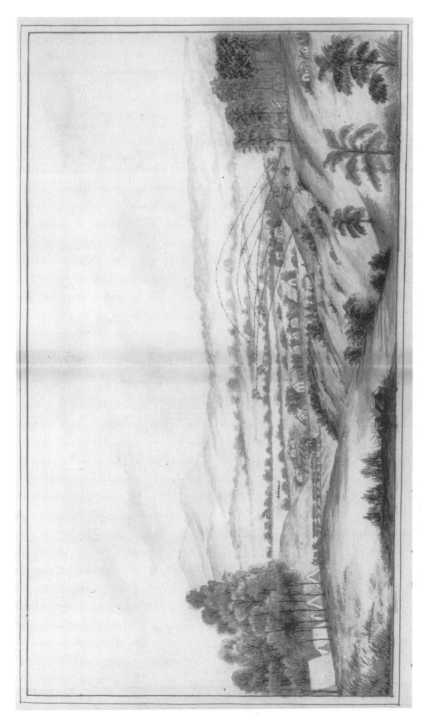

"Camp on Rapidan river near Orange C.H. Oct. 1863. Yankee camp at foot of Mountain."

"Permanent Winter Quarters. Near Orange C.H. 1863."

[Uncaptioned: Probably Leinbach's brief experience as a bugler.]

"Our Cabin. One mile of Orange C.H., Va. Dec. Slept in 3 nights only!"

"John Henry about to 'devour' an egg."

"D— the Smoke! Dec. 1863."

"Thinking of Home. New Year's [Eve] Night 1863."

"Pioneer asleep. <u>Worn out!</u> In Chickahomine [*sic*] Swamp. June 1864."

"Elephant [Transou?] under his fly, studying music Scores.
Behind the bomb-proof hill."

"Aleck's Hat, after a hard rain. Aug. 1864."

"Aleck's Lodging Behind bomb-proof hill."

"Schnirtz [Gus?] and John Henry hunting a new camp ground."

"Schnirtz studying Macbeth. 'Ye secret, black and midnight hags!'"

"A Mishap in the Swamps."

[Unidentified cavalrymen.]

The Letters of Edward Peterson: Selected Extracts

Of the countless sources of historical information on the life and times of the Civil War soldier—soldiers of any conflict for that matter—none are more interesting and revealing than those time-worn, fading letters written to friends and loved ones back home. The letters of James Edward Peterson (1827–1906), member of the Twenty-sixth Regimental Band, are a collection of priceless gems.

Peterson, mainly a trombonist, joined the Twenty-sixth bandsmen while they were at home on their first furlough in August 1862. His letters, approximately sixty-two pages (or fragments), were written primarily to his sister Theressa in Salem and comprise a collection covering the period September 1862 to October 1864. There were no doubt others of which there is no apparent record. (It will be recalled that the original letters of Julius Leinbach, quoted in his narrative, seem to have long since disappeared.)

The present collection, preserved by the late Mrs. Thomas J. Boyd of Winston-Salem, great-niece of Peterson, is designated the Agnes Peterson Boyd Material, at the Moravian Music Foundation, Winston-Salem. The author's extracts are based on two sources: (1) his own notes (early 1960s) taken from the original letters; and (2) a transcription by an unidentified worker about the same time. Permission to use this material is granted by the Moravian Music Foundation.

Reflecting a variety of subject matter, and sprinkled with numerous personal opinions, the Peterson letters are exceptionally long and show considerable interest in how things were going at home. Most were written in sections defined by inserted changes of dates. The majority were written to Ed's sister, but several were for "Siss [Sievers]," a favorite niece. Upon completion over a period of days, the letters were either mailed or entrusted for delivery to someone leaving on furlough for Salem.

The letters reveal two distinctive characteristics. First, in order to conserve space, Peterson would double-space between the lines and, upon reaching the bottom of a page, reverse direction and fill in the

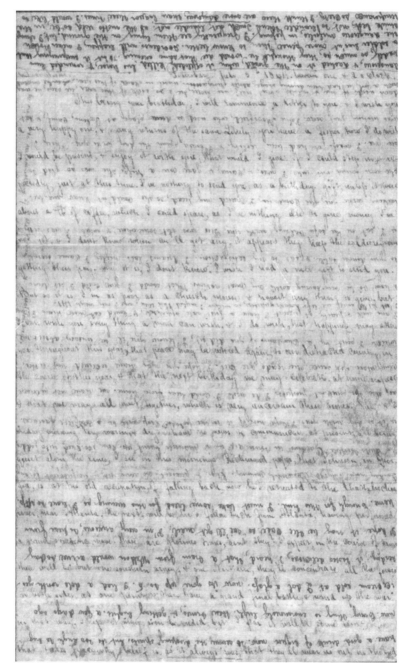

Letter from Ed Peterson to his sister Theressa, July 5, 1864, showing his method of writing to conserve paper. From the Agnes Peterson Boyd Collection, Moravian Music Foundation.

spaces on the way back to the top of the page. In many instances
some of the writing would appear in the margins—sides and top.
This procedure, together with the general physical appearance of the
pages, has made present-day reading and transcribing a problem—
often an impossibility!

A second interesting twist was to intersperse German words,
phrases, or sentences throughout the English text, although there was
an admitted lack of proficiency in Edward's use of the German
language. The switch was simply a reflection of Peterson's German-
American background rather than an attempt to be pretentious. In
several instances, this bilingual ability was put to good use when Ed
encountered German-speaking citizenry while the band was on the
march through various localities.

Surprisingly, the voluminous content of the letters includes
relatively little about music and musical activities. One important
omission is a statement on the band's role as musicians/medics at
Gettysburg. In fact, there is a noticeable gap in writing for nearly a
month during this critical period, which leads to the belief that any
letters written then (and at some other times) have either been lost or
destroyed.

The author has refrained from editing these excerpts, except when
deemed absolutely necessary for clarity or for adding presently
known facts, in order to preserve the original "flavor" of the writing.
The numerous errata—spelling, punctuation, and run-on sentences—
are for the most part left as they are. These may well have been due
to the adverse conditions under which many of the letters were
written. To include all needed editorial markings would create too
much clutter.

Edward Peterson was a humble but well-educated man who
wrote for the benefit of his immediate family—he frequently stressed
this point—and not for general consumption, especially not for
publication!

First in the collection is a letter to his sister Theressa, written at
Camp French, Petersburg, Virginia, on September 28, 1862.

Dear Sister,

I hope you will soon write. How I so wish I could be with you today; such beautiful weather too, always makes me wish for <u>home</u> <u>sweet</u> <u>home</u>. I am sometimes quite homesick, & its no wonder either, to think to have to stay in this accursed war for months & years perhaps, or forever, is killing. . . . Yesterday evening in particular I was thinking much of home; how I wished I could be there & go squirrel hunting like I used to, last fall, over on Staub's hill. If I ever get home again, I know I shall enjoy home life better than ever. . . . I was glad that our regiment was transferred out of [Robert] Ransom's brigade, otherwise we would have been in some of those fights up on the Potomac. I noticed [General] Ransom was wounded, *it's a pity he wasn't killed, such a mean man as he* [author's italics]. But that is rather a hard wish; I'll take it back. We serenaded gen. Pettigru [*sic*] last Thursday night, on my birthday; he stops about a mile from our camp, at a house; he called us in & treated us to whiskey & brandy. . . . Why don't Uncle write more? . . . I hope he'll get out of the conscript; he'll soon be 45. If I had only been 45 last Thursday, I guess I could have slipped out now. Do make Siss write oftener, & write closer, & fill up every space like I generally do.

This is an exceptionally long letter, as most of them are, and it continues with an explanation of the band's duties and location, and comments on the general state of things.

I must give you some idea how we spend our Sundays; we get up about 6, take breakfast about 1/2 past 6, at 1/2 past 7 the drum beats for guard mounting; you will wonder what that is; its all tomfoolery in my eyes; it consists of this, some 25 or 30 men standing in 2 rows & we marching by them playing a tune & back again, that is about all. I don't see any sense in it; after that we had inspection of arms; the whole regiment is marched out into the field 7 the colonel inspects one company after the other, while we play; this takes about 3/4 of an hour. In the evening at 1/2 past 5 dress parade come off; at this we play about 4 pieces, the regiment is formed into line, & we march down the line slow time, coming back in quick time. This closes the performances of the day. In the evening after supper we generally play a few pieces for the benefit of the Col. You can imagine what our occupation is in the week; every morning, guard mounting at 1/2 past 7, & in the evening at 1/2 past 5 dress parade unless when on a march. This morning I heard our chaplain preach for the 1st time, he is quite a good speaker; he preached here for the 1st time when we were at Raleigh. Since he is here, the soldiers sing methodist songs of an evening; it sounds strange, of an evening, the singing, drumming & fifing, all at the same time, all mixed up together. . . . I hav'nt described to you where we are camped now, since we came back from Raleigh, not at the same old place, on the hillside, but about a mile from there, 4 miles from Petersburg, right on the main road to Norfolk, in the pine woods; since its cleaned out, it's a pretty place. . . . You ought to see what breastworks have been thrown up about here, to fall behind, in case the Yankees come to attack Petersburg. Woods have been chopped down to stop the progress of the Yankees, & everything else done, but I fear if they were to come, all this work would be of no avail. It wouldn't surprize me any, at all, if they get Petersburg & Richmond before winter. I am no prophet, nor the son of a prophet, but what I look at is this; money is the object now, to make money & nothing else & if the south don't fall on that account I am mistaken, mark my words. . . . I notice in the papers Georgia is kicking up on account of the conscript law; one of the ablest judges has pronounced the law unconstitutional & therefore null & void, in that state. What will be the consequence she will have to be <u>coerced</u> & if they do that she will seceed from the confederacy, & that she has a right to do, because we are fighting for that very right, with the U.S. This is strange work is'nt it? How I wonder how it will end? I hope you are all well, as this sheet finds me. How are all the friends in Salem, that is *sympathizing* [author's italics] friends.

In closing there was a request for occasional copies of the local newspaper (*People's Press*), as there had been no opportunity to see many state papers: "I sometimes see the [Raleigh] *Standard* [author's italics]. I remain yours Ed." Afterthoughts included concern about correspondence, a persistent thread running throughout the letters, as well as a clear distaste for military life and a repeated longing for home.

You asked what we did with the money that we received at concerts. There was not much left after paying such enormous bills at the hotels; 3 dollars a day for each one & the railroad fare too. I hope the time will come when I can say home sweet home. There is a sweetness in the sound that is only appreciated when distance separates us from it. Is'nt it true? I am so disgusted with military life I don't know what to do, & for all I ought not complain, as we have it like kings to what the privates have it[.] I can't content my self to this life; if it wasn'nt for Gust R[eich] I don't know what I would do. That is so; we take walks together every day. Give my respects to Gust's folkes, & Gust likewise; he is well. How I wish I could go with this letter, & stay with it. Vain wish.

The general tone is set in these first few letters. Peterson had an obvious bent—it appears almost an obsession—for letter writing. There are, however, the usual conspicuous "gaps" throughout the sequence of writings.

Still located in Petersburg on October 12, as the fall days gradually became shorter and signaled the approach of winter, Ed began to think about when or if he would receive a furlough. Believing that his close friend "Gust" had probably already reached Salem on leave, he stated that "I have no idea, now, when we'll get a furlough; not before Christmas, I don't think." The same letter also singled out their young Colonel Burgwyn for comment.

I think the Col. has quite a different opinion of our abilities in giving exibitions & concerts. I believe the reason that he didn't go over the 1st night was he was fearful we could not perform what our bills stated; he said, too, he was agreeably surprised. I have quite a different opinion of him since our concert. I think a great deal of him; he is a good looking man, only 21 or 22 years of age; he is very strict with his officers & men. He is a strict drill master. I am glad that I am no private. . . . We have just been practicing about an hour. Tell [brother] Wm. we practiced old 48 in our old band, its been set a tone lower for us. Its an excellent piece; we have a good many new pieces since we left home. One by the name of "Here's your mule" a very good one. Tell siss to learn it till I get back. I think Ed Leinbach said one of the [Salem] Academy girls had it for the piano.

Voicing one of many requests that his sister refrain from showing the letters to anyone, as well as expressing satisfaction with their present location, Peterson wrote:

I wonder if you show my letters to any one but our own family. If I knew you did I would'nt write any more, as I write . . . stuff that I should'nt like for everybody to see or hear. Please don't show to any body. . . . I am in hopes that we will not leave here for some time. I am under lasting obligations to you for all the letters you send. Write often. Tell Wm. so too, & Sis. . . . I guess you talk a good deal about me today, don't you, as Gust has been to see you, at any rate I hope he has, but I must stop, as my paper is giving out. Accept my sincere love from your most affectionate brother. Eddy. We are all well, an hav'nt had to play any since Gust left [us with no drummer] except for our own satisfaction; we practiced some pieces we got from this other band this morning. Sam is copying some now.

During the early months of 1863, the Twenty-sixth Regiment and band returned from Virginia to eastern North Carolina, generally in the familiar area of Goldsboro and Kinston, where the boys remained fairly active with concerts and serenades. Although there was heavy fighting around New Bern, the band boys managed to live fairly well and found their surroundings bearable—even pleasant at times—as spring approached.

Experiencing a second taste of war, the bandsmen were again occupied with caring for the wounded following the Confederate retreat from New Bern. The trying duties were described as having a marked effect on their appearance; at the same time, some thought and expression were given to more pleasant aspects of the moment.

Whenever I have an opportunity of sending this scrawl, I'll do so, & don't think hard of it, if it is'nt closer, as I wish to write still more, if anything transpires. . . . I doubt whether you can make out to read the other half sheet; excuse its being so dirty, as I am very dirty & greasy; our faces are very black from the pine smoke, & washing does no good. I had'nt washed my face while marching for 2 or 3 days. I wish you could see me. I was wishing your eyes could see what I saw the other day; that is the beautiful scenery, along a certain creek, by the name of Contenty [Contentnea] Creek; I call it a river; the road ran all along this creek, & it was towards evening when we passed it the mossy trees, & evergreens in the swamp opposite, contrasting beautifully; it was really worth seeing. . . . I could have enjoyed it more, if I hadn't been so tired. At another time we passed several swamps, there it look like middle of summer, everything green, so many different kinds of evergreen & vines, the yellow jasimine being almost in bloom; it must really be beautiful here in the spring; so many flowers; no wonder they say the whole air is fragrant with the smell of the jasimine & other flowers; if we should stay in this part of the state I intend trying to send some roots & bulbs home; but as to our staying where we are now, is out of the question, at any rate, to my opinion. Give my love to all.

By the middle of May, the band was back in Virginia, at Hanover Junction just north of Richmond where, within a few weeks, Lee would begin assembling his troops for the forthcoming campaign into Pennsylvania. (Even then there appears to have been heavy fighting going on around Fredericksburg.) Meanwhile, Edward took advantage of several days' layover to write an unusually long letter covering two weeks (May 18–30). He had much to say; on the twentieth he began:

It seems death is busy everywhere, & Charley Clauder I suppose was killed in the recent battle on the Rappahannic. Poor fellow. He is the first Salem boy, that sacrificed his life in this accursed war. I'm afraid the young boys will be thinned out more & more & it will be like it was after the French revolution, a curiosity to see a young man.

Subsequent comments described one of many tragedies of wartime, to which the Civil War was no exception. In this instance, Ed directed a full-blown outburst of rage toward several prominent Salemites who, taking advantage of the times, were engaged in unethical business practices. One merchant was singled out for a questionable transaction involving the writer's brother.

Wm. Wants to know about the bran? Tell him he can have it, & allow me what it is selling at; how do my hogs thrive. I am sorry Wm. Vogler, I hope, will some day or other get his doom allotted, & I don't care how severe it may be; these men like he, that brot' on this war, or helped bring it on, & now extortion, & remain at home & make their money off the soldiers wives & families ought to be killed, no, they ought to be "like Mrs. Denke said of Abe Lincoln" tortured by fastening fish hooks all over them & have lines attached & drag them from Virginia to Texas; that would not be too severe. I would like to see that curly headed rascal served in that way & let me play Dixie as he would pass me. Don't show this to any one. I cant see what the end of these men will be, like Fries, Vogler, V. C.[,] that encouraged volunteering at the commencement of this war & are now at home, amassing fortunes. Justice ought to be meted out to them in full. . . . I wouldn't like to see the Yankees get to Salem, or the army get there, but I would delight to see them get there & destroy the property of these extortioners, hypocrites [*sic*], & scoundrels, & see them flee; that, I think would be just & right, if the country could be drained of such scum & off-scoring of creation. I think we might prosper here after, but not before, these very men have made all they possess thro' the North & now are for prosecuting the war & force the conscripts to go & fight & lose their lives, but they themselves cant leave home; no, they have too much business to attend to, or shirk out of it, in about every conceivable way. Wo unto you hypocrites. I do hope they may get their doom in this world already. Enough, you will please excuse my writing in this strain. I can't help it. I have to be out in this detestable war, & they growing rich, & at the same time are at home, in peace; if there is justice in that, I for my life, cant see it. . . . We are all well at present, with the exception of colds, we cant complain. We are in a healthy country, have excellent water; were we in eastern N.C. the water would be bad by this time. Altho we are farther from home here, I would prefer staying than to return to sandy eastern N.C. again, the country of ticks, & musketoes, & swamps. . . . I fear we'll be ordered up to the Rappahanock before long. . . . Wednesday evening at dusk. I must add a few lines this evening yet; . . . I heard thro Joe's [Joe Hall] letter that you received those Yankee shinplasters, & by that, you received my letter. I am glad for it; tell Siss I will try & get *Wash[ington] Greys* [author's italics] arranged for her, if I can by Neave.

By the twenty-second, orders had been received and perceived as a probable move toward Fredericksburg, as "troops were moving up that way." An unusual tone of optimism (or perhaps cynicism?) was sounded in what might be considered tongue-in-cheek remarks.

I expect there is to be a forward movement made, & invade Maryland again; they were on the way to Hamilton's Crossing, not far from Fredericksburg. If we take Wash, Baltimore, Philad. Bethlehem, & all these different cities and towns, I will let you know. I could send you some coffee then, how much would you want; perhaps Levien would like to engage some. N. Y. is bound to be taken, & boston too. I will send you some soda too, <u>if</u> we conquer the North we are bound to play smash with all the free states; there is no other chance for them. I am a little uneasy about Canada; we'll be in such a sweep when we take N. Y. that we cant stop ourselves, & we'll be apt to take Canada & that will be accomplished in a short time. England will then kick up, but I think we can soon put her down; we'll tell her she shant have any cotton anymore, & then all will be right, & you know, "Cotton is king" so we'll have a powerful time; from now till cool weather, you know the northern army is almost disbanded, all gone home, so we'll not find any opposition, & it will be quite an easy task to annihilate the vandals. I feel for them, the south is bound to have her rights; had the north let the south alone, we would now show mercy, but that day is past, if we shouldn't succeed in annihilating the north, we'll starve them out, & that we can do before fall. . . . Tell Siss she must do better [writing] or I cant have that music arranged for her.

Continuing the letter on Sunday morning, May 24, Ed again touched on the subject of keeping his letters within the family: "I have charged you over & over again not to show my letters to anyone, but I am afraid you don't stick up to it, so I cant write as I would like to. Who is it at Salem that rejoiced to hear that Jackson was killed?"

The final section of this letter to his sister was written on Saturday morning, May 30. There was mention of having received a letter from his niece Siss, something he considered a rarity.

Tell her I was well pleased with it; she wrote on the envelope she had received music from [William?] Neave; tell her she need not write to Neave about it; write me all about it, if you please. I only sent for *Wash Greys* [author's italics]; if he don't charge much, I will get him to arrange the others.

(According to Sam Mickey, the band had acquired this piece in February.)

There was growing concern about major events in the West, as well as conjecture about the forthcoming plans of Lee. Portions of the letter read:

Maybe Vicksburg has fallen, & they don't like to acknowledge it. I will not close this till in the morning; perhaps I may get some news yet. . . . Gen. Steward [J. E. B. Stuart] was at the Junction this morning & has gone up towards Fredericksburg, it is reported with the intention of making a raid into Pennsylvania, therefore look out. . . . I must stop with this half sheet, or the letter will get too thick, with the money. . . . Todays papers have it that Vicksburg still holds out, & that the feds have been repulsed with tremendous slaughter; so much so that Pemberton [Lt. Gen. John C. Pemberton, commander of the Confederate forces at Vicksburg] had to burn tar to purify the air, the stench being so great from the dead Yanks, outside of his fortifications. I cant believe such as that, altho' it may be true; it no doubt was a desperate fight, & not over yet; time will show whether it falls.

In writing that evening on a half sheet of paper, one of many, Edward closed by stating the amount of money he enclosed: "I wish I could be at home tomorrow, I would give all that [is] in this letter. Good night. Edw. 20 dollars in this; altogether 70 dollars; all 5 dol. bills, except 1, & that is a $10 bill."

Following a brigade review on June 1, the troops broke camp and headed toward Fredericksburg. This had been expected, but there was regret in having to leave the relatively peaceful camp at Hanover Junction. For the next month, while on the move, there was little time for writing letters; at the same time, several bivouacs offered some respite, though brief, from the rigors of march. There would seem to have been time for at least short notes, but posting them would have presented a problem. There is thus far no explanation for the lack of communication from Peterson from May 30 until after Gettysburg.

As Lee's forces retreated from Pennsylvania, Pettigrew's brigade and its decimated Twenty-sixth Regiment—the band members were now stragglers—headed for Hagerstown. Along the way, Edward underscored the ravages of war in his letter of July 9:

Enclosed you will find a piece of moss, grown not far from the battlefield at Gettysburg; also a yellow flower I plucked at Fayetteville. . . . I pity the people where an army passes; they were enjoying peace out in Penn., like you at home, & all at once an army of 100 thousand passes thro' & devastates the country; . . . How can private citizens help it, that this war is carried on, & why should their property be taken from them; . . . & they call it pressing them [livestock], is nothing but what I call stealing them; . . . How can we expect to succeed in carrying on such a war; the prayer of the helpless children & women, is bound to be heard; . . . It almost makes me cry to think of all this, I am innocent of such as this, all that I have trespassed [is] that I eat a few cherries passing along the road. . . . P.S. I guess we'll go to our reg about tomorrow; they are at Hagerstown. . . . The people living there are removing their household property today, . . . it is said the Cavalry were fighting yesterday to the right of Hagerstown; also reported the Yankee army at Gettysburg has fallen back to Baltimore & I wouldn't be surprized if they meet Lee in Va.

Continuing the retreat southward, the troops established camp at Bunker Hill, West Virginia, on July 14. Nearly a week's layover allowed time for rest and no doubt attention to music. Resuming the march on the twenty-first, the troops crossed the Blue Ridge into Virginia and arrived at Culpeper on Saturday, the twenty-fifth. By August, most of Lee's army had crossed the Rapidan River and was stretched out on either side of the Orange and Alexandria Railroad. The Twenty-sixth Regiment and band, together again, were stationed in the vicinity of Orange and Spotsylvania Court House until the mid-spring of 1864. Several inscriptions in the Twenty-sixth's band books indicate music received or copied while in this area.

After having enjoyed a lengthy furlough in February, including a political junket to Wilkesboro with Governor Vance, the band returned to camp near Orange in March. The boys then enjoyed a two-month period of inaction, ample time for rest and musical pursuits.

A return to the serious business of war in May witnessed the group again actively serving as musicians/medics during the engagements of the Wilderness and Spotsylvania. Some of the bloodiest fighting of the war occurred during these hard-fought battles. North Carolina suffered heavy losses in troops killed, wounded, and captured. Although the musicians were at times at the breastworks playing, they miraculously came through with hardly a scratch!

Despite unfavorable circumstances, Ed found time to write a number of letters during "off" hours. One to his brother on May 11, from the hospital camp near Spotsylvania Court House, gave a good description of the hard fighting in the area.

It was on last Saturday, that I sent a short epistle to Sister, in order to let her know, that we were all safe, at that time, we are still safe, but at present, we don't know what a day may bring forth. Death is busy all around, members have been killed & died around us, since last I wrote, & we are still being killed, & crippled. While I am seated writing, to you, the artificial thunder is heard, as well as the thunder of the skies, the air has been very hot, ever since the campaign opened, which is one week already. . . . May 12th We marched pretty much all day; towards evening pretty heavy skirmishing commenced, in front of us, we had to pass on that road, immediately behind our line of battle almost in sight of the Yankees. . . . I was so exhausted & over heated, I felt like dropping any moment. Gust & myself were together, the rest being on ahead of us; we at length caught up with them & found them resting. . . . We are getting somewhat used to hearing shell whistling thru the air & also musketry firing; while I am writing, those discordant sounds fill the air, heavy firing. Monday night we passed about a mile from Spotsylvania C. H. Tuesday morning we left; taking the road, we came marching about 6 or 8 miles when our train halted; skirmishing commenced again, on the road we came the day before. There a fight took place, our division being engaged, which lasted until night. The Yankees had thrown up breastworks & lines which our men had to charge, they succeeded in charging them out of them & drove them back, we had a good number killed & wounded in our division. . . . Just before dark we got orders to move all the wounded to the hospital near Spotsylvania C. H. some 6 miles distant. . . . Yesterday we removed to another hospital, or to a new place. Such a nice place in a shady pine grove, but little fighting was done, today, some skirmishing however. . . . Thousands & ten of thousands have fallen this day. The Yankees have made repeated charges this day, & have been repulsed, it is said with immense slaughter, the artillery firing was almost equal to Gettysburg, . . . I was frightened, for once, I'll must admit, as the shells commenced falling not a great ways from us. . . . A Yankee prisoner told me, Grant had 275 thousand to operate against Richmond. . . . All the boys are well, Sam, Julius, & Henry joined us yesterday again. Elic [Alex Meinung] left us, when we started on this campaign, being sick, left for the hospitals. . . . I wish I could talk with you all, I have lots to talk. I remain your affectionate brother Edw.

A subsequent letter to his sister was begun on May 17 from a slightly different location, but the message was practically the same: intense fighting with numerous casualties.

The whole country around here is one vast hospital. We have had our hands full, attending to the wounded. May 19th. Thursday morning after breakfast. . . . I wrote to Wm., on where our brigade, or our regiment are stationed; you will know before this thro' the papers, that our men have breastworks or fortifications too behind, as well as the Yankees, we are frequently ordered up to the breastworks to play for the reg. So we have the opportunity of knowing how it looks there. . . . Spotsylvania C.H. is a small village, has 2 churches, a C.H. & a few private houses, a large hotel too. Before the war, I guess it was a very neat little village, now its pretty much deserted, only a few citizens remaining. . . . These people living here had planted their gardens, in vegetables, & how does it look now, all the fences torn down, & burnt up, the gardens, all tramped down, & horses hitched in the gardens, rosebushes all eat off & everything else gone to destruction. These people feel the effects of this war, more than anybody else. They are to be pitied. May 20, Friday morning. . . . Clear & beautiful spring morning, how nice it would be, at home, on such a morning no doubt everything looks beautiful there vegetables growing finely, flowers blooming, bees working busily, & everything doing well. . . . I heard today, that last night the Yankee bands played most beautifully along the lines. When we were up there the other evening, we could hear them in the distance, but couldn't distinguish the air they played. I heard some one say they heard them play "Hail Columbia" the other evening. . . . We whip the Yankees or our army does it but they don't stay whipped, they will come again & again isn't it strange, like it was at Fort Donelson [Tenn.], they were whipped there, but they kept coming, as it is here. Grant won't go back to where he came from. I don't understand[;]. . . I'm not so very sanguine about our keeping Grant back, he's undoubtedly the ablest Gen. they've yet sent. . . . On the first days fight at the wilderness, before we had put up a hospital, when tremendous fighting was going on, we stopped with the ambulances, along the road, & as it happened Gen. Lee, Stewart [J. E. B. Stuart], Wilcox, A. P. Hill, Pendleton, & a lot of the other generals, were consulting together, just there, several of us lay down immediately behind them, in the pine thicket where we could see all their movements. I was intending to look on, they seemed to be considerably excited & at one time, I believe, they were somewhat nonplused. It appeared so to me, as the firing at one time, seemed to be almost in our rear. . . . My sheet is full, & not much of interest in it, at that. . . . Accept lots of love from your ever affectionate, tho' absent brother. Edw. P.S. I'll try, & do better the next time. . . . Please excuse this. Don't show it to anyone if you please, outside of our family. . . . I must stop for today, I don't know yet when I'll get the chance to send this, I may add a few lines, before I'll send it. Good bye. Some body stole Sam's Mickeys [*sic*] horn the other night, he had it hanging on a tree aside of his tent. He's had to borrow ever since, when we have playing to do. I doubt whether he'll ever see it again. It was a genuine silver instrument.

As the Confederates were gradually, relentlessly pushed further southward, Edward and his companions were once again in the Petersburg area by mid-summer, where they would remain until the spring of 1865. Although Lee established quarters there over the winter, the situation was nonetheless fluid. Grant kept the Rebs constantly engaged in moves and countermoves.

By then, Edward Peterson was one among many Johnnies becoming increasingly disillusioned about the war who felt strongly that the string was running out for the South. For some, desertion offered a means of escape; others gave vent to their feelings in a less drastic fashion. Peterson, never one to suppress his views, let his thoughts be known through letters. One, begun on July 5, opened with a personal note to his sister:

This being your birthday, I will commence a letter to you & wish you a very happy one, & many happy returns of the same. . . . These are glorious times, ain't they? I expect, in the course of time there will be but one southern army, & one Northern, they'll concentrate all the forces on both sides, at one front, & then have a grand final battle, & wind up the war in that way, I hope it may soon be ended, but I fear it will be some time before that takes place. My belief is as it always was, that they'll wear us out, in the end. I don't see how it can be otherwise, I look at the case, with an unprejudiced mind, some are so bereft of reason, they don't want to see the case, as it actually is & go it blindly. I am none of those! I want to know how my case, & condition really is. I have often studied, how the South is to get out of this scrape, she got herself in, but I can't for my life see, how she is to do it. She'll come out at the little end of the horn, any way you take it. This is the view I take of it. Some believe that we'll whip the north, in the end. I've never had such an idea. There is some talk at this time, of invading Penn. If we do, the war will end the sooner, that's my candid opinion. . . . July 9th Saturday afternoon. . . . I think these [unexploded shells] are more dangerous, than liquor these times. I would like to have a good drink of liquor now. To service the drooping spirits, but its too high to buy now. Everything is enormously high these times, & getting higher.

Also expressing frustration over the sporadic mail service—the situation would become worse—there followed a comparatively short letter written to Siss from the hospital camp at Petersburg on July 14:

My ever dear niece,

I received your welcome letter of the 18th inst. On Friday June 24th & for which, I thank you very much. I'm sorry that communication has been interrupted, so that I can't write as often, as I would wish to, & at the same time, get no letters from home, or you, at all. Yesterday it was three weeks, since I received the last letter from home. You can imagine, how anxious I am to hear from there, as well as from you.

A letter to his sister on July 31 included some interesting comments of a political nature:

Tell Wm. I voted for Vance, not because I liked him so well, or his principles, but being situated as I am I couldn't do otherwise, tell him to keep this dark, I have a good position, in the army & so I voted as I did, if I was a private in ranks, I would have voted for Holden, all the time. Vance received a large vote in the army it seems [approximately thirteen thousand out of fifteen thousand votes cast by N.C. troops], but I believe that the people at home will elect Holden, at any rate. Time will show, [and] a week from now, we'll know who is Gov., unless the vote be very close.

Vance won convincingly with a total of more than fifty-five thousand votes when all were counted. The news of the election brought the following comments in a letter to Theressa on August 10:

Had vance got a majority in Forsyth, I was surprized to hear that, I thought surely Holden will get a majority there. The result of the election was entirely different to what I expected, a change must have taken place in N.C. since we were there [playing for Vance] in March.

More expressions of Peterson's disaffection with the way things were going and his support of any peace movement at home were expressed the next day in a continuation of the above letter:

I received the *Press* [author's italics] of last week today. Levy is still for peace, but don't believe in the peace movement of the north; north will continue the war, that I fully believe, & therefore I see no prospect of peace whatever. Fight on, fight on is the motto. Vance doctrine. They'll see what the end will be, utter annihilation, to my opinion. We'll be utterly ruined in the end; mark my words, next year there will be another campaign, & can we hold out. Time will show. I wish I could get out of the war, I would do it; in a few days it will be two years that I've wasted in my life, all to no purpose. How profitably I could have spent it at home. What a fool I was, that I didn't get into some kind of government work. Aug. 13. Now is the time to act at home; hold peace meetings & call a convention of the state; the army is in favour of peace, certain & sure. I hope you may do something to stop the war, at home.

Writing from Petersburg on Sunday afternoon, August 28, Edward took special notice of attending a local church service.

My ever dear & affectionate Sister,

Abe [Gibson] and myself got a permit to go to church this morning, which paid us well. I hadn't been to church for some time, as I hadn't the opportunity, or for other reasons too. We went to the same church, I was at, last Feb., when we were on our way home, on furlough, and were delayed at this place; I think I told you of the fine music I then heard, and today we heard most delightful music again. Oh, how I wished you could enjoy it with me; we took our seat on the gallery, and saw the congregation coming in; a great many soldiers were present, not near as many ladies were present as there were last Feb., a great many having left the city, on account of the shelling; as the organist commenced his prelude, I can't tell you how it made me feel, it remind me so much of Salem church; he played most beautifully, and the organ being most a capital one, tuning excellently as powerful an organ as I ever heard I believe; such a bass I never heard before, so deep, and powerful, and the performer was what you may call No. 1. The choir was not as full as before, but they sang well; it almost appeared like heaven to me, to be seated on nicely cushioned seats, and in a fine church. I wished to myself, we were all in heaven together, out of this miserable world, so full of trouble and sorrow, enjoying the celestial music there; we did not suit in this church with our old dirty lousy clothes but for all, I felt as if I had my nice Sunday clothes on, altho at time, the lice would trouble me, so I'd have to scratch, and then I would recollect that I was seated in my old clothes, however no one I suppose knew us, and if they did I didn't care. Three ministers officiated in the services; it being an Episcopal church they have a good deal of ceremony about their mode of worship; Gen. Pendleton preached, at any rate, I took it to be him; when he came in, I took it to be Gen. Lee as they favour a great deal, in fact I frequently take one for the other. I was surprised to hear him preach, I don't think it proper for a minister, to be a general; its out of place; there was Polk who was killed; it looked odd to see a man preach, in military clothes; his sermon was but short and not a very eloquent one either.

Some of Edward's most pointed comments are about fellow band members. In a letter begun to his sister on September 12, he continued the next day:

I hope soon to hear from Gust, as I dropped him a few lines the other day with those letters of his. Only don't let Elic impose on you when he gets well; you know how I mean. . . . We got a letter from him, the other day from Richmond, and such a fuss as he had, according to his letter, no one ever was as sick as he, but then you must recollect, how he magnifies. He was sick when he started from our hospital, but I had my own thoughts, about his actions; he fell down, and went on at a dreadful rate, you have no idea; how glad I was when he was sent to the corps hospital, to get rid of his fuss; he wrote us, that when he got to the corps hospital that he crawled about on his hands and feet, in search of water. Sein fass ist kotzer lich. [Another one of his acts.] He got a furlough of 60 days, I'm told. Enough of him. We don't miss him, much in the band, in the way of playing, he does us but little good. What a pity, that we did not get Sam Brietz in place of C[harlie] Transou, so we could now have two trombones and Elic might have played second alto. . . . [In German: young Transou has little talent, nor does he have an ear for music; his horn doesn't contribute anything.] The truth of it is this, he does us more harm than good, that is in the musick; otherwise he is a good fellow, he is so thoughtless; "abwesend" [absentminded].

In the same letter he included his longest, most informative reference to musical activities.

Proff. Hartwell was with us the other day and requested me to assist in giving a series of concerts, to be given at Petersburg, some time before long; for the benefit of the poor of that place. He wants me to play trombone, the performances are to consist of instrumental and vocal, brass, string, and piano forte music. I expect it will be worth going to, not because I'm to figure in it, but because the performers are, as much as I know, professors or teachers of music, with the exception of my humble self. Hartwell is teacher in a Miss. Band; he arranged several pieces for us; one he arranged which I sent to Siss. "Dearest I think of thee." [Charlie] Siegel [leader] of the 14th S.C. band is also a proff; he is to play flute; they say he plays finely. Hagedorn, another teacher of music, plays clarionet; Rudolf, another one, I wrote the other day I got acquainted with him; and Lackey [Charles Jacke, leader] of the 55th band, also teacher of music; and who else I've not heard yet. The string music will be nice, I expect, to consist of violins, flute, clarionet with violincello, and contrabrass, and trombone. It was to have come off last night, but as some are absent at present, it has not come off yet. There is to be a rehearsal one of these days. Gaufrebeau [Eugene Geauffretean] of the 55th band, I think is one of the number too. None of our crowd, but myself are to assist. I don't like the idea much, but I told Hartwell, I would willingly assist, provided I could play their music; if it is not too difficult. He said that was sufficient, just so I was willing. Enough of this. Where is the 21st band at present; I heard the other day they were trying for a furlough; have you heard anything of it. They have had an easy time of it, this summer in eastern N.C. I will stop now, and see if I receive a letter today. [See Appendixes A and B for information on some of the above-mentioned players and their bands.]

On September 16, in camp five miles from Petersburg, Peterson addressed another letter to his niece. He left no doubt as to the deteriorating state endured by band members at that time, including the band's inability to perform and, no doubt, his own disappointment at probably being unable to play with Hartwell and the other musicians in the concert in Petersburg.

Dear Niece, . . . We have left Petersburg, as you will perceive by the heading of this letter. . . . Our crowd is getting smaller & smaller; only seven of us on this trip; Dan C[rouse] & Joe H[all] remained at the brigade hospital, Dan being very poorly & Joe has been unwell a few days ago & I suppose did not feel able to make a march, so he also remained. . . . Dan ought to be sent home; he looks very bad. We were called upon to play last night but as we had no bass [played by Hall] we could not; the 11th and 44th bands let loose; they play poorly; their music tunes miserable. About this concert I wrote about being given at Petersburg, I fear I'll not be able to take part in it, in case we remain down here any time. But I guess we'll go back before many days. . . . Enough for today.

Conditions were unsettled and would remain so as Grant jockeyed for position and Lee kept moving his troops around. On Monday morning, September 19, Edward wrote:

When will it stop, there is no prospect, at present. In case McClellan is elected at the north, I fear it will help us nothing; those in office will not listen to any terms short of separation, which you know the north will never give up to. If Lincoln is defeated, which I fear he will not be, McC. will manage the way much better and in the end ship us out, sure snough. So what are we to do? I cant understand. Some hope that Lincoln may be reelected; it would be better for the South as he has mismanaged so much already. . . . I wish you could see how it looks in camp just now, & what we are doing; the reg is all gone, & we are left, with a few others, in camp. Bill Lemly I hear about a hundred yds. from camp practicing on his drum & in another direction I hear C. Transou practicing, on his horn. Abe, & H. Siddall are baking their flour up. Sam Mickey is sitting aside of me copying out a new piece, J. Leinback is talking & I am writing; so we are employed, at present; my cold is better today.

The last letter in the collection was written from Petersburg on October 3, 1864:

Dear Sister,
Soon another week will have elapsed since I addressed you last, & an active one it has been with us; you no doubt are aware of it, that fighting has been going on here for nearly a week, more or less. . . . I look for hard fighting this week; hope your are all well; my health is only tolerably at present. I hope soon to hear from you again, as we are situated now; we don't get mail regularly, as we are not with the reg. And the mail carrier don't come to the hospital, so our mail is left with the reg; most of our wounded have been sent off to the camp hospital. I've no more news to communicate at present. . . . I would like to see a Richmond paper, but I've not had the opportunity. I don't know how, or what has been transpiring on the north side. It was reported on Friday that they had been repulsed with heavy slaughter up there; how true I can't say. This is miserable paper. I intend to sell this, and buy me good as quick as I get the chance. I remain yours, Ed.

Even in the absence of more Peterson letters, we are able to indicate some of the more important events as they happened. These are largely derived from Julius Lineback's record. Lee's troops established winter quarters in the Petersburg area until February 1865. There was no Christmas furlough this time for the band, and by mid-February the prevailing thought of defeat was growing stronger. The Federal attack at Hatcher's Run (February 5-6) threatened the Confederate supply route on the Weldon Railroad. Following an unsuccessful attempt to dislodge the Yanks from Fort

Stedman, just east of Petersburg, the subsequent engagements of Dinwiddie Court House and White Oak Road (March 31) and the Battle of Five Forks (April 1) set the Reb wheels in motion.

The band, having spent the preceding night with some of the Twenty-sixth troops in the breastworks, cleared out when the place was overrun by Billy Yank on April 1. From this time forward the boys became separated once again. The bandsmen's wartime service ended with eventual capture, imprisonment, then release after the surrender at Appomattox.

Ed Peterson and Gus Reich were forced to surrender their instruments—trombone and bass drum—when captured. Ed is reported to have been paroled at Burkeville Junction, Virginia, during the middle of April. He and Joe Hall made it back home several days later.

Notes

Chapter 1

1. *Diarium der Gemeine zu Herrnhut* (Herrnhut Congregation Diary) in Wilhelm Bettermann (former Archiv-Direktor der Brüder-Unität), "Wie das Posaunenblasen in der Brüder-gemeine aufkam," *Jarbuch der Brüder-gemeine, Jahrgang* 33 (Herrnhut: Rudolf Winter, 1937-1938), 24.

2. Excerpt from a letter of Peter Böhler, December 25, 1739; filed in the Archiv der Brüder-Unität, Herrnhut, Germany, R.14.A Nr.6.3., 710-713. Letter from Richard Träger, archivist at Herrnhut, to the author, May 31, 1960.

3. Joseph Mortimer Levering, *A History of Bethlehem, Pennsylvania, 1741-1892, with Some Accounts of its Founders and Their Early Activity in America* (Bethlehem, Pa.: Times Publishing Co., 1903), 40.

4. Adelaide L. Fries et al., eds., *Records of the Moravians in North Carolina*, 12 vols. to date (Raleigh: Division of Archives and History, Department of Cultural Resources, 1922-), 1:80.

5. *Records of the Moravians*, 1:134.

6. *Records of the Moravians*, 1:146, passim. Of particular interest are the two trumpet players, the first names thus far identified with the North Carolina wind music tradition. Gottfried Aust was a potter who moved from Bethabara to Salem in July 1771, and died sometime later while on a visit to Lititz, Pa. Carl Opitz, Bethabara's cobbler, moved with his family to Bethania, where he died in 1763.

7. Research Files, Museum of Early Southern Decorative Arts (MESDA), Old Salem, Inc., Winston-Salem, N.C.

8. *Records of the Moravians*, 1:361, 378.

9. Portion of a letter (n.d.) from the *Aufseher Collegium* [Central Board] *to the Aeltesten* [Elders] *Conferenz*, entered in "Minutes of the *Aufseher Collegium*," December 1, 1772. Quoted in *Records of the Moravians*, 2:708-709.

10. The inside cover of each book bears an inscription by the late Bernard J. Pfohl, "Moravian Trombone Choir Books (about 1780)." Examined by the author in the late 1950s and later published as Edward H. Tarr and Stephen L. Glover, eds., *The Moravian Brass Duet Book* (Nashville, Tenn.: The Brass Press, 1976).

11. Located by Donald M. McCorkle in the late 1950s and subsequently examined by the author. The first modern performances were the writer's editions of Sonatas No. 1, 3, and 8 on a program of Tower Music, Smithsonian Institution, Washington, August 3 and 10, 1965. They were performed again at the Eighth Early American Moravian Music Festival and Seminar, Winston-Salem, N.C., June 12-19, 1966. Published editions in two sets appeared as Edward H. Tarr and Harry H. Hall, eds., *Weber Sonatas No. 1, 2, 3, 4,* and *Weber Sonatas No. 5, 6, 7, 8* (Nashville, Tenn.: The Brass Press, 1977).

12. Discovered by the author in the late 1950s. His edition of Sonata No. 1 also received its first modern performance at the Smithsonian Institution in 1965, and later at the Moravian Music Festival in 1966. The third piece in this group of six has been published as Edward H. Tarr and Harry H. Hall, eds., *Cruse Sonata No. 3* (Cologne, Germany: Wolfgang G. Haas-Musikverlag Köln, 1997). Regrettably, the soprano parts to Sonatas 4, 5, and 6 remain missing.

13. *Records of the Moravians*, 5:2088. An expense note in the Salem records dated December 8, 1785, stated that these instruments had come from Herrnhut via Altoona (a small town serving as Hamburg's shipping port for several years) and Charleston, S.C. This note is in a miscellaneous collection of music receipts, expenses, and orders filed in the archives of the Moravian Music Foundation, Winston-Salem, N.C.

14. "Minutes of the Elders' Conference," November 30, 1785, Research Files, MESDA.

15. *Records of the Moravians*, 5:2088.

16. For details of orders and purchases of instruments for Salem, Bethabara, and Bethania during this period, see Harry H. Hall, "The Moravian Wind Ensemble: Distinctive Chapter in America's Music" (2 vols., Ph.D. diss., George Peabody College for Teachers, 1967), 1:144-151.

17. See the informative discussion in Donald M. McCorkle, "The Collegium Musicum Salem: Its Music, Musicians, and Importance," *North Carolina Historical Review* 33 (October 1956): 483-498; reprinted as *Moravian Music Foundation Publications*, No. 3 (Winston-Salem, N.C.: Moravian Music Foundation, Inc., 1956).

18. The organization appears to have passed into history with a second performance of Haydn's *The Creation* on October 17, 1835—possibly a few years earlier. McCorkle, "The Collegium Musicum Salem," 498.

Chapter 2

1. Extract from "Salem Board Minutes," in *Records of the Moravians*, 7:3237.

2. *Records of the Moravians*, 7:3256.

3. *Records of the Moravians*, 7:3257.

4. *Records of the Moravians*, 7:3297.

5. "Minutes of the *Aufseher Collegium*," Salem, April 15, 1822; translated excerpts (typed) from the original German. Research Files, MESDA.

6. The nineteenth-century bands of the three major Moravian communities in Pennsylvania—Bethlehem, Nazareth, and Lititz—also began as community organizations, as did other bands in this country. These and their counterparts in Wachovia, descended from their eighteenth-century religious tradition, nevertheless kept pace with changing times. In keeping with their secular contemporaries in America, the Moravian bands, also affected by current events, became militia adjuncts around the second decade of the century. (The Pennsylvania Moravians antedated the military image of the Salem Band in North Carolina by almost fifteen years.) For a

detailed account of the early Moravian band tradition in Pennsylvania, see Hall, "The Moravian Wind Ensemble," 198-240.

7. For a list of the *Collegium musicum* singers and likely orchestral personnel, see McCorkle, "The Collegium Musicum Salem," 497-498.

8. Johann Leinbach was a cobbler who, like other businessmen of Salem, experienced financial difficulty around the mid-thirties. In addition to his duties with the band as leader and flute player, he also played flute with the *Collegium musicum* orchestra. (McCorkle also mentions the violin.) One entry in the journal states that he was "beginning to play the viola." One son of John Henry, Edward W. Leinbach (1823-1901), was a prominent local musician, reputedly the most influential musician in Salem during the late nineteenth century. He is later recognized for his musical contributions to the Twenty-sixth band. John Henry's other sons included Julius, James, Henry, and Parmenio.

9. The membership of the band at this time included some or all of the following: *Flute*: John Henry Leinbach (leader) and Samuel Ephraim Brietz; *Clarinet*: Heinrich Schultz (1st), Nathanael Zevely (2nd), Samuel William Leinbach, William Praetzel Peterson, and Lewis Ephraim Belo; *Trumpet* and/or *Bugle*: Henry Ruede and Heinrich Edward Reich; *Horn*: George Foltz (1st), Rudolph Christ (Crist), and Theophilus Vierling; *Bassoon*: Joshua Boner and Charles Joseph Levering; *Bass Trombone*: Traugott Leinbach or Friedrich Meinung; *Bass Drum*: Timothy Holder. This list is based on information in *Records of the Moravians*, 8: passim; Johann Heinrich (John Henry) Leinbach Journal, Archives of the Moravian Church in America, Southern Province, Winston-Salem, N.C., passim; Research Files, MESDA; and a handwritten list of Salem musicians (1830-1850), compiled ca. 1850 by Edward Leinbach and located in Miscellaneous Collection, Moravian Music Foundation.

10. For additional information, see Appendix B.

11. Reprinted from *Miner's and Farmer's Journal* (Charlotte), n.d., and appearing in *Farmer's Reporter and Rural Repository* (Salem), June 6, 1835. The latter succeeded Salem's first newspaper, *Weekly Gleaner*.

12. These three pieces, as well as many others of the period, are among the Salem Band Collection of manuscripts, Moravian Music Foundation.

13. *Farmer's Reporter and Rural Repository*, July 11, 1835.

14. Joshua Boner (1809-1881). In 1839 he served as assistant to August Shulz, director of the congregation's music. In 1842 he succeeded Schulz as director, a position he held for only about eight months. *Records of the Moravians*, 8: passim. There is no indication when Boner assumed leadership of the band, or if he succeeded Leinbach. Two other likely directors during this period would have been Heinrich Shultz (recognized organist, singer, and teacher in the Boys' School) or Freidrich Christian Meinung (1782-1851). (See previous listing of likely band personnel.) Meinung, the leading figure of secular music in the community, is reputed to have been the foremost Salem musician during the first half of the century. He was the father of Alexander Meinung, member of the Twenty-sixth Regimental Band and a talented artist.

15. "Minutes of the Provincial Elders' Conference," Salem, July 28, 1841. Translated from the original German (typed) by Dr. Edmund Schwarze. Research Files, MESDA.

16. Probably the first time the musicians received "pay for play" was in the spring of 1831, during examination days at Salem Female Academy. The subject of pay had nothing to do with the school and thus posed no problem; however, there was a discussion with school officials about the propriety of performing at this special time. Leinbach's journal entries for May 19 and 20 indicate that the band did play and received $13.50!

17. Reprinted from *Register* (Raleigh), n.d., and appearing in *Patriot* (Greensborough [Greensboro]), April 6, 1844.

18. Reprinted from *Register*, n.d., and appearing in *Patriot*, April 12, 1844.

19. Reprinted from *Star* (Raleigh), n.d., and appearing in *Patriot*, April 20, 1844.

20. "Minutes of the Provincial Elders' Conference," April 15, 1846.

21. "Minutes of the *Aufseher Collegium*," April 17, 1846, Research Files, MESDA.

22. Just when Salem began to make use of the nineteenth-century innovations within the brass family, especially the switch from "natural" trumpets and horns to those with valves, is not known. Brass bands had made their appearance on the American scene in the 1830s, so Salem probably followed suit soon thereafter, prior to 1850, about the time Edward Leinbach possibly succeeded Joshua Boner as leader of the band.

23. *People's Press* (Salem), February 22, 1851.

24. *People's Press*, July 5, 1851.

25. *People's Press*, May 7, 1853.

26. *People's Press*, February 25, 1854.

27. *People's Press*, June 19, 1857. It appears that the society had been organized for several years but still was having a difficult time attracting public attention. If there had been a lack of support for earlier concerts, inclusion of the popular band on this date—it was absent from a performance by the society in December 1854—probably ensured the large attendance at this latest concert. Additional information, including a copy of the program, is found in Hall, "The Moravian Wind Ensemble," 329-330.

Chapter 3

1. *Records of the Moravians*, 12:6219-6220. The notes of Julius Leinbach and Sam Mickey supply the majority of quotations in this chapter. Unless otherwise identified, all quoted material in subsequent chapters is from Leinbach and may or may not be so indicated.

2. The regiment was commanded by Col. William W. Kirkland; the muster roll indicates that the original band consisted of eight members. Muster roll of the Field, Staff and Band of the Eleventh Regiment N.C. Volunteers, May 24–August 31, 1861 (Record Group 109, War Department Collection of Confederate Records, National

Archives, Washington, D.C.). For a list of personnel and other information, see Appendix A.

3. Special Order No. 222, Adjutant and Inspector General's Office, November 14, 1861, cited in Louis H. Manarin et al., comps., *North Carolina Troops, 1861-1865: A Roster*, 15 vols. to date (Raleigh: Office of Archives and History, Department of Cultural Resources, 1966-), 3:xi-xii; 6:530.

4. "General Order No. 30, April 28, 1862, Adjutant and Inspector General's Office, issued in accordance with an act of Congress, ordered all units of twelve-month volunteers to re-enlist and reorganize within forty days from April 16, 1862, or be drafted." Quoted in William H. Runge, ed., *Four Years in the Confederate Artillery: The Diary of Private Henry Robinson Berkeley* (Chapel Hill: University of North Carolina Press, 1961), 15 n. 10. April 21 is the date given for status change of the Twenty-sixth North Carolina. See *North Carolina Troops*, 7:456.

5. The change occurred while the division of Maj. Gen. Richard S. Ewell was halted briefly at Gordonsville, Virginia. *North Carolina Troops*, 3:66.

6. *North Carolina Troops*, 3:69, 78-83. For personnel, see Appendix A.

7. Muster rolls of the Twenty-first Regiment N.C. Troops, Sept. 1-Oct. 31, 1861; Dec. 31, 1862-Feb. 28, 1863; Feb. 28-Apr. 30, 1863; Dec. 31, 1864-Feb. 28, 1865, National Archives.

8. The history of the regiment by Maj. James F. Beall failed to identify the Twenty-first as formerly the Eleventh Regiment, North Carolina Volunteers, nor is there any mention of a band. See Walter Clark, ed., *Histories of the Several Regiments and Battalions from North Carolina in the Great War, 1861-'65*, 5 vols. (Goldsboro, N.C.: Nash Brothers, 1901), 2:129-146.

9. Letter by Nathaniel ("Nat") Shober Siewers (private in Company A, First Battalion, North Carolina Sharpshooters), written from Kinston, May 7, 1864. From typescripts of "Photocopies of Civil War Letters (1856-1869) of Nathaniel Shober Siewers," Archives of the Moravian Church.

10. Lee Sherrill, "Kirkland's Confederate Band," a study of the Twenty-first Regiment and Band prepared for and on file with the Forsyth County Genealogical Society, Winston-Salem. Sherrill's extensive research brings to public notice, for the first time, much information about the band and its place in the history of Salem's musicians during the war.

11. See *North Carolina Troops*, 10:220. For additional information on this regiment, including two rosters of personnel, see Appendix A.

12. Oliver J. Lehman information in possession of the Bethania Historical Association, Bethania, N.C. Letters to the author from Ms. Louise B. Kapp, Bethania, N.C., November-December, 2001.

13. See Appendix A.

14. *Western Sentinel* (Winston), August 30, 1861.

15. *Western Sentinel*, September 6, 1861.

16. For an informative discussion of the psychological connection between war and music, including especially the propaganda aspect, see James Stone, "War Music and War Psychology in the Civil War," *Journal of Abnormal and Social Psychology* 36 (October 1941): 543-560.

17. Zebulon Baird Vance (1830-1894), former captain, Buncombe County "Rough and Ready Guards," became commander of the Twenty-sixth North Carolina Infantry, a regiment organized at Camp Crabtree, Raleigh, August 27, 1861. Vance remained with the regiment until leaving the troops in August 1862, to assume his duties as the recently elected governor of the state. For the historical sketch of the Twenty-sixth, see Clark, *North Carolina Regiments*, 2:303-423.

18. Clark, *North Carolina Regiments*, 2:398.

19. Quoted, reputedly, from the missing portion of the Samuel Timothy Mickey Diary, Archives of the Moravian Church. Clark, *North Carolina Regiments*, 2:398.

20. From the Leinbach account. Mickey included the same personnel in his diary, although there were some differences in the "matching" of personnel and instruments. Oddly, neither Leinbach nor Mickey indicated that Crouse had at one time been identified with the band of the Eleventh Volunteers, although his name appeared on the single roster of this unit (May 14–August 1, 1861). His enlistment date is given as May 24, 1861, and the date of his assignment to the band is indicated as July 14, 1861. See *North Carolina Troops*, 6:575. See further comments in Appendix A.

21. There appear to have been no tables of organization specifying the instrumentations for Confederate bands, although most if not all, were typical brass groups. Confederate army regulations did stipulate, however, that "*when it is desired* [author's italics] to have bands of music for regiments, there will be allowed for each, sixteen privates to act as musicians, in addition to the chief musicians authorized by law, provided, the total number of privates in the regiment, including the band, does not exceed the legal standard." *Army Regulations, Adopted For the Use of the Army of the Confederate States* (Richmond: West and Johnston, 1861), 6. A second edition of these regulations that appeared in 1863 reads the same.

22. See Robert Garofalo and Mark Elrod, *A Pictorial History of Civil War Era Musical Instruments and Military Bands* (Charleston, West Virginia: Pictorial Histories Publishing Co., 1985), 35.

23. A roster of the band lists Hackney with the field and staff of the Twenty-sixth Regiment. The names of Long and Boyd appear on the rosters of Companies I and K, respectively. See Appendix B.

24. The Fries brothers, Francis and Henry W., were prominent manufacturers of cotton and woolen goods in Salem during this period. Their "jeans" were in great demand. No doubt these were tailor-made for the Twenty-sixth musicians, whose caps were purchased later in New Bern.

25. Regulations specified a double-breasted tunic of gray cloth; trousers of light (or sky) blue; double-breasted, cadet overcoat with cape; French-style caps; black leather tie; and Jefferson-style boots "according to pattern." *The War of the Rebellion: A Compilation of the Official Records of the Union and Confederate Armies*, 150 vols. (Washington: Government Printing Office, 1880-1901), ser. 4, pt. 1:369-372.

26. For an interesting discussion of the prescribed uniform for the Confederate soldier, see Bell Irvin Wiley, "From Finery to Tatters," in *The Life of Johnny Reb, The Common Soldier of the Confederacy* (Indianapolis: Bobbs-Merrill Co., 1943), 103-122.

27. A letter from the War Department, April 18, 1861, stated that "volunteer companies will be mustered in for a term of service of twelve months. . . . Said volunteers shall furnish their own clothes." *Official Records*, ser. 1, 51, pt. 2:15.

28. One account indicated that Vance "marched into Kinston with colors flying, preceded by his band playing 'Dixie.'" See John W. Moore, *History of North Carolina from the Earliest Discoveries to the Present Time*, 2 vols. (Raleigh: Alfred Williams and Co., 1880), 2:160. Leinbach stated that the band met the regiment on the edge of town and escorted it to the courthouse square but, like Mickey, failed to mention any music.

29. Wiley, *Life of Johnny Reb*, 175.

30. Clark, *North Carolina Regiments*, 2:330. *North Carolina Troops*, 7:535, indicates that the Blaylocks were in service for one month, from March 20 to April 20, 1862.

31. This unit had been engaged in the Battles of Roanoke Island (February 7 and 8) and New Bern (March 14), and was apparently encamped at this time near Union headquarters in the vicinity of New Bern.

32. Gilmore (1829-1892) was probably the outstanding bandleader in America at this time, and certainly the most colorful. He entered active service in 1861 as director of the Twenty-fourth Massachusetts Band. In 1863 he was assigned superintendence over all Union bands in the Louisiana theater of operations. Additional items of interest about this renowned bandleader are to be found in *Dictionary of American Biography*, s.v. "Gilmore, Patrick Sarsfield."

33. "John" to Fannie L. Partridge, April 19, 1862; quoted in Bell Irvin Wiley, *The Life of Billy Yank, The Common Soldier of the Union* (Indianapolis: Bobbs-Merrill Co., 1952), 158. Many of the military bands of this era, Union and Confederate, were small, varying from eight to sixteen pieces with all-brass instrumentations. Gilmore and his grandiose group must have proved something of a treat to the Yankee soldiers and anyone within earshot!

34. The brigade then consisted of six North Carolina regiments: Twenty-fourth, Twenty-fifth, Twenty-sixth, Thirty-fifth, Forty-eighth, and Forty-ninth. *North Carolina Troops*, 7:456.

35. This was probably the same instrument later mentioned as having been given away near the war's end by bassist Joe Hall because it was "too heavy to carry home." It is very likely that the bass of the Twenty-sixth shown in the accompanying photograph is the original instrument that the Twenty-sixth musicians took with them into service; however, it was actually used very little, only as a matter of convenience whenever the boys visited Salem on their furloughs. (This instrument was reconditioned, but not authentically restored, in the early 1960s.)

36. An interesting collection of Reich's paraphernalia is on display in the Wachovia Museum of Old Salem, Winston-Salem, N.C. For more information on Reich, see Appendix B.

37. For an extended discussion of the Moravian wind-music tradition, especially in connection with death announcements and funerals, see Hall, "The Moravian Wind Ensemble," 98-181.

38. Vance, a Democrat, was running against William J. Johnston, the Confederate (Republican) Party nominee.

39. Agnes Peterson Boyd Material, Moravian Music Foundation. For selected extracts of these letters, see Appendix D.

40. Brietz was in the band for just a short time. By July 1, 1863, he had become a lieutenant in one of the companies and was captured immediately following the Gettysburg battle. The remainder of his army career is revealed in the following quotation of a Yankee Moravian: "More than a thousand wounded prisoners passed [Bethlehem, Pa.] last Saturday and Sunday [July 19-20] on their way to New York . . . but only one of them Mr. Edward Brietz, of Salem, was recognized and spoken to by acquaintances here." *The Moravian* (Bethlehem), July 23, 1863.

41. Clark, *North Carolina Regiments*, 2:334. The soldiers of the Twenty-sixth had come to respect and like Burgwyn and were highly indignant at this remark by Ransom. Leinbach, on behalf of the band, immediately applied for a transfer; Ed Peterson expressed a strong opinion regarding Ransom. See Appendix D.

42. Pettigrew's brigade, then composed of the Forty-fourth, Forty-seventh, and Fifty-second North Carolina Regiments, was stationed at Petersburg in August 1862, when joined by the Twenty-sixth. Clark, *North Carolina Regiments*, 2:334-336; see also *North Carolina Troops*, 7:457.

43. According to Donald McCorkle, Edward Leinbach rose to musical prominence in Salem in the mid-forties and reportedly became the most influential musician in the community during the second half of the nineteenth century. Donald M. McCorkle, "Moravian Music in Salem: A German-American Heritage" (Ph.D. diss., Indiana University, 1958), 194. A partial catalog of the band's repertory includes several pieces composed and/or arranged by Edward: *Dead March*, *Easter Galop*, *Col. Hoke's March*, *Ever of Thee* (arr.), *Gov. Vance's Inauguration March*, *Marseilles* (arr.), *Serenade Waltz* (arr.), *Carolina March* (arr.), and *Parting* (arr.). See Julius A. Leinbach, "Regiment Band of the Twenty-sixth North Carolina," ed. Donald M. McCorkle, *Civil War History* 4 (September 1958): 225-236; reprinted as *Moravian Music Foundation Publications*, No. 5 (Winston-Salem, 1958), 234-236. Edward may well have composed—or at least arranged—other tunes in these books, especially those having a direct association with the band: e.g., *21st Regiment Quickstep*, *Col. Kirkland's March*, *Col. Vance's March*, and *26th Regiment Quickstep*.

44. The Pettigrew Brigade then consisted of the Eleventh, Twenty-sixth, Forty-fourth, Forty-seventh, and Fifty-second North Carolina Regiments. See *North Carolina Troops*, 5:2.

45. The Eleventh Regimental Band was a large group of about fourteen members who, according to records, were primarily from the Charlotte-Lincolnton area. See Appendix A. There is no explanation for the confusion on the part of Leinbach and Mickey; perhaps this is another example of statements based on recall.

46. The two quotations by Leinbach and Mickey are the first time the Salisbury native is mentioned by either Moravian bandsman. Leinbach's reference to Neave as a composer, here and later, raises an interesting point: Nowhere in the Twenty-sixth band books is E. B.'s name identified with any compositions; rather, the initials of his half brother (W. H.) appear as composer and/or arranger on several pieces. When subsequently mentioning Neave, the author has elected to retain Leinbach's reference. For additional information and commentary on the Neaves, including the personnel of the Fourth Regiment band led by Edward, see Appendixes A and B.

47. An unusual amount of sickness continued to plague the bandsmen, and for the past few months one or more members were usually at home on sick leave. On returning to camp, Leinbach and his companion spent Saturday, May 16, in Petersburg, where a B-flat tenor saxhorn was purchased for Siddall.

48. Jackson's funeral was held in his own Presbyterian church in Lexington, Virginia, on Friday, May 15, five days following his death from complications from pneumonia at Guiney's Station, just south of Fredericksburg. The occasion of which Leinbach speaks was perhaps one of a number of memorial services being held that Sunday for the mourned general.

49. Heth's division then consisted of the brigades of Pettigrew, Col. John M. Brockenbrough's "Virginia," Brig. Gen. James J. Archer's "Tennessee," and Brig. Gen. Joseph R. Davis's "Mississippi." (Archer's brigade also included two Alabama regiments, and Davis's the Fifty-fifth North Carolina.) Added to these forces was the artillery battalion of Lt. Col. John J. Garrett. See "The Opposing Forces at Gettysburg," in Robert U. Johnson and Clarence C. Buel, eds., *Battles and Leaders of the Civil War*, 4 vols. (New York: The Century Co., 1888), 3:439. In addition to Heth's troops, the composition of Hill's corps, then and for the duration, included the divisions of Maj. Gen. Richard H. ("Dick") Anderson (five brigades and one artillery battalion); Maj. Gen. William Dorsey Pender (four brigades and one artillery battalion); and Maj. Gen. James E. B. ("Jeb") Stuart's cavalry (five brigades); as well as the special cavalry detachments commanded by brigadier generals Albert G. Jenkins and John D. Imboden. *Battles and Leaders*, 3:437-439.

Chapter 4

1. The fate of the Confederacy, some believe, hinged on the untimely deaths of perhaps its two foremost generals: Jackson, a victim of friendly fire at Chancellorsville, and Albert Sidney Johnston at the Battle of Shiloh (or Pittsburgh Landing) in western Tennessee on April 6, 1862. Johnston, reportedly within an hour of capturing the Western Army under Grant, suffered a wound in the leg that subsequently proved fatal. See statement of former North Carolina Supreme Court chief justice Walter Clark in Glenn Tucker, *Front Rank* (Raleigh: North Carolina Confederate Centennial Commission, 1962), 38. Unless indicated otherwise, all remaining quotations in this and subsequent chapters are from Leinbach.

2. Longstreet believed strongly in pushing the war in the West by relieving hard-pressed Vicksburg from Grant's impending threat. This could best be achieved by initiating an active campaign into Ohio, even at the expense of dividing and weakening Lee's forces in Virginia. For a review of this proposal, see Douglas Southall

Freeman, *Lee's Lieutenants: A Study in Command*, 3 vols. (New York: Charles Scribner's Sons, 1944), 3:39-50.

3. According to Col. A. L. Long, then military secretary to Lee, it was Lee's intention to draw the capital city's defenders away from their positions and engage them on a field of his choosing. At the time he seriously considered York or Gettysburg as likely possibilities. See "Causes of the Defeat of Gen. Lee's Army at the Battle of Gettysburg," *Southern Historical Society Papers* 4 (August 1877): 49-87.

4. Hanover Junction marked the convergence of the Virginia Central and the Richmond, Fredericksburg and Potomac Railroads.

5. This order affected the Eleventh, Twenty-sixth, Forty-seventh, and Fifty-second North Carolina Regiments in Pettigrew's brigade. The Forty-fourth, then commanded by Col. T. C. Singletary, was deployed to assist in guarding the vulnerable approaches to Richmond and did not rejoin the brigade until the retreat of Lee's army following the defeat at Gettysburg. Clark, *North Carolina Regiments*, 3:24-25.

6. The Fifty-fifth North Carolina and Eleventh Mississippi were in Davis's brigade of Heth's division. See *Battles and Leaders*, 3:439.

7. Freeman, *Lee's Lieutenants*, 3:74, quoting James FitzJames Caldwell, *A History of a Brigade of South Carolinians Known First as Gregg's and Subsequently McGowan's Brigade* (Philadelphia: King and Baird Printers, 1866), 91.

8. The broad Rappahannock offered an ideal margin of safety for such diversions. Interestingly, this sector had been the scene of similar events after the Battle of Fredericksburg on December 13, 1862. One in particular was by a Federal band playing Northern airs, as well as the Rebel favorites *Maryland, My Maryland, Bonnie Blue Flag*, and *Dixie*, reported by Maj. G. Moxley Sorrel, a Confederate staff officer. There is no mention, strangely, of Confederate bands, although it is reasonable to think that they were quick to answer the challenge. See Douglas Southall Freeman, *R. E. Lee: A Biography*, 4 vols. (New York and London: Charles Scribner's Sons, 1934-1935), 2:496.

9. A sampling of the Twenty-sixth's extensive repertory is in the band's original books, located in the manuscript collection, Moravian Music Foundation.

10. Hooker succeeded Maj. Gen. Ambrose E. Burnside as commander of the Army of the Potomac following the Union debacle at Fredericksburg in December. With a degree of reservation, President Lincoln informed the new leader of his appointment in a letter dated January 26, 1863. Charles F. Benjamin, "Hooker's Appointment and Removal," in *Battles and Leaders*, 3:239-243. One source suggests that Hooker *let* Lee's army advance well into Pennsylvania and predicted "two weeks in advance that Gettysburg would be the battleground." *Dictionary of American Biography*, s.v. "Hooker, Joseph."

11. Upon learning of Lee's movements northward, Hooker had proposed to Lincoln on June 10 that he be allowed to overrun Hill's troops opposite his position at Fredericksburg and bring the Army of the Potomac to bear on Richmond. Refusing to agree to this proposal, the president directed Hooker to pursue Lee. On June 13, the Union forces began their march, parallel to Lee and east of the Blue Ridge. They

crossed the Potomac at Edward's Ferry near Leesburg on June 25, reaching Frederick, Maryland, the following day. For the preliminary movement of troops from June 3 to July 1, 1863, see W. C. Storrick, *Gettysburg, the Place, the Battles, the Outcome* (Harrisburg, Pa.: Horace McFarland Co., 1957), 5-10.

12. Since early June, the Third Corps had the responsibility of covering the bulk of Lee's army as it moved out of Virginia; at the same time, it was to counter any surprise move that the enemy might initiate against Richmond. Freeman, *Lee's Lieutenants*, 3:73.

13. Ewell's troops set the pace from Culpeper on June 10, crossed the Blue Ridge Mountains at Front Royal, and proceeded down the Shenandoah Valley. Simultaneously, Longstreet moved northward east of the Blue Ridge as far as Snicker's Gap, then crossed into the valley, forded the Potomac at Williamsport, and joined Hill's corps near Hagerstown. In the meantime, Hill had moved rapidly along the course taken by Ewell a few days after leaving Culpeper and had passed Longstreet. A variety of sources offer interesting descriptions of this itinerary and the circumstances that dictated specific maneuvers along the march. See James Longstreet, "Lee's Invasion of Pennsylvania," in *Battles and Leaders*, 3:244-251; Freeman, *Lee's Lieutenants*, 3:1-77; Glenn Tucker, *High Tide at Gettysburg: The Campaign in Pennsylvania* (Indianapolis and New York: Bobbs-Merrill Co., Inc., 1958), 15-79.

14. Anderson's First Division included Brig. Gen. Carnot Posey's Sixteenth Mississippi Regiment. Its band is of particular interest in that the Twenty-sixth musicians enjoyed a close association with the Mississippians and their distinguished leader, William H. Hartwell. See subsequent references to Hartwell and, especially, Appendix B.

15. Freeman, *Lee's Lieutenants*, 3:27; Tucker, *High Tide*, 27.

16. The fact that Lee traveled with the Third Corps for several days sparked many rumors concerning the army's mission. He divulged few details to his subordinates; therefore, there was considerable speculation as to his plans. Nevertheless, the significance of the advance was obvious; feelings of optimism were evident among the men. High expectations were being voiced also by certain Southern newspapers. Freeman, *Lee's Lieutenants*, 3:75-77.

17. Leinbach's identification of units throughout his diary coincides, generally, with those cited in various histories and records. In this instance, however, he appears to be in error and leaves us to speculate. The Eleventh Regiment and Band, along with other South Carolinians of the Twenty-first, Twenty-fifth, and Twenty-seventh Regiments, comprised Brig. Gen. Johnson Hagood's brigade of Maj. Gen. Robert F. Hoke's division—not Pender's, and not components of Lee's army on the Pennsylvania march. *Battles and Leaders*, 3:437-439. Perhaps Leinbach inadvertently mentioned the Eleventh Band when he was thinking of the Fourteenth South Carolina that, at the time, *was* in Pender's division (Col. Abner Perrin's First Brigade). Furthermore, the Fourteenth is subsequently referred to several times, but there is no other mention of the Eleventh. Julius's reference to "professional musicians" brings to mind another possibility: he may have been thinking of the Twenty-fifth South

Carolina of Pender's division, a band of excellent German musicians mentioned in a later chapter.

18. The top strength of Lee's army during the campaign has been estimated at 75,000, with approximately 20,000 casualties. Storrick, *Gettysburg*, 51.

19. In addition to Leinbach's statement, the histories of the Forty-seventh and Fifty-second Regiments indicate that at least Heth's division must have made the crossing at Shepherdstown. Clark, *North Carolina Regiments*, 3:88, 235. According to Longstreet, Hill's *entire* corps crossed at this point, and his own troops forded the Potomac at Williamsport. *Battles and Leaders*, 3:249.

20. William Miller Owen, *In Camp and Battle with the Washington Artillery of New Orleans* (Boston: Ticknor and Co., 1885), 239-240.

21. Across the Potomac on Antietam Creek, an undermanned Confederate army (more than one-fourth of whom were North Carolinians) made its first invasion of the North against a superior Federal force commanded by the overly cautious Maj. Gen. George Brinton McClellan. For the series of reports on this battle (referred to in the South as the Battle of Sharpsburg), see *Battles and Leaders*, 1:630-682.

22. Before entering Pennsylvania, Lee had his aide, Col. Charles Marshall, issue a number of important marching orders. At Berryville, Virginia, he had expressed a wish, tantamount to an order, to General Trimble, his topographical expert, that the Pennsylvania campaign must not be one marked by "wanton injury to private property." Though it is evident that the various subordinates were duly informed, no written order to this effect was issued until the general's staff reached Chambersburg on June 27. See Maj. Gen. Isaac R. Trimble, "The Campaign and Battle of Gettysburg," *Confederate Veteran* 25 (May 1917): 209-210.

23. Arthur Crew Inman, ed., *Soldier of the South: General Pickett's War Letters to His Wife* (Boston and New York: Houghton Mifflin Co., 1928), 43, 48.

24. An interesting account of this episode is in Robert Stiles, *Four Years under Marse Robert*, 3d ed. (New York and Washington: Neale Publishing Co., 1904), 202-203.

25. John B. Hood, *Advance and Retreat: Personal Experiences in the United States and Confederate States Armies* (New Orleans: G. T. Beauregard, 1880), 54; see also Tucker, *High Tide*, 41.

26. A lack of food apparently posed no problem for the South Carolinians of Brig. Gen. Abner Perrin's brigade (Pender's division of Hill's corps) and Brig. Gen. Jerome B. Robertson's Texas-Arkansas Brigade (Hood's division of Longstreet's corps). Tucker, *High Tide*, 38-39, 42.

27. Against his objections to taking over an army faced with yet another turnover in command—the fifth within the last ten months—Meade, commander of the Federal Fifth Corps was, nevertheless, named head of the Army of the Potomac on the morning of June 28. Lee, unlike some of his officers, had an excellent opinion of Meade. He reportedly considered him "the most dangerous man who had as yet been opposed to him; that he was a . . . soldier of intelligence and ability," and would take full advantage of any mistakes the Confederates might make. Stiles, *Four Years under Marse Robert*, 228.

28. It was not until June 28 or 29 that Lee, based on intelligence furnished by one of Longstreet's spies, was aware that the Federals had crossed the Potomac and were in a threatening position to the south. (Three corps had been reported in the vicinity of Frederick, Maryland.) See Longstreet, in *Battles and Leaders*, 3:250; *Lee's Lieutenants*, 3:34-38, 48-50. The Confederate forces in Pennsylvania were then strung out along a line extending, west to east, from Chambersburg to York, slightly over fifty miles: Longstreet's corps was in the vicinity of Chambersburg; Hill was at the base of South Mountain near Cashtown; and two divisions of Ewell's troops had reached York, while the remainder had proceeded from Chambersburg to Carlisle, approximately twenty-five miles north of Gettysburg. See Heth's report in "Causes of the Defeat of Gen. Lee's Army at the Battle of Gettysburg," *Southern Historical Society Papers* 4 (September 1877): 157.

29. Clark, *North Carolina Regiments*, 2:398.

30. Most of Maj. Gen. Robert E. Rodes's division of Ewell's corps had reached Carlisle, approximately twenty miles from Harrisburg, on June 27. With a plentiful supply of U.S. government whiskey on hand, the troops wasted little time in throwing a big one! Musical entertainment was furnished by bands of the Fourteenth and Twenty-third North Carolina Regiments of the brigades of Stephen D. Ramseur and Alfred Iverson, respectively. Tucker, *High Tide*, 62.

31. Cf. Freeman, *Lee's Lieutenants*, 3:77; Tucker, *High Tide*, 82-83; Heth's report, in "Causes of the Defeat of Gen. Lee's Army," 157.

32. These works, which were never too profitable, were owned by the fiery politician and zealous Rebel-hater, Thaddeus Stevens, and located near Greenwood, about fifteen miles west of Gettysburg. On the morning of June 26, as Early's troops moved toward Gettysburg on their way to York, the sight of Stevens's foundry stirred "Old Jube" to repay the Yanks, in part, for some of their destructive incursions on Southern soil. Accordingly, his men applied the torches. Carefully noting that the burning was entirely his own idea, he later wrote that "I did [it] on my own responsibility, as neither General Lee nor General Ewell knew I would encounter these works." It was an act, nevertheless, not to be forgotten by Stevens when he unleashed his virulent wrath against the South during the postwar Reconstruction. For an account of the incident, see Jubal Anderson Early, *Autobiographical Sketch and Narrative of the War Between the States* (Philadelphia and London: J. B. Lippincott Co., 1912), 255-256.

33. On the evening of June 29, Heth's division in advance of Hill's corps camped near Cashtown on the Chambersburg Turnpike. Clark, *North Carolina Regiments*, 1:589.

34. It seems that Leinbach was in error, for the troops were approaching Gettysburg from the northwest.

35. This mission, the well-known "quest for shoes," initiated the chain of events that precipitated the Battle of Gettysburg. General Heth stated that on the morning of June 30, upon "hearing that a supply of shoes was to be obtained in Gettysburg, . . . and greatly needing shoes for my men, I directed General Pettigrew to go to Gettysburg and get these supplies." "Causes of the Defeat of Gen. Lee's Army," 157. Pettigrew took with him three regiments (the Eleventh, Forty-seventh, and Fifty-second North Carolina); the Twenty-sixth moved out in the afternoon "to within

about three and one-half miles of Gettysburg, just this side [west] of a little creek [Marsh], crossed by a stone bridge, where . . . [it] filed to the right and bivouacked in a beautiful grove." Clark, *North Carolina Regiments*, 2:842-843. The three regiments leaving Cashtown for Gettysburg that morning were mustered preparatory to being paid; "the [Twenty-sixth] regiment was mustered as it bivouacked [at Marsh's Creek] after the day's march." Clark, *North Carolina Regiments*, 2:342, 370.

36. The Twenty-sixth Band and other Confederates were unaware of the change in command that had taken place in the Union army the preceding day.

37. Pettigrew's advance skirmishers encountered forward elements of Brig. Gen. John Buford's cavalry division in or near Gettysburg. In the meantime, the North Carolina troops had been halted less than a half-mile west of the town. Heth, continuing his account, stated that on June 30, Pettigrew "did not enter the town, returning the same evening to Cashtown, reporting that he had not carried out my orders, as Gettysburg was occupied by the enemy's cavalry, and that some of his officers reported hearing drums beating on the farther side of town; that under these circumstances he did not deem it advisable to enter Gettysburg." "Causes of the Defeat of Gen. Lee's Army," 157.

38. Shortly after 5:00 A.M. on July 1, Third Corps commander A. P. Hill, on the basis of Pettigrew's report the previous day, sent the divisions of Heth and Pender, together with Maj. William J. Pegram's artillery battalion, on a reconnaissance toward Gettysburg. See Tucker, *High Tide*, 100-105.

39. The mention of Hood's division is an obvious error, for these troops were not engaged. At the time of the encounter they, together with Maj. Gen. Lafayette McLaws's division, were moving from their position at Greenwood. Hood arrived at Lee's headquarters on Seminary Ridge, just west of Gettysburg, about sunrise on July 2. Tucker, *High Tide*, 225.

40. Obviously, the Federals were just as inclined to exaggerate as were the Rebs, and it also appears that they were equally uninformed as to their army's leader. McClellan was not among the Union commanders at Gettysburg.

41. July 1 was a day of momentary glory, yet ultimate tragedy, for the brigade of James Johnston Pettigrew. In view of the signal role played by these North Carolinians in gaining a costly, short-lived victory, it is difficult to understand why the excellent coverage by Douglas Southall Freeman limits praise to only two brigades of Heth's division, Archer's and Davis's. Freeman, *Lee's Lieutenants*, 80-89. For a more balanced view of Pettigrew's brigade in the first day's action, see Tucker, *High Tide*, 139-150. Detailed, vivid accounts of the distinguished action of the regiment and brigade in the sanguinary charge across Willoughby Run in the afternoon are in Clark, *North Carolina Regiments*, 2:343-361; 5:113-120.

42. The records list him as the regimental surgeon for the Twenty-sixth. His name is on the parole list of the regiment at Appomattox. Clark, *North Carolina Regiments*, 2:371; 5:529. Marshall was colonel of the Fifty-second North Carolina. On the third day, while in temporary command of Pettigrew's brigade during the famous Pickett-Pettigrew-Trimble assault on Cemetery Ridge, he was fatally shot from his horse. Tucker, *High Tide*, 370. Heth remained with Lee's headquarters for the remainder of the Confederate retreat to Virginia.

43. This was evidently Capt. S. W. Brewer of Company E, acting commander of the Twenty-sixth Regiment. Clark, *North Carolina Regiments*, 5:365.

44. The Federals were not the only ones to take note of Rebel band music during the second day's fight. British Lt. Col. Arthur J. L. Fremantle of the Coldstream Guards, traveling with the Confederate army and viewing the action from atop a tree at Lee's headquarters on Seminary Ridge, made the following entry in his diary: "When the cannonade was at its height [ca. 5:00 P.M.], a Confederate band of music between the cemetery [toward the southeast] and ourselves, began to play polkas and waltzes, which sounded very curious, accompanied by the hissing and bursting of the shells." Arthur J. L. Fremantle, *Three Months in the Southern States, April-June, 1863* (New York: John Bradburn, 1864), 260. Circumstantial evidence suggests that Fremantle may have heard music by North Carolina's Eleventh and Twenty-sixth bands. Though Leinbach mentions their having played in the morning, it is reasonable to assume that the all-day visit to the troops would have included some music in the afternoon. The time element of these performances and Fremantle's observation would appear to coincide. Furthermore, the two bands were within earshot of the British visitor in the area of Lee's headquarters.

45. For a special account of this melee, see Capt. Samuel A'Court Ashe of Pender's brigade, "The Pettigrew-Pickett Charge," in Clark, *North Carolina Regiments*, 5:137-158; also, see the extensive discussion by Tucker, *High Tide*, 331-382. The attack is perhaps more commonly known as "Pickett's Charge"; however, convincing evidence suggests some bias in this respect. In total number of Confederate troops engaged, Pickett commanded slightly over one-third; in depth of penetration, Pettigrew's North Carolinians (very likely Capt. E. Fletcher Satterfield's company of the Fifty-fifth Regiment) moved deeper within the enemy fortifications; finally, having to charge almost twice as far, the depleted brigades of Pettigrew and Trimble (in the stead of the wounded Pender) were exposed to the enemy's devastating fire of musketry and artillery for a longer period of time than were the fresh troops of the jaunty Virginian. Fortunately, some erroneous impressions arising from the Pickett label have been rectified, or at least modified—but not all. The commentator on a televised special in December 2003, recounting the Gettysburg encounter, repeatedly referred to the third day's bloody episode as "Pickett's Charge." This bears out a statement made by one authority more than forty years ago that "the true story has lagged hopelessly for the casual writer and reader. First impressions have been lasting." Glenn Tucker, "Some Aspects of North Carolina's Participation in the Gettysburg Campaign," *North Carolina Historical Review* 35 (April 1958): 196.

46. Casualty statistics for the third day's battle reveal that Pettigrew's brigade suffered 300 killed and wounded, with 288 listed as missing. If the figures seem small for brigade casualties, these troops had experienced a loss of 1,105 killed and wounded on the first day in the action in and around McPherson's Woods. Figures for the Gettysburg casualties of the Twenty-sixth Regiment alone are staggering: "The muster rolls for 30 June, 1863, make the aggregate present for duty, enlisted men, 885; allowing 10 percent for extra duty and details [including the band], it would leave about 800 muskets taken into battle at Gettysburg on the first day. Of this number 708 were killed, wounded and missing as the losses in the first and third day's

fighting. . . . Over 88 percent—and of the officers, 34 out of 39 were killed or wounded. Over 87 percent." Clark, *North Carolina Regiments*, 2:361, 373, 867.

Chapter 5

1. During the Gettysburg Campaign, Imboden's brigade of cavalry had operated as an independent raiding party and, in fact, had experienced relatively little action. Having taken no part in the three-day battle, these troops were fresh and would be of great assistance in conducting the army's withdrawal from Pennsylvania. See John D. Imboden, "The Confederate Retreat From Gettysburg," in *Battles and Leaders*, 3:420.

2. *Battles and Leaders*, 3:422.

3. The entire column, once under way, was seventeen miles in length. The effectives began their withdrawal from the ridge that same murky evening. Hill's corps led, followed by Longstreet, then Ewell. Their route was by way of Fairfield, southward along the Hagerstown road, thus establishing a protective line for the wagon train, then proceeding by way of Chambersburg. *Battles and Leaders*, 3:423; Tucker, *High Tide*, 385.

4. Imboden's firsthand, vivid description provides perhaps one of the more valuable sources of detail regarding the retreat. *Battles and Leaders*, 3:420-429.

5. Maj. John T. Jones of the Twenty-sixth North Carolina was placed in temporary command of the leaderless Pettigrew Brigade following the third day's encounter at Gettysburg. Clark, *North Carolina Regiments*, 2:349.

6. Brietz, the former band member, is listed on the Twenty-sixth's muster roll of June 30, 1863, as a second lieutenant in Company B. Clark, *North Carolina Regiments*, 2:371.

7. Constant attacks by enemy cavalry forced the men to do much of their traveling at night, and frequently the band members were separated from one another, as well as from the wagons, during this phase of the retreat.

8. Unbeknown to the band members at the time, Hall had been captured in Greencastle on July 6, when the Confederate wagon train and its escort were attacked by a heavy body of Union cavalry.

9. Leinbach obviously is referring to Martinsburg, West Virginia.

10. With the fall of Vicksburg to Grant on July 4, the Confederates had suffered two major disasters almost simultaneously.

11. This was probably Major William J. Baker, commissary of subsistence for Pettigrew's brigade.

12. Pettigrew's brigade was serving as rear guard for Heth's decimated division. The handsome young Pettigrew, having resumed personal command of his troops, was fatally wounded by an attacking band of Sixth Michigan Cavalry on the morning of July 14. Three days later he died at Bunker Hill. The loss of this extremely capable and well-liked officer, referred to as "probably the last casualty of the Southern army in the campaign," was also among the first in a series of tragic blows to strike the chain of

command in Lee's army following Gettysburg. See Clark, *North Carolina Regiments*, 1:591; Tucker, *High Tide*, 388-389.

13. Clark, *North Carolina Regiments*, 2:399. These and other performances by the Twenty-sixth Band that General Lee heard were perhaps responsible for impressing upon the Confederate commander the value of music to his troops.

14. Siegel was the leader of the Fourteenth South Carolina Regimental Band, something Leinbach failed to mention. A rather interesting remark by Julius identified Charlie as a "tuba" player in this band. (Leadership in those days normally fell to the first cornettist, usually a skilled E-flat player.) For a roster of Siegel's band, see Appendix A.

15. In addition to the Twenty-sixth Band, the bands of the Fourteenth South Carolina and the Thirty-third North Carolina obtained many of the same pieces from Neave. See Appendixes A and B.

16. Although Leinbach failed to identify the sender or addressee of this letter, it probably was one that he had just received from his family. There is no explanation for the apparently miraculous one-day delivery from Salem to Culpeper.

17. Leinbach noted that the band of the Thirty-third also had its request for a furlough rejected, the reason stated that "the order to grant furloughs was to apply only to men in active service and not to details."

18. From the beginning, the bandsmen had been paid in this manner, although Julius never indicated any of the amounts.

19. In seeking a transfer through proper channels, the Moravian musicians' request was in sharp contrast to that of many Rebs, who were taking their furloughs practically at gunpoint. Wiley, *Life of Johnny Reb*, 144-148.

20. Mallett was conscription officer for North Carolina at the time.

21. Freeman, *Lee's Lieutenants*, 3:289.

22. Longstreet, now in the western theater, was still pressing for an all-out offensive in Tennessee, and argued strongly in favor of reinforcing Bragg for an immediate attack on William S. Rosecrans's Army of the Cumberland. Freeman, *Lee's Lieutenants*, 3:220-221, 238.

23. *Official Records*, ser. 1, 39, pt. 2:701.

24. During the battle of Bristoe Station on October 14, 1863, the brigades of Kirkland and Cooke were in the vanguard of Lee's forces. Losses were heavy, and Kirkland was seriously wounded. He returned to the brigade in the spring of 1864 in time for the four-day engagement at Cold Harbor (May 31-June 3). He was wounded again on June 2; the brigade was placed under the command of Col. (temporary brigadier general) William McRae of the Fifteenth Regiment on June 22, 1864. McRae's promotion was made permanent on November 4, and he led the brigade as part of Heth's division for the remainder of the war.

25. It is indeed unfortunate that some American historians have criticized the Confederate bands as having been highly inferior groups. See, for example, Freeman, *R. E. Lee*, 2:496; Wiley, *Life of Johnny Reb*, 157. Much of the criticism by these and

other writers probably stems from statements, accepted without question, of a few Europeans who were visiting the camps during the war. For example, a British lieutenant colonel on duty in Montreal wrote that "almost every regiment had a small band of brass instruments. I cannot say much for the music, but it was at least enlivening." G. J. Wolseley, "A Month's Visit to the Confederate Headquarters," *Blackwood's Edinburgh Magazine* 93 (January 1863): 23. Another British officer, Arthur Fremantle, while visiting in Texas, also wrote disparagingly of a Confederate band— "eight or ten instruments braying discordantly" as they fronted a four-hundred-man regiment. Fremantle, *Three Months in the Southern States*, 71. Johnny Reb's bands and many of those of Billy Yank could hardly be expected to compete with those practitioners of a time-honored European tradition, and particularly the excellent British ensembles (e.g., the Coldstream Guards and Grenadier Guards). The Confederates, nevertheless, probably did field more good bands than credited with. The Salem Band was rooted in a distinguished musical heritage. Its musical achievements, as well as favorable comments by contemporary bandsmen, are links in the chain of evidence that should flash caution to those who readily dismiss all Johnny Reb bands as mediocre or inferior groups.

26. An entry of January 19 in Julius's handwritten notebook stated that "the time of Prof. Hartwell's engagement [with us] having expired, he left us, & returned to his own band." The good opinion of the Sixteenth Band held by Leinbach, a talented musician himself, contrasts with that of a private in the Mississippi regiment who stated that "our band is a great institution. It always keeps its numbers undiminished, and labors with the greatest assiduity at 'tooting.' Their music, however, is never the sweetest nor most harmonious." Diary of James J. Kirkpatrick, entry of October 30, 1863; quoted in Wiley, *Life of Johnny Reb*, 157.

27. For additional information on Hartwell, including some of his music in the Twenty-sixth's band books, see Appendix B.

28. Near this Virginia hamlet, approximately thirty miles southwest of Alexandria, on the Orange and Alexandria Railroad, the Confederates engaged Meade's Second and Third Corps on the afternoon of October 14. Many Rebs still had fond memories of their success in this locale more than a year before (Second Manassas or Bull Run, late August 1862). But this time the story was different—disaster rather than triumph. The brigades of Cooke and Kirkland suffered heaviest. Casualties of the former numbered about seven hundred and those of the latter approximately six hundred. Both Cooke and Kirkland sustained severe wounds; Mississippi's Carnot Posey received a wound from which he succumbed a month later. Freeman, *R. E. Lee*, 3:183. The defeat has been attributed to a gross blunder by Third Corps commander A. P. Hill, a misjudgment as to the enemy's strength and position. The day following the battle, while being briefed by Hill as to what had happened, Lee remarked tersely: "Well, well, General, bury these poor men and let us say no more about it." Freeman, *Lee's Lieutenants*, 3:247.

29. It is interesting to note that there appeared to be some change in the bandsmen's attitude. Now that their status as the Twenty-sixth Band had become official, the word "belonged" seems significant. Could it be that the boys were taking some pride

in their new identity? Perhaps they would use it to their advantage—mainly to retain their present situation with the regiment.

30. This and subsequent statements concerning the bandsmen's clothing raise an interesting question: generally, just how well provided *were* the North Carolina soldiers? Some writers have claimed that Governor Vance's Tar Heel troops were "all comfortably clad." See F. L. Owsley, *States Rights in the Confederacy* (Chicago: University of Chicago Press, 1925), 126. Another source stated: "More carefully uniformed than the other troops were the North Carolinians in Lee's army." Tucker, "North Carolina's Participation in the Gettysburg Campaign," 198. Remarks by Leinbach throughout his narrative suggest that both claims are perhaps a bit exaggerated. If Vance hoarded clothing for his own troops, who, then, were the beneficiaries? Surely those with whom he had so closely served, especially his band, were not among the fortunate.

31. The closing sentence poses another of many intriguing questions: was the Twenty-first Band, as Leinbach and others continued to identify the group, now actually serving as a brigade band, while operating as a unit of the First Battalion Sharpshooters and serving, at times, the regiment? We do know that after being detached from the regiment and made a separate command in May 1862, the battalion (with the band) operated as such, as well as an adjunct to the regiment. By the time of the Bristoe Campaign (October 9-November 9, 1863), "the activities of the battalion are not known, but it appears to have remained with the brigade and did not see any action." *North Carolina Troops*, 3:67. Could this be the situation that prompted Leinbach's remark? The state of flux characterizing Lee's troops following Gettysburg prevailed throughout the command, and no doubt many regimental bands were unable to function. Those that were operational, including the Twenty-sixth, were called on to serve the musical needs of brigades—at least for a time. More research is needed.

32. Absenteeism continued to be a problem throughout the armies of the Confederacy, and it grew worse as the months wore on. Wiley, *Life of Johnny Reb*, 143-145.

33. Freeman, *Lee's Lieutenants*, 3:219.

34. Such structures sprung up almost overnight when it became evident that the troops were to be located in one area for the winter months. The typical hut was built of logs, mud-chinked, to a height of six to eight feet and was usually covered with planks or a tent fly. Built to house from four to six men, these abodes very often included elaborate amenities—brick fireplaces, plank floors, and various items of cleverly constructed furnishings. Interesting descriptions of such improvised residences are to be found in Wiley, *Life of Johnny Reb*, 59-65.

35. Specifically mentioned in this instance are serenades to the colonels of the Forty-seventh (G. H. Faribault) and Fifty-second (James K. Marshall) Regiments. For their performances, the boys netted fifty dollars from each officer. In calling on the Twenty-sixth for music, the colonels of these regiments probably had no band—at least an insufficient number to make a creditable showing—at that particular time. Records in this respect are inconclusive but appear to support this assumption. Three names, identified as "Musicians," are included with the field and staff of the Forty-

seventh Regiment. Identified as "Band" with the field and staff of the Fifty-second Regiment are four listed as musicians—two are noted as having been chief musicians. *North Carolina Troops*, 11:247; 12:417. For additional information, see Appendix A.

36. The Army of Northern Virginia now consisted primarily of the Second and Third Corps of Ewell and Hill, respectively; Longstreet's corps had been removed to the western theater. Freeman, *Lee's Lieutenants*, 3:217-228, 269.

37. Early was in command of the Second Corps, as Ewell was absent because of a severe wound suffered at Second Manassas. Freeman, *Lee's Lieutenants*, 3:269.

38. Actually, the heaviest fighting of the entire operation was at this time, with Maj. Gen. Edward "Allegheny" Johnson's division of the Second Corps most heavily engaged. Freeman, *Lee's Lieutenants*, 3:270-273.

39. Leinbach mentioned going to the Fifty-fifth Band to copy music for Charlie Transou; on another occasion, he and Mickey paid the Twenty-seventh North Carolina a visit to obtain music for the band.

40. Clark, *North Carolina Regiments*, 1:593.

41. Lane had been recovering from the severe wound received at Gettysburg.

42. Clark, *North Carolina Regiments*, 2:380-381.

43. For interesting highlights concerning the all-important subject of rations and food-getting in the Confederate army, see "Bad Beef and Corn Bread," in Wiley, *Life of Johnny Reb*, 90-107.

44. Miss Amelia A. Van Vleck (1835-1929), a resident of Salem, inherited her musical talent largely from her father and grandfather. Three compositions represent her known contributions to the music of the Twenty-sixth: *Salem Band Waltz*, *Serenade Waltz*, and *Carolina March*. Her piano copies were arranged for the band by Edward Leinbach. Leinbach, "Regiment Band of the Twenty-sixth North Carolina," 232 n. 2.

45. The Moravian love feasts, patterned after the early Christian *agapae,* were instituted at Herrnhut, Germany, in 1727, as informal, socio-religious gatherings. The inclusion of a simple meal on these occasions became a distinctive feature of the service. For the American congregations, the love feast denoted a time when the entire congregation would gather in the church for a service of prayer, song, and Christian fellowship, and coffee and buns were served. McCorkle, "Moravian Music in Salem," 32.

46. Throughout his narrative, Leinbach mentioned such instances of social diversion, and each time he made a point of stating that he and his fellow bandsmen took no part in the dancing. This abstention was a matter of principle and wholly in keeping with the Moravian belief at the time.

47. Tune 146 in the *Moravian Hymnal.*

48. Indicative of the physical deterioration of the bandsmen, according to Leinbach, is the record of their respective weights as of January 1, 1864: Mickey, 164; Transou, 157; Crouse, 153; Peterson, 152; Joe Hall, 150; Gibson, 150; Siddall, 146; Meinung, 142; Reich, 142; and at the little end of the list, Leinbach, 129.

49. A roster of the fourteen-piece band that enlisted in 1861 indicated four members were from Guilford County, but not specifically from Greensboro. See Appendix A.

50. Feelings of disaffection against the Confederacy had been gaining momentum in North Carolina since mid-1863. Championing the peace movement being voiced from many corners was William W. Holden, editor of the Raleigh *Standard* and organizer of the state's Conservative Party. One of Vance's greatest tasks at that time was to counteract the pacifist feeling and the criticisms from Holden. With this thought in mind, he opened his campaign for re-election in late February, selecting as his springboard for attack the small western North Carolina town of Wilkesboro, in the heart of the dissentient region. There, on February 22, Vance announced his firm stand with the cause of the Confederacy and urged his listeners, estimated at two thousand, to do likewise. For an excellent digest of the political currents at that time, see Richard E. Yates, *The Confederacy and Zeb Vance*, Confederate Centennial Studies, ed. William Stanley Hoole, no. 8 (Tuscaloosa, Ala.: Confederate Publishing Co., Inc., 1958), 85-107.

51. Specifically mentioned are J. E. Mickey, James Fisher (appearing in the Twenty-sixth Band photograph), and the diarist's brother, Henry. At Teaguetown, the party was joined by two of Julius's other brothers, Edward and Parmenio.

Chapter 6

1. The year 1864 witnessed a gradual change in Leinbach's way of gathering and reporting information, although the narrative continues to include considerable material apparently taken from contemporaneous notes and/or his pocket diary. Of special interest, however, is the inclusion of several quoted letters, beginning with this one, which Julius wrote to his family in Salem. Many of these—at least ten—are specifically identified as "Quotations from a letter." (Other passages appear only in quotes without source identification and without a clue as to their origin.) Thus far, regrettably, none of the war letters appear to have survived. Their discovery would of course be a valuable find, particularly to the bandsman's descendants.

2. A similar account of this foray may be found in Clark, *North Carolina Regiments*, 2:379-380. Such encounters appear to have been a popular diversion, even for units stationed as far south as Georgia. Wiley, *Life of Johnny Reb*, 63-67.

3. In several instances instruments were taken to Culpeper for repairs. The musicians' problems in this respect were minimized, though, as no woodwinds were used by the band during the war.

4. Vance carried his vigorous campaign for re-election to the troops, and his visit at that time, though purely political, was a potent stimulant to Lee's disconsolate command. In fact, the commander remarked enthusiastically that the governor's "visit to the army was equivalent to a reinforcement of fifty thousand men. " See Samuel A'Court Ashe, *History of North Carolina*, 2 vols. (Raleigh: Edwards and Broughton Printing Co., 1925), 2:880. Vance's visit apparently paid off, for on July 28 North Carolina troops gave him 13,209 out of a total of 15,083 votes cast. On August 4, the home vote increased the governor's total to 57,878, giving him an overwhelming victory. Interestingly, one of three counties that gave Holden a small

majority was Republican Wilkes, where Vance had opened his campaign in February. Ashe, *History of North Carolina*, 2:106.

5. Some months later the boys learned that it had been their own Colonel Lane who had stopped Meinung's petition for a transfer. That Alex would have been well qualified for this new position is evident from the accompanying examples of his artistic ability and beautiful penmanship. See Appendix C.

6. Reflecting upon the scenic beauty, Leinbach indicated that, with a little persuasion, he would *almost* be willing to establish residence in this inviting locale.

7. See especially Grant's own narrative, "Preparing for the Campaigns of '64," in *Battles and Leaders*, 4:97-117.

8. May 2 was the date on which the order was issued for the movement of Union forces from Culpeper. See Andrew A. Humphreys, *The Virginia Campaigns of 1864 and 1865*, Campaigns of the Civil War, vol. 12 (New York: Charles Scribner's Sons, 1883), 18.

9. Freeman, *Lee's Lieutenants*, 3:345; see also Maj. Gen. E. M. Law, "From the Wilderness to Cold Harbor," in *Battles and Leaders*, 4:118.

10. Ewell's corps, led by Early's division, followed by the divisions of Rodes and Johnson, moved off eastwardly along the Orange-Fredericksburg Turnpike. Simultaneously, two divisions of Hill's corps (Heth and Wilcox) proceeded in the same direction along the Orange Plank Road toward Verdiersville. (Anderson's division of Hill's troops remained at its position along the Rapidan, joining the main body on May 6.) Around 4:00 P.M. on May 4, Longstreet's troops, returned from Tennessee and stationed at Gordonsville, followed the route taken by Hill. This was essentially the same course taken in the November Mine Run operation, only now the forces were moving more rapidly. Freeman, *Lee's Lieutenants*, 3:346; *Battles and Leaders*, 4:119-121.

11. At that time, Hill's corps had drawn abreast of Ewell's, the left of the former joining the right of the latter approximately midway between Parker's Store and the Orange Turnpike. Both commands were heavily engaged. Aptly named after the nature of the terrain in which it was fought, the engagement took place in a densely entangled mesh of underbrush and scrub trees. There were few clearings, and the roads were nothing more than narrow trails. The engulfing mass of greenery made it practically impossible for gunners to locate their targets. *Battles and Leaders*, 4:122; Freeman, *Lee's Lieutenants*, 3:850.

12. Sometimes referred to as the Wilderness-Spotsylvania Operations (see map in Freeman, *Lee's Lieutenants*, 3:847), the campaign moved southeastward about eight miles from Wilderness Tavern to Spotsylvania Court House. In the latter location, there was almost continuous fighting during the period May 7-19, with the heaviest engagements occurring on May 11-12.

13. Mickey made a special trip to Orange and had a coffin sent back to the bivouac area. Jones's death was just one instance during the campaign when the boys were touched closely by the loss of loved ones—friend and kin. Mentioned at this time also was the wounding of John Atwood, who was from near Salem, and the death of Capt. Henry Belo of the Moravian village. A few days later, on May 11, the band was to

bury Abe's brother. As Leinbach refers only to the death of "Captain Gibson, brother of our Abe," it is assumed that this was Capt. Leonidas R. Gibson of Company I, Fifty-second Regiment, North Carolina Troops. He is listed as having been killed at Spotsylvania on May 11, 1864. Clark, *North Carolina Regiments*, 3:246; *North Carolina Troops*, 12:447.

14. The general area of battle was a "U"-shaped salient referred to as the "Mule Shoe." The major focus of the attack that day occurred at an angle point on the slightly elevated position of the breastworks, just north of Spotsylvania Court House. Commonly known as the "Bloody Angle," the fighting there was reputedly one of the more bloodletting contests fought by the opposing armies. Defending this sector, Maj. Gen. Edward Johnson's division of Ewell's corps was overrun, and the general and most of his command, nearly three thousand troops, were captured. See *Battles and Leaders*, 4:130-132; Freeman, *Lee's Lieutenants*, 3:407.

15. *Battles and Leaders*, 4:135. Telegraph Road lay about three miles to the east of Spotsylvania Court House and extended from Fredericksburg southward through Chilesburg and across the North Anna River.

16. At this location, approximately ten miles northeast of Richmond, Lee's well-entrenched army repulsed Grant's massive blow on June 8. Estimated casualties were about 1,500 for the Confederates in contrast to nearly 7,000 for the Union. It was slaughter, pure and simple. No advantage was gained, and Grant later remarked that he regretted having ordered the final attack. Freeman, *Lee's Lieutenants*, 3:508.

17. These troops were formed in line of battle facing the Union Sixth Corps of Maj. Gen. Horatio G. Wright, about midway between Gaines's Mill and Old Cold Harbor. See the map locations in Clifford Dowdey, *Lee's Last Campaign: The Story of Lee and His Men against Grant—1864* (Boston and Toronto: Little, Brown and Co., 1960), 295. The Twenty-fifth South Carolina (Hagood's brigade, Hoke's division) had just joined Lee's troops at Cold Harbor. The division, having been detached from its position in the Richmond-Petersburg defenses (under Gen. P. G. T. Beauregard) was moved to reinforce Lee. Dowdey, *Lee's Last Campaign*, 281-282.

18. Freeman, *Lee's Lieutenants*, 3:536-537.

19. Freeman, *Lee's Lieutenants*, 3:536.

20. Freeman, *Lee's Lieutenants*, 3:533.

21. Freeman, *Lee's Lieutenants*, 3:537.

22. The brigade had been without a permanent leader since Cold Harbor, where General Kirkland had received another serious wound. Toward the last of June, Col. William McRae of the Fifteenth North Carolina Regiment was placed in command of the former Pettigrew Brigade and served as its leader until the war's end. He was promoted to brigadier general in November 1864. Clark, *North Carolina Regiments*, 3:29.

23. Though Leinbach refers to "the band," it may reasonably be assumed that several musical units were involved in this bit of strategy. The ten or twelve (probably less) healthy members of the Twenty-sixth Band could hardly have made an impressionable demonstration—or could they?

24. Some of the important engagements included Globe Tavern (August 14-16); Reams Station (August 24-25); the September 29 attack on Fort Harrison (southeast of Richmond on the north bank of the James River); and a second, unsuccessful assault against this line in October. Freeman, *Lee's Lieutenants*, 3:593-594.

25. As numerous as they were varied, the demands of duties continued to have a telling effect upon the physical well-being of the musicians. During the late summer of 1864, practically all were sick at one time or another. Gus Reich, after having spent some time in the hospital, was sent home for a brief spell.

26. The troops were quickly made aware of their new commander's demands. In one instance, reflecting his reputation as a strict disciplinarian, McRae imposed a stern penalty on the Twenty-sixth Regiment for not participating in a scheduled dress parade—the punishment: to parade one day "every hour from 3 a.m. to 6 p.m." The band participated in only three or four of these because of sickness. The ranks were so depleted on September 1 that Leinbach mentioned having to call on their "Greensboro" friends in the Twenty-seventh Band to assist in playing for a parade. For additional information, including the significance of the word "Greensboro," see comments in Appendix A.

27. Kirkland, having returned to duty in August, was placed in charge of James G. Martin's old brigade, now a part of Robert Hoke's division. Clark, *North Carolina Regiments*, 4:537. The review of which Leinbach speaks was a division affair, and General Kirkland had invited his former bandsmen to play for his brigade. As the parade ground was located some distance away (near Petersburg), the boys failed to arrive in time to participate.

28. Generally, Lee's army occupied a line extending from its southern position at the Claiborne Road crossing of Hatcher's Run to White Oak Swamp, slightly southeast of Richmond, a distance of about thirty-seven miles. Hill's corps occupied the southern section of this line southwest of Petersburg, about one mile east of the Boydton Plank Road and extending northward for about five miles to Fort Gregg. Humphreys, *The Virginia Campaign*, 310.

29. Not until December 27 did the boys learn that their furloughs had been denied. This action on the part of McRae may well have stemmed from his having learned of attempts to exert outside pressure in the matter. That is exactly what had happened. Leinbach mentioned having received two letters written on their behalf by one A. C. Hege of Lexington. Earlier in the month, Julius's brother James had succeeded in getting Governor Vance to petition General Lee in the bandsmen's interest.

30. Some of these troubles may have been averted, or at least minimized, by some commanders. For example, John B. Hood had engaged the enemy in a foolhardy, wasteful assault at the Battle of Franklin, Tennessee. Other miscalculations are also a matter of record. A particularly alarming event was the fall of Savannah to Sherman on December 27.

31. On the night of December 27, General McRae issued a directive to the effect that the three bands in the brigade would perform every night, alternatingly, between the hours of 8:00 and 10:00. (Though not specified, this would have included the bands of the Eleventh, Twenty-sixth, and either the Forty-seventh or Fifty-second North

Carolina Regiments.) Concerning this extra demand, Julius remarked that "we have reason to think that this order had its origin in a feeling of unfriendliness on the part of the commanding officer." By now it had become apparent, at least in the musicians' minds, that McRae was no particular fan of theirs.

32. The Twenty-seventh, still in Cooke's brigade and having undergone no disruption in command, very likely suffered no drastic changes in routine and policy as were affecting the Twenty-sixth.

33. Fort Fisher, located near the mouth of the Cape Fear River, was practically the South's last contact with the outside world; by its loss, a vital source of supply had been severed. Freeman, *Lee's Lieutenants*, 3:657.

34. Freeman, *Lee's Lieutenants*, 3:645.

35. Freeman, *Lee's Lieutenants*, 3:655.

36. Humphreys, *The Virginia Campaign*, 316. The move had been anticipated as early as March 14; orders were issued on March 24, and the movement began on March 29.

37. Humphreys, *The Virginia Campaign*, 334-362.

38. McRae's brigade, on the morning of March 8, was entrenched along White Oak Road below Hatcher's Run, between Claiborne's Road and the Boydton Plank Road. Humphreys, *The Virginia Campaign*, 326.

39. Next to the regular profusion of rousing, patriotic airs, J. P. Webster's *Lorena,* first published in Chicago in 1857, became one of Johnny Reb's favorites. Of the many tunes that Hartwell composed, only one appears to have been published: *Confederates Grand March.* See Richard B. Harwell, *Confederate Music* (Chapel Hill: University of North Carolina Press, 1950), 86. This piece was not positively identified among the Mississippian's music in the Twenty-sixth's band books.

40. Possibly between Hatcher's Run and White Oak Road.

41. About that time, Peterson and Reich fell behind the others and were soon picked up by the enemy. Gus had to give up his drum and Ed his trombone. (This is the only reference to a trombone throughout Leinbach's entire account.) The Yanks, after detaining the two boys momentarily, told them to go their way. They soon became separated, however—Gus finally reaching the regiment, and Ed joining Joe Hall, who had become separated from the band by now. Leinbach said that Gus was paroled with the band. His name is not among those on the parole list of the Twenty-sixth Regiment. Clark, *North Carolina Regiments*, 5:531-553. Ed and Joe made it home on their own and are reported to have reached Salem a few days after Gus. During this time, Meinung and Julius Transou were already at home on sick leave.

42. Leinbach stated that, in order to not attract attention, they made their trips singly because it was discovered that the Federals were using the house for the same purpose.

43. Leinbach's arrival was timely; five days later his mother passed away. The Twenty-sixth Regiment's historian is apparently in error when stating that Mickey arrived in Salem on July 3, 1865 (Clark, *North Carolina Regiments*, 2:400). Julius would be in a better position to know when the bandleader reached home, i.e., on July 1.

Epilogue

1. Clark, *North Carolina Regiments*, 2:305.

2. *People's Press*, May 20, 1870.

3. *People's Press*, May 27, 1870.

Bibliography

Primary Sources

Manuscript Collections

Archiv der Brüder-Unität, Herrnhut, Germany.

> Peter Böhler letter, December 25, 1739. R.14.A, Nr.6.3.

Archives of the Moravian Church in America, Southern Province, Winston-Salem, N.C.

> Johann Heinrich (John Henry) Leinbach Journal.
> Samuel Timothy Mickey Diary.
> Nathaniel Shober Siewers Civil War letters.

Bethania Historical Association, Bethania, N.C.

> Oliver J. Lehman Letters and associated material.

Mississippi Department of Archives and History, Archives and Library Division, Jackson, Miss.

> Confederate Military Records.
> Death certificate and grave registration of William H. Hartwell.

Moravian Music Foundation, Winston-Salem, N.C.

> Agnes Peterson Boyd Material, including the letters of James Edward Peterson (1827-1906).
> Miscellaneous Collection.
> Salem Band Manuscript Collection.

Museum of Early Southern Decorative Arts (MESDA), Winston-Salem, N.C.

Research Files:

> "Minutes of the *Aufseher Collegium*," Salem, April 15, 1822, April 17, 1846; Translated excerpts (typed) from the original German by Erika Huber and Dr. Edmund Schwarze.
> "Minutes of the Elders' Conference," November 30, 1785.

"Minutes of the Provincial Elders' Conference," Salem, July 28, 1841, April 15, 1846; Translated from the original German (typed) by Dr. Edmund Schwarze.

Miscellaneous entry, August 14, 1766, Research Card File.

National Archives, Washington, D.C.

Record Group 109, War Department Collection of Confederate Records:

Muster roll of the Field, Staff and Band, Eleventh Regiment N.C. Volunteers, May 24–August 31, 1861.

Muster rolls (3) of the Eleventh Regiment N.C. Troops, August 31, 1864–February 21, 1865.

Muster rolls (4) of the Twenty-first Regiment N.C. Troops, 1861–1865.

Muster rolls (13) of the Thirty-third Regiment N.C. Troops, 1861–1865.

South Carolina Department of Archives and History, Columbia, S.C.

Muster roll of the Fourteenth Regiment S.C. Volunteers, May 1, 1863–June 30, 1863.

Muster rolls (2) of the Twenty-fifth Regiment S.C. Volunteers, November 1–December 31, 1862, and July 1–August 31, 1863.

Southern Historical Collection, Manuscripts Department, Wilson Library, University of North Carolina at Chapel Hill, Chapel Hill, N.C.

Julius A. Lineback Papers.

Newspapers

The City Itemizer, Water Valley (Yalobusha County), Miss., March 12, 1914.

Farmer's Reporter and Rural Repository (Salem), June 6, July 11, 1835.

The Moravian (Bethlehem, Pa.), July 23, 1863.

Patriot (Greensborough [Greensboro]), April 6, 12, 20, 1844.

People's Press (Salem), February 22, July 5, 1851; May 7, 1853; February 25, 1854; June 19, 1857; May 20, 27, 1870.

Western Sentinel (Winston), August 30, September 6, 1861.

Printed Documentary Sources

Army Regulations Adopted For the Use of the Confederate States. Richmond: West and Johnston, 1861.

Davis, George B., et al. *Atlas to Accompany the Official Records of the Union and Confederate Armies.* Washington: Government Printing Office, 1891-1895.

Fremantle, Arthur J. L. *Three Months in the Southern States, April-June, 1863.* New York: John Bradburn, 1864.

Fries, Adelaide L., et al., eds. *Records of the Moravians in North Carolina,* 12 vols. to date. Raleigh: Division of Archives and History, Department of Cultural Resources, 1922-.

Inman, Arthur Crew, ed. *Soldier of the South: General Pickett's War Letters to His Wife.* Boston and New York: Houghton Mifflin Co., 1928.

Manarin, Louis H., et al., comps. *North Carolina Troops, 1861-1865: A Roster.* 15 vols. to date. Raleigh: Office of Archives and History, Department of Cultural Resources, 1966-.

Runge, William H., ed. *Four Years in the Confederate Artillery: The Diary of Private Henry Robinson Berkeley.* Chapel Hill: University of North Carolina Press, 1961.

The War of the Rebellion: A Compilation of the Official Records of the Union and Confederate Armies. 150 vols. Washington: Government Printing Office, 1880-1901.

Wolseley, G. J. "A Month's Visit to the Confederate Headquarters." *Blackwood's Edinburgh Magazine* 93 (January 1863): 1-29.

Secondary Sources
Books and Articles

Ashe, Samuel A'Court. *History of North Carolina.* 2 vols. Raleigh: Edwards and Broughton Printing Co., 1925.

Bettermann, Wilhelm. "Wie das Posaunenblasen in der Brüder-gemeine aufkam." *Jarbuch der Brüder-gemeine, Jahrgang* 33. Herrnhut: Rudolf Winter, 1937-1938.

"Causes of the Defeat of Gen. Lee's Army at the Battle of Gettysburg." *Southern Historical Society Papers* 4 (August 1877): 49-87; 4 (September 1877): 97-160.

Clark, Walter, ed. *Histories of the Several Regiments and Battalions from North Carolina in the Great War, 1861-'65.* 5 vols. Goldsboro, N.C.: Nash Brothers, 1901.

Connor, R. D. W., et al. *History of North Carolina.* 5 vols. Chicago and New York: Lewis Publishing Company, 1919.

Dowdey, Clifford. *Lee's Last Campaign: The Story of Lee and His Men Against Grant—1864.* Boston and Toronto: Little, Brown and Co., 1960.

Early, Jubal Anderson. *Autobiographical Sketch and Narrative of the War Between the States.* Philadelphia and London: J. B. Lippincott Co., 1912.

Freeman, Douglas Southall. *Lee's Lieutenants: A Study in Command.* 3 vols. New York: Charles Scribner's Sons, 1944.

———. *R. E. Lee: A Biography.* 4 vols. New York and London: Charles Scribner's Sons, 1934-1935.

Garofalo, Robert, and Mark Elrod. *A Pictorial History of Civil War Era Musical Instruments and Military Bands.* Charleston, W. Va.: Pictorial Histories Publishing Co., 1985.

Harwell, Richard B. *Confederate Music.* Chapel Hill: University of North Carolina Press, 1950.

Hood, John B. *Advance and Retreat: Personal Experiences in the United States and Confederate States Armies.* New Orleans: G. T. Beauregard, 1880.

Humphreys, Andrew A. *The Virginia Campaigns of 1864 and 1865.* Campaigns of the Civil War, vol. 12. New York: Charles Scribner's Sons, 1883.

Johnson, Robert U., and Clarence C. Buel, eds. *Battles and Leaders of the Civil War.* 4 vols. New York: The Century Co., 1888.

Leinbach, Julius A. "Regiment Band of the Twenty-sixth North Carolina," ed. Donald M. McCorkle, *Civil War History* 4 (September 1958): 225-236; reprinted as *Moravian Music Foundation Publications*, No. 5. Winston-Salem, N.C.: Moravian Music Foundation, Inc., 1958.

Levering, Joseph Mortimer. *A History of Bethlehem, Pennsylvania, 1741-1892, with Some Accounts of its Founders and Their Early Activity in America.* Bethlehem, Pa.: Times Publishing Co., 1903.

McCorkle, Donald M. "The Collegium Musicum Salem: Its Music, Musicians, and Importance." *North Carolina Historical Review* 33 (October 1956): 483-498; reprinted as *Moravian Music*

Foundation Publications, No. 3. Winston-Salem, N.C.: Moravian Music Foundation, Inc., 1956.

Moore, John W. *History of North Carolina from the Earliest Discoveries to the Present Time*. 2 vols. Raleigh: Alfred Williams and Co., 1880.

Olson, Kenneth E. *Music and Musket: Bands and Bandsmen of the American Civil War*. Westport, Conn.: Greenwood Press, 1981.

Owen, William Miller. *In Camp and Battle with the Washington Artillery of New Orleans*. Boston: Ticknor and Co., 1885.

Owsley, F. L. *States Rights in the Confederacy*. Chicago: University of Chicago Press, 1925.

Pfohl, Bernard J. *The Salem Band*. Winston-Salem, N.C.: n.p., 1953.

Raynor, George. "The Brothers Neave: Professional Musicians." *Piedmont Passages*. 6 vols. Salisbury, N.C.: *Salisbury Post,* 1990-1991. 5:48-60.

Sherrill, Lee. "Kirkland's Confederate Band" (Part One). *Forsyth County Genealogical Society Journal* 22 (winter 2004): 105-129.

Stiles, Robert. *Four Years under Marse Robert*. 3d ed. New York and Washington: Neale Publishing Co., 1904.

Stone, James. "War Music and War Psychology in the Civil War." *Journal of Abnormal and Social Psychology* 36 (October 1941): 543-560.

Storrick, W. C. *Gettysburg, the Place, the Battles, the Outcome*. Harrisburg, Pa.: Horace McFarland Co., 1957.

Tarr, Edward H., and Stephen L. Glover, eds., *The Moravian Brass Duet Book*. Nashville, Tenn.: The Brass Press, 1976.

Tarr, Edward H., and Harry H. Hall, eds. *Cruse Sonata No. 3*. Cologne, Germany: Wolfgang G. Haas-Musikverlag Köln, 1997.

———, eds., *Weber Sonatas No. 1, 2, 3, 4*, and *Weber Sonatas No. 5, 6, 7, 8*. Nashville, Tenn.: The Brass Press, 1977.

Trimble, Isaac R. "The Campaign and Battle of Gettysburg." *Confederate Veteran* 25 (May 1917): 209-213.

Tucker, Glenn. *Front Rank*. Raleigh: North Carolina Confederate Centennial Commission, 1962.

———. *High Tide at Gettysburg: The Campaign in Pennsylvania*. Indianapolis and New York: Bobbs-Merrill Co., Inc., 1958.

———. "Some Aspects of North Carolina's Participation in the Gettysburg Campaign." *North Carolina Historical Review* 35 (April 1958): 191–212.

Wiley, Bell Irvin. *The Life of Billy Yank, The Common Soldier of the Union.* Indianapolis: Bobbs-Merrill Co., 1952.

———. *The Life of Johnny Reb, The Common Soldier of the Confederacy.* Indianapolis: Bobbs-Merrill Co., 1943.

Yates, Richard E. *The Confederacy and Zeb Vance.* Confederate Centennial Studies, ed. William Stanley Hoole, no. 8. Tuscaloosa, Ala.: Confederate Publishing Co., Inc., 1958.

Unpublished

Dumond, Mathilde, comp. "Research on William Augustus Reich (1833–1917)," 1987. Typescript copy on file at Research Center, Museum of Early Southern Decorative Arts (MESDA), Winston-Salem, N.C.

Hall, Harry H. "The Moravian Wind Ensemble: Distinctive Chapter in America's Music." 2 vols., Ph.D. diss., George Peabody College for Teachers, 1967.

McCorkle, Donald M. "Moravian Music in Salem: A German-American Heritage." Ph.D. diss., Indiana University, 1958.

Sherrill, Lee. "Kirkland's Confederate Band," n.d. Copy on file with the Forsyth County Genealogical Society, Winston-Salem, N.C.

Index